THE COMPLETE GUIDE TO

"S" Corporations

Ted Nicholas

Enterprise · Dearborn

a division of Dearborn Publishing Group, Inc.

While a great deal of care has been taken to provide accurate and current information, the ideas, suggestions, general principles and conclusions presented in this text are subject to local, state and federal laws and regulations, court cases and any revisions of same. The reader is thus urged to consult legal counsel regarding any points of law—this publication should not be used as a substitute for competent legal advice.

Publisher: Kathleen A. Welton
Acquisitions Editor: Patrick J. Hogan
Associate Editor: Karen A. Christensen
Senior Project Editor: Jack L. Kiburz
Cover Design: The Publishing Services Group

Published by Enterprise • Dearborn,
a division of Dearborn Publishing Group, Inc.

Printed in the United States of America

94 95 10 9 8 7 6 5 4 3

Library of Congress Cataloging-in-Publication Data

Nicholas, Ted, 1934
  The complete guide to "S" corporations / Ted Nicholas.
    p.   cm.
  Includes bibliographical references and index.
  ISBN 0-79310-613-3 (pbk.)
  1. Subchapter S corporations—Taxation. I. Title.
KF6491.N53 1993
343.7306′7—dc20
[347.30367]   92-47263
                                                  CIP

Books by Ted Nicholas

The Complete Book of Corporate Forms

The Complete Guide to Business Agreements

The Complete Guide to Consulting Success (coauthor, Howard Shenson)

The Complete Guide to Nonprofit Corporations

The Complete Guide to "S" Corporations

The Executive's Business Letter Book

43 Proven Ways To Raise Capital for Your Small Business

The Golden Mailbox: How To Get Rich Direct Marketing Your Product

How To Form Your Own Corporation Without a Lawyer for under $75

How To Get a Top Job in Tough Times (coauthor, Bethany Waller)

How To Get Your Own Trademark

How To Publish a Book and Sell a Million Copies

Secrets of Entrepreneurial Leadership: Building Top Performance Through Trust and Teamwork

Contents

1

How the "S" Corporation Works for You

Nearly forty years ago President Dwight D. Eisenhower, in his Budget Message to Congress, made the point that: "Small businesses should be able to operate under whatever form of organization is desirable for their particular circumstances, without incurring unnecessary tax penalties. To secure this result, I recommend that corporations with a small number of active stockholders be given the option to be taxed as partnerships."

President Eisenhower recognized the difficult choice facing entrepreneurs when they embark on a new venture: to opt for the favorable tax advantages available to individuals and partnerships and risk the vast potential for personal liability to which every business is exposed in our litigious society, or to choose the security of the corporate form and expose the profits of their labors to double taxation.

Four years after President Eisenhower's recommendation Congress finally acted: In 1958 the subchapter "S" corporation was created. Today, the "S" corporation, in most respects, is taxed as if it were a partnership.

This means that the profits of an "S" corporation are taxed only once, when the profits are received by the corporation's shareholders. A "C" corporation's profits, on the other hand, are taxed twice: as a profit to the corporation and as a dividend when that profit is disbursed to its shareholders.

Despite some early claims that the Revenue Reconciliation Act of 1993 dealt a severe blow to the "S" corporation, that simply is not the case. Most leading tax experts still recommend the "S" corporation as the singlemost valuable tool entrepreneurs can use to eliminate the harsh impact of the double taxation imposed on regular "C" corporations.

In fact, as important as the "S" corporation was in the 1950s, it is even more meaningful to many of today's businesspeople. In order to understand just how valuable an "S" corporation can be, you need only consider these results of the 1993 tax changes:

- If a "C" corporation has annual profits of more than $75,000 and less than $250,000, it will pay a top tax rate of at least 3 percent and can be as much as 8 percent *higher* than the tax imposed on individuals who form an "S" corporation—and the "C" corporation's profits will be taxed twice.
- Even if your corporation's profits are less than $75,000 or more than $250,000, *you will always pay less taxes if you form an "S" corporation.* This is because regular "C" corporation profits are subject to double taxation, whereas an individual or partner is taxed only once.
- If a "C" corporation has profits that range between $100,000 and $335,000, its tax rate is 39 percent.

THE CONCEPT OF DOUBLE TAXATION

When a regular, or "C," corporation, finishes up the year in the black, it pays a corporate income tax on its profits. If those profits are to go to the corporation's owners, its shareholders, then the corporation must declare a dividend. The corporation's shareholders must include the dividend as part of their income, and that money is taxed again. This stems from the fact that, for tax purposes, the "C" corporation is a taxable entity.

Assume that you operated your business as an individual or as a partnership. The profits of the business would not be taxed. Rather, the business would file a tax return showing income, deductions, losses and credits for the year. Those items are then passed through to the partners who report them on their returns and either pay a personal income tax on the profit or take the benefit of the loss, if there is one. These results stem from the fact that a partnership is not a taxable entity.

HOW THE "S" CORPORATION WORKS FOR YOU

The "S" corporation creates the best of all possible worlds: the limitations on investor liability associated with incorporation and the "pass through" taxation attribute of a partnership—single, not double taxation.

The tax benefits that flow from using the "S" corporation mean that any loss suffered by the corporation is not wasted and that profits made by the corporation are taxed once, not twice. Let's look at three examples:

> *Example No. 1:* Assume John Investor forms a regular "C" corporation in 1993. Given high costs—particularly in start-up years when a

loss is most likely to occur—the business absorbs a $20,000 loss its first year. That loss is useless to Mr. Investor. He cannot claim it on his return since it is the corporation's loss. He can only carry the loss forward and use it to offset corporate profits in 1994.

If we assume Mr. Investor has other net taxable income of $90,000, the "S" corporation loss would reduce his other income to $70,000. With $90,000 of net taxable income, he would be in the 31 percent tax bracket and would pay $27,900 in taxes in 1993. If he formed an "S" corporation, his net taxable income would have been only $70,000, and he would have been in the 28 percent tax bracket. His tax bill would have been only $19,600. Mr. Investor will keep an extra $8,300 simply because he chose "S" over "C" incorporation.

Example No. 2: Jane Businessperson, a married woman who files a joint return, formed a "C" corporation in 1993. The corporation was immediately successful and Jane drew a salary of $75,000 in 1993. In addition, the corporation had $100,000 in profits at the end of the year. The corporation would pay $22,250 in taxes on those profits (15 percent on the first $50,000, 25 percent on the next $25,000 and 34 percent on the next $25,000). The corporation's after-tax profits will be $77,750.

Now assume she takes the $77,750 out of the business as a dividend. We will also assume that she or her spouse has other income that brings their combined income to $89,150, the point at which the 31 percent tax rate begins. Their total income will be $166,900, including the $77,750 dividend. The first $50,850 will be taxed at 31 percent; the next $26,900 (the amount over $140,000) will be taxed at the rate of 36 percent. The tax on the $77,750 will come out to $25,448.

The total tax bite will have been $47,698 ($22,250 in corporate taxes plus $25,448 in personal income taxes)—almost half of the business profits will be lost to taxes.

Now, let's assume that Jane had formed an "S" corporation when she went into business. The $100,000 in profits would not have been taxed at the corporate level. Instead, it would flow through to her, and she would pay a personal income tax on it. In her case that tax would total $33,458 (remember we are assuming that she and her spouse have additional income over her $75,000 to bring their income up to $89,150, at which point the 31 percent tax bracket begins). Since Jane and her spouse will have total joint income in excess of $140,000 (at which point the 36 percent bracket begins), the first $50,850 of the $100,000 in profits will be taxed at 31 percent and the remaining $49,150 at 36 percent, a total of tax of $33,458.

Ms. Businessperson would have saved $14,240 by opting for "S" incorporation. And she has all of the protection and benefits offered by the corporate form of business organization to boot.

Example No. 3: Let's assume that five years go by and Ms. Businessperson sells the business assets at a $1,000,000 gain, liquidates the corporation and distributes the proceeds to herself. The corporation will be taxed at a 34 percent rate on its gain, and she will be taxed on the remainder. Translated into actual dollars, $340,000 of the money paid to the corporation will be lost to taxes. Of the remaining $660,000, an additional $232,890 will be lost to personal income taxes when the money is distributed to her. The bottom line is that $572,890 of the $1,000,000—well over half her profit—will be lost to taxes.

What would have happened if Ms. Businessperson had formed an "S" corporation? She would have paid a total of $367,528 in personal income taxes on her $1,000,000 gain—a savings of $205,362 because she chose "S" incorporation.

THE NUMBERS THAT WORK FOR YOU

You may have read that because some personal income tax rates are higher than corporate rates, it may not pay for certain individuals to form an "S" corporation. That simply is not true. In fact, in Example 3 above, Ms. Businessperson, as the shareholder of an "S" corporation, was taxed at the top rate of 39.6 percent on $750,000 of her profits—well above the corporate tax rate, which averages out to 34 percent. Nevertheless, she still ended up having a total tax bill that was $200,000 less than if she had formed a "C" corporation. That is because she paid a single tax that averaged 36.7 percent, instead of a corporate tax of 34 percent, followed by a personal income tax that would have taken an additional 35 percent.

The reason an "S" corporation is always the better choice for most entrepreneurs is that its profits are taxed only once. Furthermore, for taxpayers with income below $335,000 annually, the tax rate imposed on the earnings of individuals is always lower than the corporate rate. That means that if your business earns $335,000 or less, not only will you pay one tax instead of two if you choose "S" incorporation, but you will pay a lower tax rate—as much as 8 percent lower. Even in those few situations where the personal tax is higher than the corporate tax, the single tax applicable to "S" corporation profits always makes it the best choice.

Finally, we should note that if you reside in a state with corporate and personal income taxes, the "S" corporation is even more attractive since many states apply their tax laws in the same manner as the federal government. That means that you will enjoy comparable "single-tax" savings on your state taxes if you opt for "S" incorporation instead of "C" incorporation.

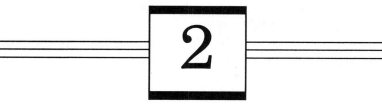

Choosing Your Business Organization

THE FOUR CHOICES

Most business advisers and lawyers if asked what choices an entrepreneur has when starting a business, list three options: the sole proprietorship, the partnership and the corporation. Actually, as countless thousands of small businesspeople know, there is a fourth choice—the "S" corporation. Let's see what each of these choices means to the businessperson embarking on a new venture.

The Sole Proprietorship

When an individual forms a business and operates it in his or her own name, or a trade name, that person runs the risk of having all of his or her personal assets exposed to creditors of the business. So, for example, if an employee accidentally or carelessly injures a customer or some other person, the owner of the business stands liable for the injury. Even if there is insurance coverage, the possibility always exists that liability may exceed the coverage provided by the policy—particularly in a society such as ours where multi-million dollar judgments are becoming commonplace.

Other drawbacks exist. If the sole proprietor becomes ill or dies, the business he or she has developed immediately loses much of its value—it becomes difficult, if not impossible, to hide the fact that the business is available under a forced sale—a situation guaranteed to get less than the best possible selling price. The chief benefit of the sole proprietorship—a benefit not to be taken lightly—is the fact that it is not a taxable entity. In other words, any gain, loss, deduction or business credit available because of the business belongs to the sole proprietor.

Overall, however, having all of one's assets (savings, home, auto and so on) at risk because of a business venture makes the sole proprietorship unattractive to many people.

The Partnership

This form of business shares many of the benefits and drawbacks of the sole proprietorship. Each partner is personally liable for all of the business debts. The partnership comes to an end whenever any partner decides he or she no longer wants to be part of the business or if a partner dies or becomes bankrupt. This means that the continuity of the business is uncertain and can end on the whim of a partner.

Other drawbacks include the difficulty of obtaining new partners, particularly if they do not share profits on an equal basis. Would you, as a partner, be willing to take less than an equal share of profits if you also had to expose yourself to the potential of 100 percent liability for the business debts?

As in the case of the sole proprietorship, the partnership is not a taxable entity. Its profits, gains, losses and credits pass through to its partners.

The Corporation

Perhaps the greatest bundle of nontax benefits is wrapped in the garb of the corporation.

The most significant attribute of the corporation is its ability to shield its investors from personal liability. The shareholder is not liable for the debts of the business. The corporation, in the eyes of the law, is an independent person held solely liable for its debts. The only exceptions to this rule occur when courts "pierce the corporate veil" because of fraud on the part of its shareholders or with respect to penalties imposed under environmental laws. Otherwise, the shareholder's maximum risk in the corporation is measured by the amount of money he or she invests in it.

Second, the corporation has perpetual life. If one of its shareholders dies, becomes incapacitated or bankrupt or just chooses to leave the business, the corporation nevertheless continues its independent existence.

Next, the corporate mode of doing business makes it easier to attract additional investors and to attract them on more favorable terms than in a partnership. A corporation with a proven track record, but which needs additional money to carry it to its next level, may find it possible to attract investors who put in more money than the original shareholders and who take back a smaller proportionate interest.

Why would an investor pay more for less? For several reasons. First, the business's proven track record indicates the nature of the expected return. Second, the business's form assures that an investor will not be putting his or her entire personal fortune at risk when investing in the corporation—unlike the investor in a partnership.

Third, the corporate form of business makes it possible to attract passive investors who will allow those entrepreneurs who have run the business profitably to continue doing so without much interference. In a partnership, where new investors have all of their personal assets at risk, these investors are more likely to demand to be kept up-to-date on all business decisions and to have an equal voice in those decisions.

Fourth, an individual can form a corporation and maintain anonymity. Consider the example of a doctor who wishes to open a copying center and may not want the general public to know of his involvement in the center. If he operates as a sole proprietor, he must be known openly as the owner; the same would probably be true if he joined with a second person in a partnership. If, however, he forms a corporation, his affiliation with the corporation need never become a matter of public record.

Finally, a corporation's shares are freely transferable. This means that any shareholder may sell his or her shares to any other person without ending the business (if the parties wish, this right can be restricted).

With all of these benefits, why isn't the corporation the perfect vehicle at all times for every investor? Because of the federal government's tax laws!

A corporation is a person for tax purposes. This means that if it has a profit, even if that profit is not distributed to shareholders, it must pay a tax on the profit. If it has a loss, that loss does not work to the benefit of its shareholders. At most the loss can be saved and applied against corporate profits in a future year. Finally, when profits are distributed to shareholders as dividends, they are taxed a second time as income to the recipient.

The "S" Corporation

Unlike the regular corporation, which is treated as a separate person for tax purposes, an "S" corporation avoids separate taxation for most purposes. Essentially, the "S" corporation more closely resembles the partnership for tax purposes because its income, deductions, losses and credits flow through to the corporation's shareholders who account for those items on their returns. The tax form filled out by an "S" corporation is, in fact, a reporting form that breaks down the various types of income, deductions, losses and business credits that will become part of the shareholders' income tax filing.

There are, however, exceptions to these rules. First, an "S" corporation may be liable for certain capital gains, usually where a regular corporation converts to an "S" corporation in order to avoid double taxation. Second, certain types of "passive income" may be subject to double taxation if the "S" corporation was previously a regular corporation. Both exceptions are discussed in the chapters on "S" corporation taxation.

Despite its favorable tax position, the "S" corporation suffers no concomitant loss of nontax benefits available to regular corporations. Its shareholders are immune from personal liability for the business debts. Shares are transferable to anyone willing to buy into the "S" corporation (although there are limits on the number of shareholders the corporation can have). Corporate existence remains perpetual, and an individual can maintain the same degree of anonymity available in regular incorporation.

What, then, are the drawbacks to "S" incorporation? There are very few. First, unlike a regular corporation, an "S" corporation may not get the benefit of a business deduction for fringe benefit payments made on behalf of its shareholder-employees. However, techniques are available to capture fringe benefit deductions while enjoying "S" corporation status (see Chapter 9).

A second perceived drawback stems from the fact that "S" corporation shareholders cannot defer business income. If an "S" corporation has two equal shareholders and a profit of $100,00, each shareholder must report $50,000 of income for income tax purposes. If a "C" corporation does not distribute its profits, then those profits will be taxed only once.

This reasoning, however, overlooks three factors. First, a corporation is only apt to retain its profits in order to reinvest them in the business. It is likely to invest the "profits" in deductible items and will do so before the close of the tax year. There is no reason an "S" corporation cannot do the same thing, so that it, too, will have no profits at the end of the year.

Second, a "C" corporation that regularly retains its profits risks being hit with the extremely expensive excess accumulated earnings penalty tax.

Third, the "S" corporation shareholder will generally pay a lower tax on undistributed profits than a "C" corporation. Under the 1993 Act, corporate tax rates are only meaningfully lower when individual income exceeds $335,000 (39.6 percent). Corporations with earnings over $335,000 are subject to tax rates from 34 percent to 38 percent. But, as noted earlier, given the double tax imposed on "C" corporation profits, you will still be far better off if you've established an "S" rather than a "C" corporation.

WHAT IF YOU HAVE AN EXISTING CORPORATION?

Even if you have already established a business that operates as a regular "C" corporation, you can obtain the benefits of "S" incorporation. The procedure for switching to "S" corporation status is quite simple and is explained in subsequent chapters. Once the switch is made, almost all "S" corporation benefits become available to your business. Furthermore, those few areas for which you do not get the benefit of single taxation are treated no worse than they would have been had you not made the switch.

3

The First Step: Creating Your Corporation

THE NEED TO INCORPORATE

In order to have a valid "S" corporation, you must first form a valid corporation under state law. Although many people believe it is difficult and expensive to form a corporation, nothing could be further from the truth. It is possible to form a corporation in Delaware for $74, and your corporation can operate anywhere in the United States. Why Delaware? Because the Delaware corporation laws take particular notice of requirements for "S" corporation status and expressly permit your business to do everything legally necessary to qualify for and maintain your company's "S" corporation status.

In addition to being one of the most favorable, if not the most favorable, taxing jurisdictions, Delaware provides a very quick, speedy and inexpensive incorporation process. You do not have to use an attorney or an accountant to incorporate your business in any state. The Company Corporation, founded to assist in low-cost incorporation in any of the 50 states, is headquartered at Three Christina Centre, 201 North Walnut Street, Wilmington, Delaware, 19801 (1-800-542-2677), and can incorporate your business for a minimum of $119.

BENEFITS OF DELAWARE INCORPORATION

In addition to the fact that Delaware's corporation laws are specifically tailored to meet the precise needs of "S" corporations, there are at least 24 other good reasons for incorporation in Delaware:

1. *There is no minimum capital requirement.* A corporation can be organized with zero capital, if desired. Many states require that a corporation have at least $1,000 in capital.
2. *One person can hold the offices of president, treasurer and secretary and can be all the directors.* Many states require at least three officers or directors, or both. Therefore, there is no need to bring other persons into a Delaware corporation if the owner(s) does not desire it.
3. *Delaware has a specific body of corporation law that permits a corporation to function through its shareholders, thereby avoiding many of the formalities of corporate operations.*
4. *An established body of laws relevant to corporations has been tested in the Delaware courts over the years.* The outcome of any legal proceedings that involve the Delaware courts is therefore highly predictable, based on past history and experience. This can be meaningful to investors in a corporation. The Court of Chancery in Delaware is the only separate business court system in the United States, and has a long record of promanagement decisions.
5. *There is no income tax for corporations that are formed in Delaware, but that do not do business in the state.*
6. *The franchise tax on corporations compares favorably with those in any other state.*
7. *Shares of stock owned by a person outside the state are not subject to Delaware taxes.*
8. *The owner of a Delaware corporation can operate anonymously if desired.*
9. *One can form a corporation by mail and never visit the state, even to conduct annual meetings.* Meetings can be held anywhere, at the option of the directors.
10. *Delaware's corporation department welcomes new corporations and is organized to process them the same day they are received.*
11. *Delaware is the friendliest state to corporations.* The reason is that the state depends on its corporation department as a prime source of revenue. The corporation revenue is exceeded by income taxes. The state, therefore, depends on attracting a high volume of corporations. Historically Delaware's laws relating to corporations are favorable to business and fees remain low.
12. *There is no inheritance tax on shares of stock held by nonresidents.* These are taxed only in the state of residence of the owners.

13. *Director(s) may fix a sales price on any stock the corporation issues and wishes to sell.*
14. *Stockholders, directors and committee members may act by unanimous written consent in lieu of formal meetings.*
15. *Director(s) may determine what part of consideration received for stock is capital.*
16. *Corporations can pay dividends out of profits as well as surplus.*
17. *Corporations can hold stocks, bonds or securities of other corporations, as well as real and personal property, within or without the state, without limitation as to amount.*
18. *Corporations may purchase shares of its own stock and hold, sell and transfer them.*
19. *Corporations may conduct different kinds of business.* If the corporate documents filed with Delaware have a "broad purpose clause" as outlined later in this book, virtually any business activity can be conducted, other than banking or insurance. More than one type of business can be conducted by the same corporation without any changes in the documents filed with the state.
20. *A corporation has perpetual existence (unless otherwise specified in its certificate of incorporation).*
21. *The director(s) has power to make or alter bylaws.*
22. *Stockholder liability is limited to stock held in the corporation (with the exception of taxes and assuming the business is conducted in a legal manner).*
23. *Only one person acting as the incorporator is required; many other states require three.*
24. *Personal liability of the director(s) is either entirely eliminated or strictly limited under the Delaware code.*

FORMING THE CORPORATION WITHOUT ENGAGING A REGISTERED AGENT

Any person can form a Delaware corporation. The owner(s) need never visit the state. Annual meetings may be held anywhere.

The following is the least costly way to accomplish the incorporation:

1. *Establish a street mailing address in Delaware.* This can be a private home or office. (Without engaging a registered agent to provide assistance, this is usually the most difficult problem to solve.)
2. *Complete the blank certificate of incorporation for a Delaware close corporation on the following pages, using the format provided on the sample form.* The language in this certificate has been prepared by the Secretary of State, Corporation Department, Dover, Delaware. Be sure

to fill in the name and address of one incorporator who resides in any state. (Two blank certificates have been included for your convenience.)

Send two signed copies of this certificate to the Secretary of State, Corporation Department, Townsend Building, Dover, Delaware 19901. Include a check in the amount of $74, which is the total cost of the incorporation and recording. (This fee breaks down as follows: $25 for filing, receiving and indexing; $15 for the minimum state filing fee; $10 for a certified copy; and $9 per page submitted, minimum $19 to record a one-page certificate and the certification page, plus a $3 document recording fee.)

If the corporate name you pick is not available, you will be notified. Otherwise you will receive notice of the date that your corporation has been filed.

3. *The certificate is recorded with the Recorder of Deeds in the county where the street mailing address of the corporation is located.* There are three counties in Delaware. The Secretary of State, Corporation Department, routinely takes care of this recording function, and costs are included in the above breakdown. The addresses for the Recorder of Deeds offices in the three counties are as follows:

Kent County—County Courthouse, Dover, DE 19901
Sussex County—Box 505, Georgetown, DE 19947
New Castle County—800 French Street, Wilmington, DE 19801

In some states, other than Delaware, a similar incorporation procedure applies. Readers interested in forming a non-Delaware corporation can obtain specific information by writing to the Secretary of State, Corporation Department, in any state, or call The Company Corporation. No state, however, has all the benefits of incorporating in Delaware.

Some legal stationery companies can supply a complete kit of the above forms, at costs ranging from $45 to $70. A corporate seal and stock certificates cost $20 to $30. The Company Corporation provides a "Corporate Kit" including a corporate seal, stock certificates, forms for minutes and bylaws for $49.95, plus $5 for U.P.S. delivery.

If you prefer to engage a registered agent to act in your behalf, such services can easily be obtained. (See "Registered Agents," later in this chapter.)

A CLOSE CORPORATION

A close corporation is one whose certificate of incorporation contains the basic elements contained in a standard Delaware corporation and provides that:

1. all the corporation's issued stock shall be held by not more than a specified number of persons, not exceeding thirty.
2. all the issued stock shall be subject to one or more restrictions on transfer. The most widely used restriction obligates a shareholder to offer to the corporation or its shareholders a prior opportunity, to be exercised within a reasonable time, to acquire the restricted securities.

Sometimes other restrictions are included in the certificate of incorporation, which:

1. obligate the corporation or any holder of shares of the corporation to purchase the shares that are the subject of an agreement regarding the purchase and sale of the restricted shares;
2. require the corporation or shareholders of the corporation to consent to any proposed transfer of the restricted shares or prohibit the transfer of restricted shares to designated persons or classes of persons, if such designation is not unreasonable;
3. state that any restriction on the transfer of shares of a corporation for the purpose of maintaining its status as an electing small business corporation under subchapter "S" of the Internal Revenue Code is presumed to be for a reasonable purpose; or
4. provide that the business of the corporation shall be managed by the shareholders. No directors need be elected so that no directors' meetings are necessary. This provision has the effect of eliminating the formality of having directors' meetings. Under this feature, the shareholders of the corporation have the powers and responsibilities that directors would normally have.

A close corporation is not permitted to make a public offering of its shares within the meaning of the Securities Act of 1933.

A close corporation is the ideal type of business form if the head of a corporation wishes to limit the number of shareholders and to give himself or herself, or other shareholders, the first opportunity to buy shares from a selling shareholder. This first option to buy shares of stock can be the key to preventing undesirable persons to become shareholders in a corporation.

An existing Delaware corporation can also elect to be a close corporation if two-thirds of the shareholders vote in favor of it. An amendment to this effect is filed with the Secretary of State in Dover, Delaware.

A close corporation can change its status to a regular or "open" corporation by filing a certificate of amendment with the Secretary of State.

On the following pages is a specimen copy and blank certificates that can be completed should a person wish to form a close corporation. It contains the provisions referred to in paragraphs 1, 2 and 6.

As with other Delaware corporations, the certificate of incorporation can be filed using any address initially. It is preferable, however, to have these filed through a registered agent, since a Delaware mailing address is necessary.

REGISTERED AGENTS

Help is available in setting up a new corporation and with all aspects of your existing corporation—through a registered agent. In Delaware, more than 30 companies provide registered agent services to corporations. Some of these companies are listed later in this section. One of the main functions these companies provide is a street address for corporations, which is important, since all corporations formed in Delaware are required to have a mailing address in the state.

Annual fees charged by registered agents for providing a Delaware address range from $75 to $250 per year. One of the largest registered agents (who owns several registered agent companies) charges $150 per year. If a lawyer's services are used, there are additional fees of $300 to $3,000. Registered agents generally charge an additional fee of $60 to $300 for the initial formation of a corporation.

The Company Corporation

One company, The Company Corporation (TCC), charges only $45 per calendar year during the first year for their annual registered agent service. This modest fee is less than that charged by others. This fee increases to $75 for the second year and $99 the third year. (Prices and fees are subject to change without notice.)

No initial fee is charged for the formation of the corporation. No legal fees are necessary, since customers of TCC complete the forms themselves. No counseling service is provided or needed if the forms are completed by the person forming the corporation.

Service is provided in a highly confidential and speedy manner. Upon receipt of your forms, TCC files them with the Secretary of State the same day.

By using the services of TCC, clients can save up to $3,000 for the initial formation of the corporation and up to $250 on an annual basis.

CERTIFICATE OF INCORPORATION

of

_____ABC Corporation_____

A CLOSE CORPORATION

FIRST: The name of this corporation is (Repeat proposed name here) _____

_____ABC Corporation_____

SECOND: Its registered office in the State of Delaware is to be located at _____

__Three Christina Centre, 201 North Walnut Street, City of Wilmington__

County of _____New Castle_____ . The registered agent in charge thereof is:

__The Company Corporation__

_____ address "same as above".

THIRD: The nature of the business and the objects and purposes proposed to be transacted, promoted and carried on, are to engage in any lawful act or activity for which corporations may be organized under the General Corporation Law of Delaware.

FOURTH: The amount of total authorized capital stock of the corporation is divided into:

(# of shares desired) i.e.1500 shares of No-par value (unless desire to establish a par value).

FIFTH: The name and mailing address of the incorporator is:

(Leave blank if using The Company Corporation as agent, otherwise your name and address)

SIXTH: The powers of the incorporator are to terminate upon filing of the Certificate of Incorporation, and the name(s) and mailing address(es) of the persons who are to serve as director(s) until the first annual meeting of stockholders or until their successors are elected are as follows:

John Doe, 1 Main Street, Atlantis, Ca.

SEVENTH: All of the corporation's issued stock, exclusive of treasury shares, shall be held of record by not more than thirty (30) persons.

EIGHTH: All of the issued stock of all classes shall be subject to the following restriction on transfer permitted by Section 202 of the General Corporation Law.

Each stockholder shall offer to the Corporation or to other stockholders of the corporation a thirty (30) day "first refusal" option to purchase his stock should he elect to sell his stock.

NINTH: The corporation shall make no offering of any of its stock of any class which would constitute a "public offering" within the meaning of the United States Securities Act of 1933, as it may be amended from time to time.

TENTH: Directors of the corporation shall not be liable to either the corporation or its stockholders for monetary damages for a breach of fiduciary duties unless the breach involves: (1) a director's duty of loyalty to the corporation or its stockholders; (2) acts or omissions not in good faith or which involve intentional misconduct or a knowing violation of law; (3) liability for unlawful payments of dividends or unlawful stock purchases or redemption by the corporation; or (4) a transaction from which the director derived an improper personal benefit.

I, THE UNDERSIGNED, for the purpose of forming a corporation under the laws of the State of Delaware, do make, file and record this certificate, and do certify that the facts herein stated are true; and I have accordingly hereunto set my hand.

DATED AT:

_____

John Doe

(Signature of person or officer of corporation named in Fifth Article.)

(Leave blank if using The Company Corporation.)

CERTIFICATE OF INCORPORATION
of

_____

A CLOSE CORPORATION

FIRST: The name of this corporation is _____

_____

SECOND: Its registered office in the State of Delaware is to be located at _____

_____

County of _____ . The registered agent in charge thereof is:

_____

_____ address "same as above".

THIRD: The nature of the business and the objects and purposes proposed to be transacted, promoted and carried on, are to engage in any lawful act or activity for which corporations may be organized under the General Corporation Law of Delaware.

FOURTH: The amount of total authorized capital stock of the corporation is divided into:

_____ shares of _____

FIFTH: The name and mailing address of the incorporator is:

SIXTH: The powers of the incorporator are to terminate upon filing of the Certificate of Incorporation, and the name(s) and mailing address(es) of the persons who are to serve as director(s) until the first annual meeting of stockholders or until their successors are elected are as follows:

SEVENTH: All of the corporation's issued stock, exclusive of treasury shares, shall be held of record by not more than thirty (30) persons.

EIGHTH: All of the issued stock of all classes shall be subject to the following restriction on transfer permitted by Section 202 of the General Corporation Law.

Each stockholder shall offer to the Corporation or to other stockholders of the corporation a thirty (30) day "first refusal" option to purchase his stock should he elect to sell his stock.

NINTH: The corporation shall make no offering of any of its stock of any class which would constitute a "public offering" within the meaning of the United States Securities Act of 1933, as it may be amended from time to time.

TENTH: Directors of the corporation shall not be liable to either the corporation or its stockholders for monetary damages for a breach of fiduciary duties unless the breach involves: (1) a director's duty of loyalty to the corporation or its stockholders; (2) acts or omissions not in good faith or which involve intentional misconduct or a knowing violation of law; (3) liability for unlawful payments of dividends or unlawful stock purchases or redemption by the corporation; or (4) a transaction from which the director derived an improper personal benefit.

I, THE UNDERSIGNED, for the purpose of forming a corporation under the laws of the State of Delaware, do make, file and record this certificate, and do certify that the facts herein stated are true; and I have accordingly hereunto set my hand.

DATED AT:

_____

_____

CERTIFICATE OF INCORPORATION
of

_____

A CLOSE CORPORATION

FIRST: The name of this corporation is _____

_____

SECOND: Its registered office in the State of Delaware is to be located at _____

_____

County of _____. The registered agent in charge thereof is:

_____

_____ address "same as above".

THIRD: The nature of the business and the objects and purposes proposed to be transacted, promoted and carried on, are to engage in any lawful act or activity for which corporations may be organized under the General Corporation Law of Delaware.

FOURTH: The amount of total authorized capital stock of the corporation is divided into:

shares of

_____ _____

FIFTH: The name and mailing address of the incorporator is:

SIXTH: The powers of the incorporator are to terminate upon filing of the Certificate of Incorporation, and the name(s) and mailing address(es) of the persons who are to serve as director(s) until the first annual meeting of stockholders or until their successors are elected are as follows:

SEVENTH: All of the corporation's issued stock, exclusive of treasury shares, shall be held of record by not more than thirty (30) persons.

EIGHTH: All of the issued stock of all classes shall be subject to the following restriction on transfer permitted by Section 202 of the General Corporation Law.

Each stockholder shall offer to the Corporation or to other stockholders of the corporation a thirty (30) day "first refusal" option to purchase his stock should he elect to sell his stock.

NINTH: The corporation shall make no offering of any of its stock of any class which would constitute a "public offering" within the meaning of the United States Securities Act of 1933, as it may be amended from time to time.

TENTH: Directors of the corporation shall not be liable to either the corporation or its stockholders for monetary damages for a breach of fiduciary duties unless the breach involves: (1) a director's duty of loyalty to the corporation or its stockholders; (2) acts or omissions not in good faith or which involve intentional misconduct or a knowing violation of law; (3) liability for unlawful payments of dividends or unlawful stock purchases or redemption by the corporation; or (4) a transaction from which the director derived an improper personal benefit.

I, THE UNDERSIGNED, for the purpose of forming a corporation under the laws of the State of Delaware, do make, file and record this certificate, and do certify that the facts herein stated are true; and I have accordingly hereunto set my hand.

DATED AT:

_____

_____

The Company Corporation operates differently than other registered agents. It operates on a volume basis and advertises for its customers on a direct basis. Its fees are substantially less than those of its competitors. All middle fees are eliminated.

The Company Corporation will provide services to customers referred by lawyers but does not require this. All that is required is that the customer complete a certificate of incorporation and signed confidential information form and send it to TCC. The certificate is then forwarded to the appropriate places. TCC handles all the rest.

The Company Corporation provides no legal advice or counseling. Only administerial functions are provided. No review or advice on the form itself can be given; however, if the form is complete (instructions are contained herein), none is necessary. If for any reason the certificate of incorporation is not accepted by the Secretary of State in Dover, Delaware, it is returned without comment by TCC, but with any of the Secretary of State's comments.

In addition to providing a permanent street address in Delaware, TCC, unlike any other registered agent, provides the following services to its customers:

Initial Services

- Acts as registered agent and provides a mailing address in Delaware. The Company Corporation provides a mailing address for the purpose of receiving and forwarding all legal documents, not general mail delivery. General mail forwarding can be arranged for an additional fee.
- Furnishes the incorporator. (Certificate of incorporation can be completed but unsigned if desired.)
- Forwards the certificate of incorporation to the Corporation Department in Dover, Delaware, for filing.
- Files a copy of the certificate of incorporation with the Recorder of Deeds.
- Prepares checks for payment of initial recording fees to the state of Delaware.
- Reserves corporate name and files documents within 24 hours of receipt of a request from a customer.
- Orders printed stock certificates, corporate seal and forms for minutes and bylaws, if the option is desired by the client.
- Supplies the appropriate forms for qualifying the Delaware corporation in any other state in the United States at the nominal handling charge—$.50 each upon request.
- Processes application for federal identification number.
- Processes application for "S" status filings with the IRS.

Continuing Services

- Acts as registered agent and provides a mailing address in Delaware.

- Forwards the corporation's annual report form to the Secretary of State. Once each year the Secretary of State sends an annual report form to the Delaware mailing address of every corporation chartered in the state. TCC will, upon request, handle all paperwork and filing through its Tax-on-Time service, or The Company Corporation forwards this to its customers. It is completed by the customer and sent to the Secretary of State for filing.
- Provides a referral service to competent Delaware lawyers, if legal counseling or advice is requested on any corporate matter. (Since the volume of corporate activity is so great in Delaware, many capable lawyers practice there.)
- Assists in locating facilities for annual meetings if the client wishes to hold them in Delaware.
- Receives legal documents served on the corporation in Delaware, including lawsuits, and forwards these to the business address of the corporation.
- Publishes a periodic newsletter dealing with helpful business ideas that can save money. This newsletter also describes other services that TCC makes available to its customers. Other services through affiliated companies include simplified bookkeeping systems, tax deductible group and individual insurance plans, helpful books and manuals, and patent and trademark searches.

In addition, TCC will furnish upon request the Delaware fee schedule for filing forms with the state. These include, but are not limited to increases of number of shares of stock, new classes of stock, amending certificates of incorporation, dissolutions and so on.

The Company Corporation has been in business for 20 years and has incorporated more than 90,000 firms in all 50 states. In Delaware alone TCC has incorporated approximately one third of all new Delaware corporations. The Company Corporation also can help get your "S" corporation and Federal ID number forms filed.

If you'd like to have TCC set up a corporation for you and get fast one-day service, complete the "Confidential Information Form" at the end of this chapter and mail it to the address listed below. Or if you prefer or have any questions, call the toll free number.

The Company Corporation	No initial fee for filing corporate documents.
Three Christina Centre	No legal fees necessary. Annual fees are:
201 North Walnut Street	$45—first calendar year
Wilmington, DE 19801	$75—second calendar year
(800) 542-2677, Ext. BSC	$99—third year and thereafter annually

Other Registered Agents

A partial list of additional companies in Delaware that are available to provide services to corporations, including acting as registered agent, follows. Most of the companies listed below require that clients be referred to them by lawyers. Their fee schedules vary in the amounts shown below:

Initial fee: $60 to $300 for filing corporate documents
Legal fees: $300 to $3,000
Annual fees: $75 to $250

American Guaranty & Trust
3801 Kennett Pike
Greenville Center
Wilmington, DE 19807

Colonial Charter Company
1102 West Street
Wilmington, DE 19801

Capital Trust Company of Delaware
4305 Lancaster Pike
Wilmington, DE 19805

Delaware Enterprises, Inc.
26 The Green
Dover, DE 19901

Corporate Registry Company
Delaware Trust Building
900 Market Street
Wilmington, DE 19801

Corporation Service Company
1013 Centre Road
Wilmington, DE 19805

Delaware Registration Trust
  Company
913 Market Street, Suite 1001
Wilmington, DE 19801

Delaware Incorporators Trust
  Company
1013 Center Road
Wilmington, DE 19805

Incorporating Services, Ltd.
15 E. North Street
Dover, DE 19901

Incorporators of Delaware
48 The Green
Dover, DE 19901

Corporation Company of Delaware
1105 North Market Street
Wilmington, DE 19899

Corporation Guarantee & Trust Co.
11th Floor Rodney Square North
11th & Market Streets
Wilmington, DE 19801

The Corporation Trust Company
1209 Orange Street
Wilmington, DE 19801

Delaware Charter Company
1105 North Market Street
Wilmington, DE 19899

Delaware Charter Guarantee
  & Trust Company
4305 Lancaster Pike
Wilmington, DE 19805

The Delaware Corporation Agency
300 Market Tower
901 Market Street
Wilmington, DE 19801

The Prentice-Hall Corp. System, Inc.
229 South State Street
Dover, DE 19901

Registrar and Transfer Company
306 South State Street
Dover, DE 19901

United States Corporation Company
229 South State Street
Dover, DE 19901

States Charter Corporation
The Green
Dover, DE 19901

Yacht Registry, Ltd.
2316 Baynard Blvd.
Wilmington, DE 19802

Changing Registered Agents

In order for an existing Delaware corporation to obtain the advantages TCC offers, a simple form is all that is necessary. The total cost to a corporation the first year is $99, the actual filing cost that is paid to the state of Delaware. The fee includes $75 to file the form with the Secretary of State and $24 to the Recorder of Deeds. This is less than existing corporations are charged by their present registered agent each year.

The Company Corporation will provide its registered agent services at no cost during the first calendar year to existing corporations. Thereafter, its annual fee is $99. This is an annual savings of at least $25 and up to $200.

To obtain this low-cost service, write or call TCC for a copy of this form in duplicate. By mailing this form and a completed confidential information form with a check for $99 (payable to The Company Corporation), the certification document will be forwarded to the Secretary of State's office in Dover, Delaware, for filing.

If the corporation has its present office in Kent or Sussex County, prepare an additional copy of the form and add $21 to the amount, making a total of $120.

The
Company
Corporation

CONFIDENTIAL INFORMATION FORM

1. Name of Corporation:_____
   (a) Alternative name if above name is reserved or already being used by another corporation:
   _____

2. Nature of business the company will transact:_____
   _____

3. State of Incorporation:_____

4. Number of shares of common stock (up to 1,500 at lowest cost): [   ]
   (These shares shall be NO-PAR VALUE unless otherwise specified.)

5. Where is the principal office outside of state of incorporation:
   _____

6. Type of corporation (✓ check one) ☐ open ☐ close ☐ non-stock/non-profit

7. Number of Directors: [   ]

8. Date and place of regular meeting of stockholders:_____
   _____

9. Date and place of regular meeting of Directors:_____

10. Name(s) and address(es) of Director(s): (Delaware requires just one who may also be an officer.)

    _____   _____

    _____   _____

    _____   _____

    _____   _____

11. Names of officer(s): (One person may hold all offices in Delaware)

PRESIDENT_____ SECRETARY_____

VICE
PRESIDENT_____ TREASURER_____

12. Any special instructions:_____

13. Please send all correspondence relevant to this corporation to:

Name:_____

Address:_____

City:_____ State:_____ Zip:_____

I certify that neither The Company Corporation nor any of its employees or agents have provided me with any personal counsel or advice.

Signature X_____ Date:_____/_____/_____

Be sure to complete both sides of this form.

CONFIDENTIAL INFORMATION FORM

State Filing Fees ($ 74.00 in Delaware; call us for other states' fees)		$
Registered Agent Fees (first calendar year service $45.00 for Delaware - $100 all other states)		$
Corporate Kit: Check one (✓)		
☐ CUSTOM (Our most popular style)	($ 79.95 + $ 5.00 UPS delivery)	
☐ DELUXE	($ 159.95 + $ 5.00 UPS delivery)	
☐ ECONOMY	($ 49.95 + $ 5.00 UPS delivery)	$
Apply for "S" Corporation Status	($ 35.00)	$
Federal Tax I.D. Number (expedited service, add $ 23.00)	($ 25.00)	$
Standard Forms for Your Corporation's Management	($ 39.95 + $ 2.00 shipping & handling)	$
Complete Book of Corporate Forms	($ 59.95 + $ 5.00 shipping & handling)	$
Tax-On-Time	($ 25.00)	$
TOTAL We'll bill you or refund the difference if under or overpaid.		$

☐ Enclosed is a check drawn on a U.S. bank payable to The Company Corporation
in the amount of $_____

☐ Charge my: ☐ Visa   ☐ MasterCard

Card Number: ▢▢▢▢▢▢▢▢▢▢▢▢▢▢   Exp. Date:_____/_____

Signature X_____

Daytime Telephone:_____

Fax Number:_____

NOTE: For rapid service, enclose a certified check, treasurer's check, money order, or credit card information. Otherwise allow fourteen (14) days for check clearance.

How did you learn of our services?

☐ Advertisement in_____

☐ Book _____

☐ Direct Mail _____

☐ Referred by_____

☐ Other_____

THE COMPANY CORPORATION
Three Christina Centre
201 N. Walnut Street
Wilmington, Delaware 19801
Telephone: (302) 575-0440
Facsimile: (302) 575-1346

Dept. BSC

Protect your corporation's valuable legal status with easy-to-use corporate kit

Contains everything that's needed. Personalized especially for you!

The complete kit includes:

1. Your personalized "Corporate Binder"— to protect your corporate records. Your corporate name will be printed on a gold inset for the spine of this handsome binder.

2. Your personalized corporate seal— can be kept in a pouch inside your binder. Use your corporate seal for completion of legal documents such as, leases and purchase agreements. Your corporate name and year of completion will be permanently etched into the dies which create a raised impression on any paper. (Seal separately is $20 for up to 45 characters.)

3. For your permanent records: minutes & by-laws— Printed on three hole paper for easy recordkeeping. Complete forms included for any corporation, along with instructions.

4. 20 personalized stock certificates— Lithographed with your corporate name on each certificate. Rich background design. Printing also includes number of shares authorized by corporation. (Additional stock certificates can be purchased. Minimum purchase is 20 @ $18.50 total; 21-99 @ $.65 each; over 100 @ $.25 each.)

5. Celluloid tab index separators— make it easy to turn to any section in your binder.

6. Stock/Transfer ledger— to keep an accurate and complete record of your corporate stock including stock transfers.

7. Extra blank pages— for any business purpose. (Additional blanks @$3.00 per 100.)

Your Choice of Three Luxurious Corporate Kits:

Economy Corporate Kit $49.95

This all-in-one kit comes with all the necessities featured above. Excellent quality and at a very modest price. Best value on the market today. Binder and slipcase are covered in durable black vinyl with a satin finish. Your corporate name is imprinted on a gold inset on the binder's spine.

Custom Corporate Kit.................$79.95

With the look and feel of real leather, this handsome binder and matching slipcase are actually made of top-grade vinyl. Luxuriously padded and quality constructed, this kit comes complete with the items featured above. Your own corporate name is imprinted on a gold inset on the spine. Makes a great addition to your organization or office.

Deluxe Corporate Kit...............$149.95

Crafted from the finest quality natural leather, this deluxe edition corporate binder with matching slipcase will become a classic addition to your office, boardroom or library. With your corporate name embossed in the binder in gold, this elegant all-in-one kit comes complete with the items listed above. When nothing but the best will suffice for your new corporation, this genuine leather kit is the choice for you.

Qualifying Your Business

THE BASIC REQUIREMENTS

Corporations that wish to enjoy traditional corporate advantages and the added benefit of single taxation must elect to become "S" corporations. The election itself is available to any "small business corporation" that satisfies the following eligibility requirements, none of which pose a burden for the average businessperson operating a business:

- There must be a corporation.
- The corporation must have no more than 35 shareholders.
- Each shareholder must be a natural person or an estate (certain trusts may be shareholders). There are limits on estates or shareholders, as outlined later in this chapter.
- The corporation may have only one class of stock, although limited exceptions to this requirement exist.
- The corporation must be a small business corporation.

With respect to the "small business corporation" requirement, it should be noted at the outset that this requirement limits neither the volume nor the scope of business that can be conducted. For the most part, it refers to the maximum number of shareholders a corporation can have (35) and the fact that it must be a corporation formed under the laws of one of the United States.

Incorporation

To qualify as an "S" corporation, a business must be incorporated. If your existing or proposed business operates as a sole proprietorship or partnership, it must first be converted to a corporation.

35 or Fewer Shareholders

The "S" corporation law's requirement that single taxation provisions be applicable to small business corporations refers, for the most part, to the number of shareholders the corporation may have. It sets no limits on the corporation's dollar volume of business, nor, for the most part, on the type of business it may conduct.

The law limits to 35 the number of shareholders a corporation may have. In calculating whether a corporation may have more than 35 shareholders, the following guidelines should be observed:

- Husbands and wives are treated as one person, even if they own stock in their own names. For example, if Mr. Smith owns ten shares of an "S" corporation in his name only and Mrs. Smith owns 12 shares in her name only, they will be viewed as one shareholder for "S" corporation purposes.
- Jointly held stock, such as shares owned by John Smith and Mary Jones as joint tenants or tenants in common, is viewed as being owned by one shareholder.
- Shares held in trust by a trustee or custodian for beneficiaries are viewed as being owned by the beneficiaries, not the custodian or trustee. For example, if a parent holds shares as trustee or custodian for each of his or her three children, there are three shareholders for "S" corporation purposes, not one.

In the event shares of an "S" corporation become owned by 36 or more shareholders, the business will lose its "S" corporation status and be treated as a regular "C" corporation, subject to double taxation. Therefore, if an "S" corporation will have more than one shareholder, all shareholders should sign a shareholders' agreement restricting the right of each person to sell his or her shares if the sale would jeopardize the business's "S" corporation status. A form for just this purpose is provided at the end of this chapter.

Qualified Shareholders

Any individual who is a citizen or resident of the United States, as well as estates and certain trusts, may hold shares in an "S" corporation. Shareholders who do not fit into any one of those categories are not qualified to be "S" corporation shareholders; if they obtain shares, the business will lose its "S" corporation status.

Citizens and U.S. Residents. Since an individual is a natural person, both partnerships and corporations are disqualified from owning shares in an "S" corporation, as are aliens visiting this country. Two cautions should be observed with respect to nonresident aliens:

- If shares are jointly held, for example, by spouses, and one spouse is a nonresident alien, the corporation will be viewed as having a disqualified shareholder; "S" corporation status will be denied to this business.
- Only residence in the United States qualifies an alien for shareholder status in an "S" corporation. Residence in a territory or a possession is not sufficient.

Estates. With respect to estates, it should be noted that a corporation will not lose its "S" corporation status if a qualified shareholder dies and his or her shares pass to the decedent's estate. Nor will such an event preclude an existing corporation from switching from regular "C" status to "S" status. Two cautions must be observed with respect to estate.

1. The shares cannot remain in the estate indefinitely. Assuming the decedent's estate is processed in the ordinary time period for processing estates in the local jurisdiction, there should be no problem.
2. Care should be taken to avoid having the shares in the decedent's estate go to a beneficiary not qualified to be an "S" corporation shareholder.

A second type of estate, the estate of a bankrupt, may also be a shareholder in an "S" corporation. If an individual shareholder files for bankruptcy, his or her assets, including shares in the corporation, are placed in the bankrupt's estate. That estate is qualified to be a shareholder in an "S" corporation. As is the case with decedents' estates, care should be taken to avoid having the shares passing to an individual or entity not qualified to be an "S" corporation shareholder.

Trusts. The matter is far more complex when it comes to trusts. Although certain trusts may qualify to become shareholders in an "S" corporation, the applicable rules are complex and highly detailed. In the event that a shareholder in an "S" corporation intends to establish a trust that includes the corporation shares, qualified legal counsel should be obtained.

Because a corporation can lose its "S" corporation status if a shareholder transfers shares to an unqualified recipient, all shareholders should enter into an agreement that would prevent this from happening. The sample shareholders' agreement at the end of this chapter was developed with this concern in mind.

One Class of Stock

An "S" corporation may issue and have outstanding only one class of stock. Essentially, this requirement means that if a corporation is authorized to create more than one class of stock and wishes to qualify as an "S" corporation, it may sell only one class of stock to its shareholders.

To determine whether a corporation has more than one class of stock, one need only ask whether, in the event of a redemption of shares or a liquidation, each shareholder is entitled to receive the same dividend and the same amount for each share he or she holds, at the same time as every other shareholder. If all aspects of each share's economic rights are the same, then the shares are considered to be of the same class.

The mere fact that shares may be differentiated as voting and nonvoting common stock will not cause the IRS to rule that the corporation issues or has outstanding more than one class of stock. Economic rights—dividend and liquidation rights—may not be differentiated.

When Debt May Be Treated as a Second Class of Stock. In a regular "C" corporation, shareholders may lend money to the corporation rather than put all of their investment in stock. Their reasons may be:

- to avoid the double tax by taking interest payments rather than dividend payments (interest is a business expense and is not taxed at the corporate level);
- to minimize the risk in their investment, since they become creditors of the corporation, and, in the event the business fails, they have a better chance to recoup part of their investment; and
- to balance control if one shareholder puts up more money than another but both want an equal number of shares.

Although the first reason does not apply to the "S" corporation, which is not subject to the double tax process imposed on "C" corporation profits, the two other reasons are equally applicable to "S" corporations.

The use of shareholder-provided loans can create a major problem for a regular "C" corporation or an "S" corporation: The IRS may treat the loan as an equity investment, i.e., an investment in shares.

When that happens in the context of a "C" corporation, the interest paid on the loan is treated as a dividend and the double taxation rule is imposed. If a shareholder loan to an "S" corporation is treated as an investment in equity by the IRS, it will be treated as an investment in a different class of stock. The result here is that the corporation will lose its "S" status and will be subject to double taxation on all its profits and gains.

To permit shareholders to lend money to an "S" corporation with a measure of security, the Internal Revenue Code provides a "safe harbor" provision, which, if followed, will ensure that an intended loan will not be treated as a second class of stock. Essentially, the safe harbor rule provides that if the loan from the shareholder is comparable to a loan that would have been offered by a stranger, it will be treated as a loan and not a second class of shares.

To be protected under the safe harbor rule, the shareholder loan must:

- be in writing;
- require the corporation to pay interest at fixed times—for example, monthly, quarterly or annually—and set a rate of interest that is in keeping with current interest rates and which does not depend on the corporation's profits, the corporation's discretion or similar factors;
- oblige the corporation to repay the entire principal amount of the loan; and
- not allow the loan to be convertible to stock at either the borrower's or lender's option.

The safe harbor rules do not present any real problem for a shareholder who seeks to hedge his or her risk by lending money to an "S" corporation. The loan terms required by the rule are exactly those that any creditor would demand before lending money.

Prudent investors will closely follow these safe harbor rules. The IRS can be quick to challenge a shareholder loan to an "S" corporation. If it finds the loan is really an investment in a second class of stock, the results can be disastrous. The actual date of the loan will become the date the second class of stock was created and, therefore, the date on which "S" corporation status ends. That might mean the corporation would owe back taxes as a "C" corporation starting from the date of the loan.

Small Business Corporation

The congressional intent behind limiting "S" incorporation to small business corporations has never really been defined by law. In fact, a definition of that term is available only by determining what kinds of enterprises cannot take advantage of the "S" corporation option.

Initially, it should again be noted that the term *small business corporation* places no restrictions on the dollar volume of business that may be done by the corporation, nor, for the most part, does it restrict the type of business in which an "S" corporation may engage.

The only forms of businesses that may not take advantage of "S" incorporation are:

- financial institutions such as banks, insurance companies, building and loan associations or mutual savings and loan associations;

- foreign corporations. (An "S" corporation must be incorporated under the laws of any state, possession or territory of the United States);
- corporations that operate in possessions of the United States and use the possessions tax credit against their United States income tax;
- domestic international sales corporations (DISCs) or former DISCs; and
- affiliated or subsidiary corporations. This follows from the fact that shareholders of an "S" corporation must be natural persons, estates or certain trusts.

With regard to the last item, a corporation that owns 80 percent or more of all of the stock of another corporation is an ineligible affiliated corporation. If, however, the second corporation has two classes of stock, such as voting and nonvoting common stock, the "S" corporation must own 80 percent or more of each class of stock in order to be disqualified as an affiliated corporation. Thus, if a businessperson wishes to set up a subsidiary for an "S" corporation, there does not appear to be any bar if that person creates one class of stock and transfers 79 percent to the "S" corporation parent and retains 21 percent individually; or creates voting and nonvoting common stock, keeping 21 percent of either class individually while transferring the rest of that class and all the shares of the other class to the "S" corporation.

ADDITIONAL REQUIREMENTS FOR EXISTING CORPORATIONS

Existing regular "C" corporations can elect to become "S" corporations. If such a corporation elects to switch to "S" status, it must satisfy the requirements discussed previously in this chapter as well as two additional requirements.

Prior Elections—The Five-Year Rule

Any regular "C" corporation that had previously been an "S" corporation and revoked or lost its "S" status within the past five years will not be qualified to become an "S" corporation for five years from the last date it was an "S" corporation. This provision exists to deter shareholders from electing "S" status only in those years during which their enterprise will lose money. In a losing year, any losses the regular "C" corporation has are of no benefit to its shareholders. In the past, shareholders would opt to have their corporation taxed as an "S" corporation for a year during which the corporation lost money. The loss, then, would flow to the shareholders, who would use it to offset other income. The next year, when the corporation became profitable, the shareholders would revoke the election, and the corporation would have its profits taxed at the lower corporate rates that existed before the Tax Reform Act of 1986.

Because of this, the IRS will not approve an election to be taxed as an "S" corporation if the shareholders of the corporation revoked or lost their "S" corporation election during the past five years. A possible exception to this rule exists if the corporation's shares (or at least a controlling interest) are held by different shareholders than those who revoked or lost the election to be treated as an "S" corporation.

It should also be kept in mind that this type of switching referred to was prevalent before the enactment of the Tax Reform Act of 1986, which created a higher maximum tax rate for corporate profits than its maximum rate for individual income. This change in tax rates removed the motive for switching out of "S" corporation status when a corporation becomes profitable, since not only will profits be subject to a double tax imposed on "C" corporations, but they will also be taxed at a higher maximum corporate rate.

Planning Note: It should be observed that there is no bar or penalty if shareholders opt to be treated as an "S" corporation during the enterprise's first year (when it is likely to lose money because of start-up costs) and switch to regular "C" status the following year. At most, the shareholders will be barred from making an "S" corporation election for another five years.

Passive Investment Income

If a "C" corporation elects to become an "S" corporation and has no accumulated earnings and profits, it can qualify for "S" status regardless of the type or sources of income the corporation had.

If, on the other hand, the regular "C" corporation does have accumulated earnings and profits when it makes its election for "S" incorporation, its election may not be recognized. Under this rule, if an "S" corporation has accumulated earnings and profits from its "C" corporation operations at the end of the "S" corporation tax year and more than 25 percent of its gross income comes from passive investment income sources (dividends, interest, annuities, rents, royalties and gain from the sale of securities), the election will be lost.

Planning Note: For the passive income rule to apply, the corporation must fall within both sides of the test for three years. In other words, during each of the first three years starting with the election year, the corporation must have accumulated "C" corporation earnings and profits and must have passive investment income that is more than 25 percent of its gross income.

If that does happen, the "S" corporation election is lost in the fourth year—but it remains valid for each of the first three years. What happens if the election is lost in the fourth year? First, the corporation profits will be taxed as if the corporation is a regular "C" corporation. Second, the ability to elect to become an "S" corporation will be lost for five years.

PROTECTING AGAINST LOSS OF ELIGIBILITY

The greatest threat to a corporation's continued eligibility as an "S" corporation stems from the possibility that an existing, qualified shareholder may sell his or her shares to an unqualified shareholder or to more than one person, thereby bringing the total number of shareholders to more than 35 persons. This threat can be effectively and safely eliminated by taking two relatively easy steps: adopting a shareholders' agreement under which each shareholder agrees not to make a transfer that would endanger the "S" status of the corporation and placing notice of the restriction on each share certificate.

The shareholders' agreement should be entered into by the corporation and every shareholder. The corporation should utilize the services of an objective third person, ideally the corporation's lawyer, to determine whether a proposed share transfer would jeopardize the company's "S" corporation standing and whether it should contain penalty provisions that give the agreement "teeth."

A notice of the restriction on share transfer should also be placed on each share certificate in order to warn innocent buyers that the corporation may not be required to issue new shares to them if that would cause the business to lose its "S" corporation status. Without such a warning, an innocent buyer who pays fair value for the shares may be in a position to force the corporation to issue new shares to him or her, even if that would disqualify it from "S" corporation status. Although a state court might order such a buyer to sell his or her share to the "S" corporation or its shareholders, the process can be costly. First, the lawsuit that must be brought to force the sale will be expensive. Second, the buyer must be paid an amount equal to the amount he or she paid for the shares, which may be more than fair market value.

Following is a sample of a shareholders' agreement and a stock certificate with a notice of restriction on share transfer.

SHAREHOLDERS' AGREEMENT

This agreement is made on the 12th day of January, 19   , by and between ABC Products, Inc., a Delaware corporation, and John Smith, Jane Roberts, and Peter Brown, who are all shareholders (Shareholders) of ABC Products, Inc.

In consideration of the facts that (a) The Corporation has elected to be taxed as an "S" corporation as permitted by the Internal Revenue Code of the United States, and that each Shareholder has consented to that election; and (b) the Shareholders believe it is in their mutual interests for The Corporation to continue as an "S" corporation as long as the holders of 51 percent of the outstanding shares of stock agree the corporation shall be an "S" corporation, it is hereby mutually agreed that:

1. Unless the approval of all of the Shareholders is obtained, no Shareholder shall sell, donate, or in any way transfer shares of stock in The Corporation without first obtaining (a) the written opinion of the legal counsel to The Corporation that the transfer will not cause The Corporation to lose its status as an "S" corporation and (b) the transferee's written consent that he or she will be bound by all the terms of this Agreement.

2. No Shareholder shall refuse to provide any consent or other document that may be required by the Internal Revenue Code, any regulations promulgated under the Internal Revenue Code or the Internal Revenue Service that may be as a condition for maintaining The Corporation election to be taxed as an "S" corporation.

3. Any actual or attempted transfer of shares of stock in violation of Paragraph One above will be null, void, and without legal effect.

4. In the event any Shareholder violates or refuses to perform in accordance with the provisions of Paragraphs One and/or Two above, the other Shareholders shall not be limited to seeking money damages, and, in addition to monetary damages, may enforce this Agreement by requesting any form of legal or equitable relief or remedy that requires specific performance from the Shareholder in accordance with this Agreement.

5. In the event that The Corporation loses its "S" corporation status and such loss is attributable in whole or in any part to the failure of one or more Shareholders to act in accordance with the provisions of Paragraphs 1 and/or 2 above, then each Shareholder who failed to comply with the provisions of Paragraphs 1 and/or 2 above shall be jointly and severally liable for all losses incurred by The Corporation and the other Shareholders.

6. Each Shareholder, upon the signing of this agreement, shall return to ABC Products, Inc., all ABC Products, Inc.'s, share certificates he or she may now own and shall receive in substitution therefor a share certificate for the same number of shares. The new certificate shall contain a printed legend stating that the shares represented by the certificate are subject to the restrictions on transfer set out in this Agreement.

7. In the event that the Internal Revenue Code provisions governing "S" corporation status are amended or changed in any way, this Agreement will be modified by the parties to comply with such changes or amendments if advised by legal counsel to The

Corporation that such modification or modifications are necessary in order for the Shareholders to continue to receive the benefits of "S" incorporation status.

8. This agreement shall end upon the happening of any one of the following events:

a. The written agreement of the holders of 51 percent of the outstanding shares of the corporation or

b. The repeal of the Internal Revenue Code provisions allowing for the election of "S" corporation status and the failure of the Internal Revenue Code, or any future law replacing the Internal Revenue Code, to provide a substitute for the single taxation approach to corporate profits and dividends currently provided by the existing "S" corporation provisions of the Internal Revenue Code.

9. This Agreement will be binding upon and exists for the benefit of the parties to this Agreement, and, subject to the restrictions set out in this Agreement, upon their heirs, legatees, distributees, assigns, personal representatives, and successors.

10. This Agreement has been entered into and will be governed by the laws of Delaware.

IN WITNESS WHEREOF, the parties have executed this Agreement on the day, month, and year first mentioned above.

ABC Products, Inc.

By _____
John Smith
President, ABC Products, Inc.

ATTEST:

By: _____
Peter Brown
Secretary, ABC Products, Inc.

WITNESS: SHAREHOLDERS:

_____   _____

_____   _____

_____   _____

SHAREHOLDERS' AGREEMENT

This agreement is made on the   day of   , 19   , by and between   , a   corporation, and   , who are all shareholders (Shareholders) of

In consideration of the facts that (a) The Corporation has elected to be taxed as an "S" corporation as permitted by the Internal Revenue Code of the United States, and that each Shareholder has consented to that election; and (b) the Shareholders believe it is in their mutual interests for The Corporation to continue as an "S" corporation as long as the holders of   percent of the outstanding shares of stock agree the corporation shall be an "S" corporation, it is hereby mutually agreed that:

1. Unless the approval of all of the Shareholders is obtained, no Shareholder shall sell, donate, or in any way transfer shares of stock in The Corporation without first obtaining (a) the written opinion of the legal counsel to The Corporation that the transfer will not cause The Corporation to lose its status as an "S" corporation and (b) the transferee's written consent that he or she will be bound by all the terms of this Agreement.

2. No Shareholder shall refuse to provide any consent or other document that may be required by the Internal Revenue Code, any regulations promulgated under the Internal Revenue Code or the Internal Revenue Service that may be as a condition for maintaining The Corporation election to be taxed as an "S" corporation.

3. Any actual or attempted transfer of shares of stock in violation of Paragraph One above will be null, void, and without legal effect.

4. In the event any Shareholder violates or refuses to perform in accordance with the provisions of Paragraphs One and/or Two above, the other Shareholders shall not be limited to seeking money damages, and, in addition to monetary damages, may enforce this Agreement by requesting any form of legal or equitable relief or remedy that requires specific performance from the Shareholder in accordance with this Agreement.

5. In the event that The Corporation loses its "S" corporation status and such loss is attributable in whole or in any part to the failure of one or more Shareholders to act in accordance with the provisions of Paragraphs 1 and/or 2 above, then each Shareholder who failed to comply with the provisions of Paragraphs 1 and/or 2 above shall be jointly and severally liable for all losses incurred by The Corporation and the other Shareholders.

6. Each Shareholder, upon the signing of this agreement, shall return to   , all   , share certificates he or she may now own and shall receive in substitution therefor a share certificate for the same number of shares. The new certificate shall contain a printed legend stating that the shares represented by the certificate are subject to the restrictions on transfer set out in this Agreement.

7. In the event that the Internal Revenue Code provisions governing "S" corporation status are amended or changed in any way, this Agreement will be modified by the parties to comply with such changes or amendments if advised by legal counsel to The

Corporation that such modification or modifications are necessary in order for the Shareholders to continue to receive the benefits of "S" incorporation status.

8. This agreement shall end upon the happening of any one of the following events:

    a. The written agreement of the holders of   percent of the outstanding shares of the corporation or

    b. The repeal of the Internal Revenue Code provisions allowing for the election of "S" corporation status and the failure of the Internal Revenue Code, or any future law replacing the Internal Revenue Code, to provide a substitute for the single taxation approach to corporate profits and dividends currently provided by the existing "S" corporation provisions of the Internal Revenue Code.

9. This Agreement will be binding upon and exists for the benefit of the parties to this Agreement, and, subject to the restrictions set out in this Agreement, upon their heirs, legatees, distributees, assigns, personal representatives, and successors.

10. This Agreement has been entered into and will be governed by the laws of

IN WITNESS WHEREOF, the parties have executed this Agreement on the day, month, and year first mentioned above.

By_____

ATTEST:

By: _____

WITNESS: SHAREHOLDERS:

_____   _____

_____   _____

_____   _____

NUMBER:

SHARES:

INCORPORATED UNDER THE LAWS OF THE STATE OF DELAWARE

TOTAL AUTHORIZED ISSUE

1,000 SHARES WITHOUT PAR VALUE

This is to Certify that _____ is the owner of

_____ fully paid and non-assessable

shares of the above Corporation transferrable only on the books of the Corporation by the holder
hereof in person or by duly authorized Attorney upon surrender of this Certificate properly endorsed.

Witness, the seal of the Corporation and the signatures of its duly authorized officers.

Dated: _____

_____
Treasurer

_____
President

THE SALE, GIFT, OR ANY OTHER TRANSFER OF THE SHARES REPRESENTED BY THIS CERTIFICATE ARE SUBJECT TO AN AGREEMENT, DATED
_____, 19 _____ . A COPY OF THE AGREEMENT IS ON FILE AND AVAILABLE FOR INSPECTION IN THE PRINCIPAL
OFFICE OF THE CORPORATION.

5

Timing and Mechanics of Filing

The mechanics of making an election are quite simple—in fact, the IRS has already done much of the work for you. The IRS Form 2553, "Election by a Small Business Corporation," contains everything most small businesses need to file their election. The key to a successful filing amounts to no more than filling in the blanks accurately and doing it on time to get the "S" corporation benefits that will save you money. These two requirements should not be taken lightly, however. If the electing corporation does not file on time, or if its filings are inaccurate, the benefits of "S" incorporation will be lost.

This chapter describes the mechanics of filing, the types of information needed and the dates by which a filing must be made, and supplies a blank Form 2553, among other forms—all to make your filing as simple as rolling off a log.

THE DOCUMENTS THAT MUST BE FILED

For most filings, only one document is needed: Form 2553. Available from any IRS office, a copy of the current Form 2553 is included at the end of this chapter and may be used for filing purposes.

To complete Form 2553, the applying corporation must supply the following information:

- The corporation name

- The corporation employer identification number (If yours is a new business and it does not yet have a number, just fill in the words "applied for" and fill out Form SS-4, available from the IRS or use the copy included at the end of this chapter.)
- The address of the corporation
- Whether the corporation has already operated as a regular "C" corporation
- If the filing is made for the corporation's first year of existence, the earliest of the dates the corporation had shareholders, had assets or began doing business
- The principal business and product or service of the corporation (This entry requires you to use the "Codes for Principal Business Activity" contained in IRS Form 1120S; a current copy of the codes is included at the end of this chapter.)
- The number of shares actually held by shareholders at the time of the election filing. (Note: The information sought here relates to the number of shares, not share certificates, held by shareholders. One shareholder, for example, may own ten shares that are represented by one share certificate. In this case, the number to fill in would be ten, not one.)
- The date and state of incorporation
- The corporation tax year (If you want a tax year other than a calendar year, Parts II, III and IV of Form 2553 must be filled out. Noncalendar years will be approved only in limited circumstances.)
- The consent of each shareholder, along with information stating how many shares each person owns, when the shares were acquired and each person's tax year

The completed Form 2553 must be signed by a corporate officer and mailed to the IRS Service Center where the corporation's tax return will be filed. A copy of the addresses of IRS Service Centers is included on the instructions page of Form 2553. A procedure followed by cautious lawyers, and one that you should adopt, involves taking two safeguards whenever you file any form with the IRS by mail. First, send it by certified mail, return receipt requested. The receipt will supply you with proof of timely filing should the question ever arise. Second, enclose a photocopy of the form together with a self-addressed, stamped envelope, and ask to have a stamped copy of the Form 2553 returned to you. This will demonstrate both timeliness and accuracy should the service ever claim you never filed.

> *Caution:* Filing does not occur until Form 2553 is postmarked by the post office. A filing that is even one day late will cause the corporation to lose the benefit of "S" incorporation for a full year. If time has run down to the last day, you may wish to consider hand-delivering your Form 2553 to the IRS rather than taking a chance on a late postmark by the somewhat erratic post office. If you do hand-carry your Form 2553, make sure you take along a photocopy and have it stamped by

the person to whom you submitted the original. Unless you take this precaution, you may run into problems if the IRS should misplace your form and later claim they never received it.

TIMING YOUR FILING

The timing of an "S" corporation election filing is strictly defined by law. If the election is to be effective for the corporation's existing tax year, Form 2553 must be filed no later than the fifteenth day of the third month of the corporation taxable year. Note that the rule refers to months and days. Timing, therefore, works as follows:

- A new corporation, with a taxable year that starts on June 6, 1993, counts two months to August 6, and adds 14 more days (August 6 was two months and one day). It must file on or before August 20, 1993.
- An existing corporation that wishes to switch to "S" corporation status in 1994 can file at anytime during 1993 and no later than March 15, 1994.

   Planning Note: It is vital that you allow yourself enough time to meet the two month and fifteen day time frame. The Internal Revenue Service will not grant an extension of time for filing the election under any circumstances. For example, if a filing is late because the accountant engaged to prepare and file Form 2553 had a heart attack, thereby delaying the filing, it would still be unacceptable to the Internal Revenue Service.

FILING AND ELIGIBILITY

For a filing to be effective, it must be made in a timely fashion, and the corporation must conform to all of the eligibility requirements described in Chapter 4 by the filing date and on every day of the taxable year for which it seeks "S" corporation treatment.

   Example: XYZ, Inc., a "C" corporation, elects to be taxed as an "S" corporation. A calendar year corporation, it files its election on March 1, 1993, in ample time to satisfy the two-month, fifteen-day requirement. Knowing it intended to make this election, XYZ, Inc., redeemed all of its preferred stock on January 1, 1993. It is not eligible for "S" corporation treatment in 1993 and must wait until 1994 to obtain the benefits of single taxation. This results from the fact that it was ineligible to be an "S" corporation in 1993 since it had two classes of stock that year, even though it had two classes for only one day. It should have redeemed its preferred stock on December 31, 1992.

SHAREHOLDER CONSENT

All shareholders must consent to the corporation election to be taxed as an "S" corporation. Equally important, shareholder consents must be filed within the time limits for a filing.

In determining which shareholders should file consents, the following rules apply:

- Every person who owned shares during the taxable year must file a consent—even if the person sold his or her shares before the election was filed.

    Example: John Doe owned three shares of XYZ Corporation, which he sold on January 3. XYZ Corporation files its election on March 1. Mr. Doe must file a consent.

- If shares are held for the benefit of a second person, the beneficiary should file a consent. A beneficial owner of stock is ordinarily held by the courts to be the person who is entitled to the financial benefits (dividends or other distributions) of the shares. A safe course to follow would be to get consents from both the beneficiary and the person who holds the stock for the beneficiary.
- Owners of nonvoting common stock should file consents.
- If stock is held jointly by husbands and wives, or others, each joint owner or tenant in common should file a consent.

    Caution: In community property states, even if shares of stock are listed in the name of only one spouse, both husband and wife should file consents.

- If shares have passed to an estate, it is generally safe to cover all possibilities by obtaining consents from the executor of the estate as well as the beneficiaries or legatees of the stock.

Although they are not available for the filing of the Form 2553 itself, extensions are available for the filing of shareholder consents. If, for example, a former shareholder whose consent is required has left the immediate area, the corporation can obtain an extension of time for the filing of that person's consent. A sample form for this purpose is included at the end of the chapter.

Filing Shareholder Consents

This process involves little if any paperwork for most corporations. Form 2553 has a section in which shareholder consents can be included.

On occasion, however, the Form 2553 consent provision may not be available. Assume, for example, that your corporation has three or four shareholders, two of whom reside in distant communities. It may not be possible for you to mail Form 2553 to different parts of the country and get it back on time to file within the two-month, fifteen-day limit. In such cases, a separate shareholder consent statement can be filed.

A sample copy of a separate statement is included at the end of this chapter.

**Department of the Treasury
Internal Revenue Service**

Instructions for Form 2553
(Revised December 1990)
Election by a Small Business Corporation

(Section references are to the Internal Revenue Code unless otherwise noted.)

Paperwork Reduction Act Notice.—We ask for the information on this form to carry out the Internal Revenue laws of the United States. You are required to give us the information. We need it to ensure that you are complying with these laws and to allow us to figure and collect the right amount of tax.

The time needed to complete and file this form will vary depending on individual circumstances. The estimated average time is:

Recordkeeping . . . . .6 hrs., 28 min.
Learning about the law or the form . . . . .3 hrs., 16 min.
Preparing, copying, assembling, and sending the form to IRS . . . .3 hrs., 31 min.

If you have comments concerning the accuracy of these time estimates or suggestions for making this form more simple, we would be happy to hear from you. You can write to both the **Internal Revenue Service**, Washington, DC 20224, Attention: IRS Reports Clearance Officer, T:FP, and the **Office of Management and Budget,** Paperwork Reduction Project (1545-0146), Washington, DC 20503. **DO NOT** send the tax form to either of these offices. Instead, see the instructions below for information on where to file.

General Instructions

A. Purpose.—To elect to be treated as an "S Corporation," a corporation must file Form 2553. The election permits the income of the S corporation to be taxed to the shareholders of the corporation rather than to the corporation itself, except as provided in Subchapter S of the Code. For more information, see **Publication 589,** Tax Information on S Corporations.

B. Who May Elect.—Your corporation may make the election to be treated as an S corporation only if it meets **all** of the following tests:

1. It is a domestic corporation.

2. It has no more than 35 shareholders. A husband and wife (and their estates) are treated as one shareholder for this requirement. All other persons are treated as separate shareholders.

3. It has only individuals, estates, or certain trusts as shareholders. See the instructions for Part III regarding qualified subchapter S trusts.

4. It has no nonresident alien shareholders.

5. It has only one class of stock. See sections 1361(c)(4) and (5) for additional details.

6. It is not one of the following ineligible corporations:

(a) a corporation that owns 80% or more of the stock of another corporation, unless the other corporation has not begun business and has no gross income;

(b) a bank or thrift institution;

(c) an insurance company subject to tax under the special rules of Subchapter L of the Code;

(d) a corporation that has elected to be treated as a possessions corporation under section 936; or

(e) a domestic international sales corporation (DISC) or former DISC.

See section 1361(b)(2) for details.

7. It has a permitted tax year as required by section 1378 or makes a section 444 election to have a tax year other than a permitted tax year. Section 1378 defines a permitted tax year as a tax year ending December 31, or any other tax year for which the corporation establishes a business purpose to the satisfaction of the IRS. See Part II for details on requesting a fiscal tax year based on a business purpose or on making a section 444 election.

8. Each shareholder consents as explained in the instructions for Column K.

See sections 1361, 1362, and 1378 for additional information on the above tests.

C. Where To File.—File this election with the Internal Revenue Service Center listed below.

If the corporation's principal business, office, or agency is located in ▼	Use the following Internal Revenue Service Center address ▼
New Jersey, New York (New York City and counties of Nassau, Rockland, Suffolk, and Westchester)	Holtsville, NY 00501
New York (all other counties), Connecticut, Maine, Massachusetts, New Hampshire, Rhode Island, Vermont	Andover, MA 05501
Florida, Georgia, South Carolina	Atlanta, GA 39901
Indiana, Kentucky, Michigan, Ohio, West Virginia	Cincinnati, OH 45999
Kansas, New Mexico, Oklahoma, Texas	Austin, TX 73301
Alaska, Arizona, California (counties of Alpine, Amador, Butte, Calaveras, Colusa, Contra Costa, Del Norte, El Dorado, Glenn, Humboldt, Lake, Lassen, Marin, Mendocino, Modoc, Napa, Nevada, Placer, Plumas, Sacramento, San Joaquin, Shasta, Sierra, Siskiyou, Solano, Sonoma, Sutter, Tehama, Trinity, Yolo, and Yuba), Colorado, Idaho, Montana, Nebraska, Nevada, North Dakota, Oregon, South Dakota, Utah, Washington, Wyoming	Ogden, UT 84201
California (all other counties), Hawaii	Fresno, CA 93888
Illinois, Iowa, Minnesota, Missouri, Wisconsin	Kansas City, MO 64999
Alabama, Arkansas, Louisiana, Mississippi, North Carolina, Tennessee	Memphis, TN 37501
Delaware, District of Columbia, Maryland, Pennsylvania, Virginia	Philadelphia, PA 19255

D. When To Make the Election.—Complete Form 2553 and file it either:
(1) at any time during that portion of the first tax year the election is to take effect which occurs before the 16th day of the third month of that tax year (if the tax year has 2½ months or less, and the election is made not later than 2 months and 15 days after the first day of the tax year, it shall be treated as timely made during such year), or
(2) in the tax year before the first tax year it is to take effect. An election made by a small business corporation after the 15th day of the third month but before the end of the tax year is treated as made for the next year. For example, if a calendar year corporation makes the election in April 1991, it is effective for the corporation's 1992 calendar year tax year. See section 1362(b) for more information.

E. Acceptance or Non-Acceptance of Election.—The Service Center will notify you if your election is accepted and when it will take effect. You will also be notified if your election is not accepted. You should generally receive a determination on your election within 60 days after you have filed Form 2553. If the Q1 box in Part II is checked on page 2, the corporation will receive a ruling letter from IRS in Washington, DC, which approves or denies the selected tax year. When Item Q1 is checked, it will generally take an additional 90 days for the Form 2553 to be accepted.

Do not file Form 1120S until you are notified that your election is accepted. If you are now required to file **Form 1120,** U.S. Corporation Income Tax Return, or any other applicable tax return, continue filing it until your election takes effect.

Care should be exercised to ensure that the election is received by the Internal Revenue Service. If you are not notified of acceptance or nonacceptance of your election within 3 months of date of filing (date mailed), or within 6 months if Part II, Item Q1, is checked, you should take follow-up action by corresponding with the Service Center where the election was filed. If filing of Form 2553 is questioned by IRS, an acceptable proof of filing is: (1) certified receipt (timely filed); (2) Form 2553 with accepted stamp; (3) Form 2553 with stamped IRS received date; or (4) IRS letter stating that Form 2553 had been accepted.

F. End of Election.—Once the election is made, it stays in effect for all years until it is terminated. During the 5 years after the election is terminated under section 1362(d), the corporation can make another election on Form 2553 only with IRS consent.

Specific Instructions
Part I

Part I must be completed by all corporations.

Name and Address of Corporation.— Enter the true corporate name as set forth in the corporate charter or other legal document creating it. If the corporation's mailing address is the same as someone else's, such as a shareholder's, please enter this person's name below the name of the corporation. Include the suite, room, or other unit number after the street address. If the Post Office does not deliver to the street address and the corporation has a P.O. box, show the P.O. box number instead of the street address. If the corporation has changed its name or address since applying for its EIN (filing Form SS-4), be sure to check the box in item F of Part I.

A. Employer Identification Number.— If you have applied for an employer identification number (EIN) but have not received it, enter "applied for." If the corporation does not have an EIN, you should apply for one on **Form SS-4,** Application for Employer Identification Number, available from most IRS and Social Security Administration offices.

C. Effective Date of Election.— Enter the beginning effective date (month, day, year) of the tax year that you have requested for the S corporation. Generally, this will be the beginning date of the tax year for which the ending effective date is required to be shown in item I, Part I. For a new corporation (first year the corporation exists) it will generally be the date required to be shown in item H, Part I. The tax year of a new corporation starts on the date that it has shareholders, acquires assets, or begins doing business, whichever happens first. If the effective date for item C for a newly formed corporation is later than the date in item H, the corporation should file Form 1120 or Form 1120-A, for the tax period between these dates.

Column K. Shareholders' Consent Statement.— Each shareholder who owns (or is deemed to own) stock at the time the election is made must consent to the election. If the election is made during the corporation's first tax year for which it is effective, any person who held stock at any time during the portion of that year which occurs before the time the election is made, must consent to the election although the person may have sold or transferred his or her stock before the election is made. Each shareholder consents by signing and dating in column K or signing and dating a separate consent statement described below. If stock is owned by a trust that is a qualified shareholder, the deemed owner of the trust must consent. See section 1361(c)(2) for details regarding qualified trusts that may be shareholders and rules on determining who is the deemed owner of the trust.

An election made during the first 2½ months of the tax year is considered made for the following tax year if one or more of the persons who held stock in the corporation during such tax year and before the election was made did not consent to the election. See section 1362(b)(2).

If a husband and wife have a community interest in the stock or in the income from it, both must consent. Each tenant in common, joint tenant, and tenant by the entirety also must consent.

A minor's consent is made by the minor or the legal representative of the minor, or by a natural or adoptive parent of the minor if no legal representative has been appointed. The consent of an estate is made by an executor or administrator.

Continuation sheet or separate consent statement.— If you need a continuation sheet or use a separate consent statement, attach it to Form 2553. The separate consent statement must contain the name, address, and employer identification number of the corporation and the shareholder information requested in columns J through N of Part I.

If you want, you may combine all the shareholders' consents in one statement.

Column L.— Enter the number of shares of stock each shareholder owns and the dates the stock was acquired. If the election is made during the corporation's first tax year for which it is effective, do not list the shares of stock for those shareholders who sold or transferred all of their stock before the election was made. However, these shareholders must still consent to the election for it to be effective for the tax year.

Column M.— Enter the social security number of each shareholder who is an individual. Enter the employer identification number of each shareholder that is an estate or a qualified trust.

Column N.— Enter the month and day that each shareholder's tax year ends. If a shareholder is changing his or her tax year, enter the tax year the shareholder is changing to, and attach an explanation indicating the present tax year and the basis for the change (e.g., automatic revenue procedure or letter ruling request).

If the election is made during the corporation's first tax year for which it is effective, you do not have to enter the tax year of any shareholder who sold or transferred all of his or her stock before the election was made.

Signature.— Form 2553 must be signed by the president, treasurer, assistant treasurer, chief accounting officer, or other corporate officer (such as tax officer) authorized to sign.

Part II

Complete Part II if you selected a tax year ending on any date other than December 31 (other than a 52-53-week tax year ending with reference to the month of December).

Box P1.— Attach a statement showing separately for each month the amount of gross receipts for the most recent 47 months as required by section 4.03(3) of

Revenue Procedure 87-32, 1987-2 C.B. 396. A corporation that does not have a 47-month period of gross receipts cannot establish a natural business year under section 4.01(1).

Box Q1.— For examples of an acceptable business purpose for requesting a fiscal tax year, see Revenue Ruling 87-57, 1987-2 C.B. 117.

In addition to a statement showing the business purpose for the requested fiscal year, you must attach the other information necessary to meet the ruling request requirements of Revenue Procedure 90-1, 1990-1 C.B. 356 (updated annually). Also attach a statement that shows separately the amount of gross receipts from sales or services (and inventory costs, if applicable) for each of the 36 months preceding the effective date of the election to be an S corporation. If the corporation has been in existence for fewer than 36 months, submit figures for the period of existence.

If you check box Q1, you must also pay a user fee of $200 (subject to change). Do not pay the fee when filing Form 2553. The Service Center will send Form 2553 to the IRS in Washington, DC, who, in turn, will notify the corporation that the fee is due. See Revenue Procedure 90-17, 1990-1 C.B. 479.

Box Q2.— If the corporation makes a back-up section 444 election for which it is qualified, then the election must be exercised in the event the business purpose request is not approved. Under certain circumstances, the tax year requested under the back-up section 444 election may be different than the tax year requested under business purpose. See **Form 8716,** Election To Have a Tax Year Other Than a Required Tax Year, for details on making a back-up section 444 election.

Boxes Q2 and R2.— If the corporation is not qualified to make the section 444 election after making the item Q2 back-up section 444 election or indicating its intention to make the election in item R1, and therefore it later files a calendar year return, it should write "Section 444 Election Not Made" in the top left corner of the 1st calendar year Form 1120S it files.

Part III

Certain Qualified Subchapter S Trusts (QSSTs) may make the QSST election required by section 1361(d)(2) in Part III. Part III may be used to make the QSST election only if corporate stock has been transferred to the trust on or before the date on which the corporation makes its election to be an S corporation. However, a statement can be used in lieu of Part III to make the election.

Note: Part III may be used only in conjunction with making the Part I election (i.e., Form 2553 cannot be filed with only Part III completed).

The deemed owner of the QSST must also consent to the S corporation election in column K, page 1, of Form 2553. See section 1361(c)(2).

*U.S. Government Printing Office: 1992 — 619-071/40536

Form 2553
(Rev. December 1990)

Department of the Treasury
Internal Revenue Service

Election by a Small Business Corporation
(Under section 1362 of the Internal Revenue Code)
▶ **For Paperwork Reduction Act Notice, see page 1 of Instructions.**
▶ **See separate Instructions.**

OMB No. 1545-0146
Expires 11-30-93

Notes: 1. *This election, to be treated as an "S corporation," can be accepted only if all the tests in General Instruction B are met; all signatures in Parts I and III are originals (no photocopies); and the exact name and address of the corporation and other required form information are provided.*

2. *Do not file Form 1120S until you are notified that your election is accepted. See General Instruction E.*

Part I   Election Information

Name of corporation (see instructions)	A Employer identification number (see instructions)

Number, street, and room or suite no. (If a P.O. box, see instructions.)	B Name and telephone number (including area code) of corporate officer or legal representative who may be called for information

City or town, state, and ZIP code	C Election is to be effective for tax year beginning (month, day, year)

D Is the corporation the outgrowth or continuation of any form of predecessor? . . ☐ Yes ☐ No

If "Yes," state name of predecessor, type of organization, and period of its existence ▶ ....

E Date of incorporation

F Check here ▶ ☐ if the corporation has changed its name or address since applying for the employer identification number shown in item A above.

G State of incorporation

H If this election takes effect for the first tax year the corporation exists, enter month, day, and year of the **earliest** of the following: (1) date the corporation first had shareholders, (2) date the corporation first had assets, or (3) date the corporation began doing business. ▶

I Selected tax year: Annual return will be filed for tax year ending (month and day) ▶ ....

If the tax year ends on any date other than December 31, except for an automatic 52-53-week tax year ending with reference to the month of December, you **must** complete Part II on the back. If the date you enter is the ending date of an automatic 52-53-week tax year, write "52-53-week year" to the right of the date. See Temporary Regulations section 1.441-2T(e)(3).

J Name of each shareholder, person having a community property interest in the corporation's stock, and each tenant in common, joint tenant, and tenant by the entirety. (A husband and wife (and their estates) are counted as one shareholder in determining the number of shareholders without regard to the manner in which the stock is owned.)	K Shareholders' Consent Statement. We, the undersigned shareholders, consent to the corporation's election to be treated as an "S corporation" under section 1362(a). (Shareholders sign and date below.)*		L Stock owned		M Social security number or employer identification number (see instructions)	N Share-holder's tax year ends (month and day)
	Signature	Date	Number of shares	Dates acquired		

*For this election to be valid, the consent of each shareholder, person having a community property interest in the corporation's stock, and each tenant in common, joint tenant, and tenant by the entirety must either appear above or be attached to this form. (See instructions for Column K if continuation sheet or a separate consent statement is needed.)

Under penalties of perjury, I declare that I have examined this election, including accompanying schedules and statements, and to the best of my knowledge and belief, it is true, correct, and complete.

Signature of officer ▶   Title ▶   Date ▶

See Parts II and III on back.   Form **2553** (Rev. 12-90)

Part II **Selection of Fiscal Tax Year (All corporations using this Part must complete item O and one of items P, Q, or R.)**

O Check the applicable box below to indicate whether the corporation is:

   1. ☐ A new corporation adopting the tax year entered in item I, Part I.

   2. ☐ An existing corporation retaining the tax year entered in item I, Part I.

   3. ☐ An existing corporation changing to the tax year entered in item I, Part I.

P Complete item P if the corporation is using the expeditious approval provisions of Revenue Procedure 87-32, 1987-2 C.B. 396, to request: **(1)** a natural business year (as defined in section 4.01(1) of Rev. Proc. 87-32), or **(2)** a year that satisfies the ownership tax year test in section 4.01(2) of Rev. Proc. 87-32. Check the applicable box below to indicate the representation statement the corporation is making as required under section 4 of Rev. Proc. 87-32.

   1. Natural Business Year ▶ ☐ I represent that the corporation is retaining or changing to a tax year that coincides with its natural business year as defined in section 4.01(1) of Rev. Proc. 87-32 and as verified by its satisfaction of the requirements of section 4.02(1) of Rev. Proc. 87-32. In addition, if the corporation is changing to a natural business year as defined in section 4.01(1), I further represent that such tax year results in less deferral of income to the owners than the corporation's present tax year. I also represent that the corporation is not described in section 3.01(2) of Rev. Proc. 87-32. (See instructions for additional information that must be attached.)

   2. Ownership Tax Year ▶ ☐ I represent that shareholders holding more than half of the shares of the stock (as of the first day of the tax year to which the request relates) of the corporation have the same tax year or are concurrently changing to the tax year that the corporation adopts, retains, or changes to per item I, Part I. I also represent that the corporation is not described in section 3.01(2) of Rev. Proc. 87-32.

Note: *If you do not use item P and the corporation wants a fiscal tax year, complete either item Q or R below. Item Q is used to request a fiscal tax year based on a business purpose and to make a back-up section 444 election. Item R is used to make a regular section 444 election.*

Q Business Purpose—To request a fiscal tax year based on a business purpose, you must check box Q1 and pay a user fee. See instructions for details. You may also check box Q2 and/or box Q3.

   1. Check here ▶ ☐ if the fiscal year entered in item I, Part I, is requested under the provisions of section 6.03 of Rev. Proc. 87-32. Attach to Form 2553 a statement showing the business purpose for the requested fiscal year. See instructions for additional information that must be attached.

   2. Check here ▶ ☐ to show that the corporation intends to make a back-up section 444 election in the event the corporation's business purpose request is not approved by the IRS. (See instructions for more information.)

   3. Check here ▶ ☐ to show that the corporation agrees to adopt or change to a tax year ending December 31 if necessary for the IRS to accept this election for S corporation status in the event: (1) the corporation's business purpose request is not approved and the corporation makes a back-up section 444 election, but is ultimately not qualified to make a section 444 election, or (2) the corporation's business purpose request is not approved and the corporation did not make a back-up section 444 election.

R Section 444 Election—To make a section 444 election, you must check box R1 and you may also check box R2.

   1. Check here ▶ ☐ to show the corporation will make, if qualified, a section 444 election to have the fiscal tax year shown in item I, Part I. To make the election, you must complete **Form 8716**, Election To Have a Tax Year Other Than a Required Tax Year, and either attach it to Form 2553 or file it separately.

   2. Check here ▶ ☐ to show that the corporation agrees to adopt or change to a tax year ending December 31 if necessary for the IRS to accept this election for S corporation status in the event the corporation is ultimately not qualified to make a section 444 election.

Part III **Qualified Subchapter S Trust (QSST) Election Under Section 1361(d)(2)** **

Income beneficiary's name and address	Social security number
Trust's name and address	Employer identification number

Date on which stock of the corporation was transferred to the trust (month, day, year) ▶

In order for the trust named above to be a QSST and thus a qualifying shareholder of the S corporation for which this Form 2553 is filed, I hereby make the election under section 1361(d)(2). Under penalties of perjury, I certify that the trust meets the definition requirements of section 1361(d)(3) and that all other information provided in Part III is true, correct, and complete.

_____   _____
Signature of income beneficiary or signature and title of legal representative or other qualified person making the election   Date

**Use of Part III to make the QSST election may be made only if stock of the corporation has been transferred to the trust on or before the date on which the corporation makes its election to be an S corporation. The QSST election must be made and filed separately if stock of the corporation is transferred to the trust after the date on which the corporation makes the S election.

Form SS-4
(Rev. April 1991)
Department of the Treasury
Internal Revenue Service

Application for Employer Identification Number

(For use by employers and others. Please read the attached instructions before completing this form.)

EIN

OMB No. 1545-0003
Expires 4-30-94

Please type or print clearly.

1 Name of applicant (True legal name) (See instructions.)

2 Trade name of business, if different from name in line 1

3 Executor, trustee, "care of" name

4a Mailing address (street address) (room, apt., or suite no.)

5a Address of business (See instructions.)

4b City, state, and ZIP code

5b City, state, and ZIP code

6 County and state where principal business is located

7 Name of principal officer, grantor, or general partner (See instructions.) ▶

8a Type of entity (Check only one box.) (See instructions.)
- ☐ Individual SSN _____
- ☐ REMIC
- ☐ Personal service corp.
- ☐ State/local government
- ☐ National guard
- ☐ Other nonprofit organization (specify) _____
- ☐ Other (specify) ▶ _____
- ☐ Estate
- ☐ Plan administrator SSN _____
- ☐ Other corporation (specify) _____
- ☐ Federal government/military
- ☐ Trust
- ☐ Partnership
- ☐ Farmers' cooperative
- ☐ Church or church controlled organization

If nonprofit organization enter GEN (if applicable) _____

8b If a corporation, give name of foreign country (if applicable) or state in the U.S. where incorporated ▶

Foreign country

State

9 Reason for applying (Check only one box.)
- ☐ Started new business
- ☐ Hired employees
- ☐ Created a pension plan (specify type) ▶ _____
- ☐ Banking purpose (specify) ▶ _____
- ☐ Changed type of organization (specify) ▶ _____
- ☐ Purchased going business
- ☐ Created a trust (specify) ▶ _____
- ☐ Other (specify) ▶ _____

10 Date business started or acquired (Mo., day, year) (See instructions.)

11 Enter closing month of accounting year. (See instructions.)

12 First date wages or annuities were paid or will be paid (Mo., day, year). **Note:** *If applicant is a withholding agent, enter date income will first be paid to nonresident alien. (Mo., day, year)* . . . . ▶

13 Enter highest number of employees expected in the next 12 months. **Note:** *If the applicant does not expect to have any employees during the period, enter "0."* . . . . ▶

Nonagricultural	Agricultural	Household

14 Principal activity (See instructions.) ▶

15 Is the principal business activity manufacturing? . . . . ☐ Yes ☐ No
If "Yes," principal product and raw material used ▶

16 To whom are most of the products or services sold? Please check the appropriate box. ☐ Business (wholesale)
☐ Public (retail) ☐ Other (specify) ▶ ☐ N/A

17a Has the applicant ever applied for an identification number for this or any other business? . . . . ☐ Yes ☐ No
Note: *If "Yes," please complete lines 17b and 17c.*

17b If you checked the "Yes" box in line 17a, give applicant's true name and trade name, if different than name shown on prior application.

True name ▶

Trade name ▶

17c Enter approximate date, city, and state where the application was filed and the previous employer identification number if known.

Approximate date when filed (Mo., day, year) | City and state where filed | Previous EIN

Under penalties of perjury, I declare that I have examined this application, and to the best of my knowledge and belief, it is true, correct, and complete | Telephone number (include area code)

Name and title (Please type or print clearly.) ▶

Signature ▶

Date ▶

Note: *Do not write below this line.* For official use only.

Please leave blank ▶	Geo.	Ind.	Class	Size	Reason for applying

For Paperwork Reduction Act Notice, see attached instructions.

Cat. No. 16055N

Form **SS-4** (Rev. 4-91)

Codes for Principal Business Activity

These codes for the Principal Business Activity are designed to classify enterprises by the type of activity in which they are engaged to facilitate the administration of the Internal Revenue Code. Though similar in format and structure to the Standard Industrial Classification (SIC) codes, they should not be used as SIC codes.

Using the list below, enter on page 1, under B, the code number for the specific industry group from which the largest percentage of "total receipts" is derived. "Total receipts" means the total of: gross receipts on line 1a, page 1; all other income on lines 4 and 5, page 1; all income on lines 2, 19, and 20a of Form 8825; and income (receipts only) on lines 3a and 4a through 4f of Schedule K.

On page 2, Schedule B, line 2, state the principal business activity and principal product or service that account for the largest percentage of total receipts. For example, if the principal business activity is "Grain mill products," the principal product or service may be "Cereal preparations."

If, as its principal business activity, the corporation: (1) purchases raw materials, (2) subcontracts out for labor to make a finished product from the raw materials, and (3) retains title to the goods, the corporation is considered to be a manufacturer and must enter one of the codes (2010–3998) under "Manufacturing."

Agriculture, Forestry, and Fishing
Code
- 0400 Agricultural production.
- 0600 Agricultural services (except veterinarians), forestry, fishing, hunting, and trapping.

Mining
Metal mining:
- 1010 Iron ores.
- 1070 Copper, lead and zinc, gold and silver ores.
- 1098 Other metal mining.
- 1150 Coal mining.

Oil and gas extraction:
- 1330 Crude petroleum, natural gas, and natural gas liquids.
- 1380 Oil and gas field services.

Nonmetallic minerals, except fuels:
- 1430 Dimension, crushed and broken stone; sand and gravel.
- 1498 Other nonmetallic minerals, except fuels.

Construction
General building contractors and operative builders:
- 1510 General building contractors.
- 1531 Operative builders.

- 1600 Heavy construction contractors.

Special trade contractors:
- 1711 Plumbing, heating, and air conditioning.
- 1731 Electrical work.
- 1798 Other special trade contractors.

Manufacturing
Food and kindred products:
- 2010 Meat products.
- 2020 Dairy products.
- 2030 Preserved fruits and vegetables.
- 2040 Grain mill products.
- 2050 Bakery products.
- 2060 Sugar and confectionery products.
- 2081 Malt liquors and malt.
- 2088 Alcoholic beverages, except malt liquors and malt.
- 2089 Bottled soft drinks, and flavorings.
- 2096 Other food and kindred products.

- 2100 Tobacco manufacturers.

Textile mill products:
- 2228 Weaving mills and textile finishing.
- 2250 Knitting mills.
- 2298 Other textile mill products.

Apparel and other textile products:
- 2315 Men's and boys' clothing.
- 2345 Women's and children's clothing.
- 2388 Other apparel and accessories.
- 2390 Miscellaneous fabricated textile products.

Lumber and wood products:
- 2415 Logging, sawmills, and planing mills.
- 2430 Millwork, plywood, and related products.
- 2498 Other wood products, including wood buildings and mobile homes.

- 2500 Furniture and fixtures.

Paper and allied products:
- 2625 Pulp, paper, and board mills.
- 2699 Other paper products.

Printing and publishing:
- 2710 Newspapers.
- 2720 Periodicals.
- 2735 Books, greeting cards, and miscellaneous publishing.
- 2799 Commercial and other printing, and printing trade services.

Code
Chemicals and allied products:
- 2815 Industrial chemicals, plastics materials and synthetics.
- 2830 Drugs.
- 2840 Soap, cleaners, and toilet goods.
- 2850 Paints and allied products.
- 2898 Agricultural and other chemical products.

Petroleum refining and related industries (including those integrated with extraction):
- 2910 Petroleum refining (including integrated).
- 2998 Other petroleum and coal products.

Rubber and misc. plastics products:
- 3050 Rubber products: plastics footwear, hose, and belting.
- 3070 Misc. plastics products.

Leather and leather products:
- 3140 Footwear, except rubber.
- 3198 Other leather and leather products.

Stone, clay, and glass products:
- 3225 Glass products.
- 3240 Cement, hydraulic.
- 3270 Concrete, gypsum, and plaster products.
- 3298 Other nonmetallic mineral products.

Primary metal industries:
- 3370 Ferrous metal industries; misc. primary metal products.
- 3380 Nonferrous metal industries.

Fabricated metal products:
- 3410 Metal cans and shipping containers.
- 3428 Cutlery, hand tools, and hardware; screw machine products, bolts, and similar products.
- 3430 Plumbing and heating, except electric and warm air.
- 3440 Fabricated structural metal products.
- 3460 Metal forgings and stampings.
- 3470 Coating, engraving, and allied services.
- 3480 Ordnance and accessories, except vehicles and guided missiles.
- 3490 Misc. fabricated metal products.

Machinery, except electrical:
- 3520 Farm machinery.
- 3530 Construction and related machinery.
- 3540 Metalworking machinery.
- 3550 Special industry machinery.
- 3560 General industrial machinery.
- 3570 Office, computing, and accounting machines.
- 3598 Other machinery except electrical.

Electrical and electronic equipment:
- 3630 Household appliances.
- 3665 Radio, television, and communications equipment.
- 3670 Electronic components and accessories.
- 3698 Other electrical equipment.

- 3710 Motor vehicles and equipment.

Transportation equipment, except motor vehicles:
- 3725 Aircraft, guided missiles and parts.
- 3730 Ship and boat building and repairing.
- 3798 Other transportation equipment, except motor vehicles.

Instruments and related products:
- 3815 Scientific instruments and measuring devices; watches and clocks.
- 3845 Optical, medical, and ophthalmic goods.
- 3860 Photographic equipment and supplies.

- 3998 Other manufacturing products.

Transportation and Public Utilities
Code
Transportation:
- 4000 Railroad transportation.
- 4100 Local and interurban passenger transit.
- 4200 Trucking and warehousing.
- 4400 Water transportation.
- 4500 Transportation by air.
- 4600 Pipe lines, except natural gas.
- 4700 Miscellaneous transportation services.

Communication:
- 4825 Telephone, telegraph, and other communication services.
- 4830 Radio and television broadcasting.

Electric, gas, and sanitary services:
- 4910 Electric services.
- 4920 Gas production and distribution.
- 4930 Combination utility services.
- 4990 Water supply and other sanitary services.

Wholesale Trade
Durable:
- 5008 Machinery, equipment, and supplies.
- 5010 Motor vehicles and automotive equipment.
- 5020 Furniture and home furnishings.
- 5030 Lumber and construction materials.
- 5040 Sporting, recreational, photographic, and hobby goods, toys and supplies.
- 5050 Metals and minerals, except petroleum and scrap.
- 5060 Electrical goods.
- 5070 Hardware, plumbing and heating equipment and supplies.
- 5098 Other durable goods.

Nondurable:
- 5110 Paper and paper products.
- 5129 Drugs, drug proprietaries, and druggists' sundries.
- 5130 Apparel, piece goods, and notions.
- 5140 Groceries and related products.
- 5150 Farm-product raw materials.
- 5160 Chemicals and allied products.
- 5170 Petroleum and petroleum products.
- 5180 Alcoholic beverages.
- 5190 Misc. nondurable goods.

Retail Trade
Building materials, garden supplies, and mobile home dealers:
- 5220 Building materials dealers.
- 5251 Hardware stores.
- 5265 Garden supplies and mobile home dealers.

- 5300 General merchandise stores.

Food stores:
- 5410 Grocery stores.
- 5490 Other food stores.

Automotive dealers and service stations:
- 5515 Motor vehicle dealers.
- 5541 Gasoline service stations.
- 5598 Other automotive dealers.

- 5600 Apparel and accessory stores.
- 5700 Furniture and home furnishings stores.
- 5800 Eating and drinking places.

Misc. retail stores:
- 5912 Drug stores and proprietary stores.
- 5921 Liquor stores.
- 5995 Other retail stores.

Finance, Insurance, and Real Estate
Code
Banking:
- 6030 Mutual savings banks.
- 6060 Bank holding companies.
- 6090 Banks, except mutual savings banks and bank holding companies.

Credit agencies other than banks:
- 6120 Savings and loan associations.
- 6140 Personal credit institutions.
- 6150 Business credit institutions.
- 6199 Other credit agencies.

Security, commodity brokers and services:
- 6210 Security brokers, dealers, and flotation companies.
- 6299 Commodity contracts brokers and dealers; security and commodity exchanges; and allied services.

Insurance:
- 6355 Life insurance.
- 6356 Mutual insurance, except life or marine and certain fire or flood insurance companies.
- 6359 Other insurance companies.
- 6411 Insurance agents, brokers, and service.

Real estate:
- 6511 Real estate operators and lessors of buildings.
- 6516 Lessors of mining, oil, and similar property.
- 6518 Lessors of railroad property and other real property.
- 6530 Condominium management and cooperative housing associations.
- 6550 Subdividers and developers.
- 6599 Other real estate.

Holding and other investment companies, except bank holding companies:
- 6744 Small business investment companies.
- 6749 Other holding and investment companies, except bank holding companies.

Services
- 7000 Hotels and other lodging places.
- 7200 Personal services.

Business services:
- 7310 Advertising.
- 7389 Business services, except advertising.

Auto repair; miscellaneous repair services:
- 7500 Auto repair and services.
- 7600 Misc. repair services.

Amusement and recreation services:
- 7812 Motion picture production, distribution, and services.
- 7830 Motion picture theaters.
- 7900 Amusement and recreation services, except motion pictures.

Other services:
- 8015 Offices of physicians, including osteopathic physicians.
- 8021 Offices of dentists.
- 8040 Offices of other health practitioners.
- 8050 Nursing and personal care facilities.
- 8060 Hospitals.
- 8071 Medical laboratories.
- 8099 Other medical services.
- 8111 Legal services.
- 8200 Educational services.
- 8300 Social services.
- 8600 Membership organizations.
- 8911 Architectural and engineering services.
- 8930 Accounting, auditing, and bookkeeping.
- 8980 Miscellaneous services (including veterinarians).

☆ U.S. Government Printing Office: 1991-285-274

SHAREHOLDERS' CONSENT

March 1, 19

Director
Internal Revenue Service Center
100 Main Street
Anytown, USA 10000

Dear sir:

I, Robert Jones, by means of this letter, state my consent to have the Ace Corporation, a Delaware corporation with offices at 123 High Street, Wilmington, DE 10000, treated as "S" corporation under Section 1362(a) of the Internal Revenue Code. In accordance with the information requested by Form 2553, I offer the following data:

1. My name is Robert Jones.

2. I own ten shares of stock of the Ace Corporation.

3. I acquired that stock on May 1, 19   .

4. My Social Security number is: 999-99-999

5. My tax year ends on December 31.

Robert Jones
Date: March 1, 19

Director
Internal Revenue Service Center

Dear   :

       I,   , by means of this letter, state my consent to have the
                    , a   corporation with offices at
          , treated as "S" corporation under Section 1362(a) of the Internal
Revenue Code. In accordance with the information requested by Form 2553, I offer the
following data:

    1. My name is

    2. I own   shares of stock of the

    3. I acquired that stock on

    4. My Social Security number is:

    5. My tax year ends on

                                        _____

                                        Date:

REQUEST FOR EXTENSION TO FILE
SHAREHOLDERS' CONSENT

March 14, 19

Director
Internal Revenue Service Center
100 Main Street
Anytown, USA   10000

Dear sir:

By means of this letter, the Ace Corporation (hereinafter, "The Corporation") requests an extension of the time for the filing of shareholder consents with respect to The Corporation's election to be subject to the "S" incorporation provisions of the Internal Revenue Code. In support of this request, the following information is provided:

1. The Corporation was incorporated under the laws of the State of Delaware on January 2, 19   .

2. The Corporation first had assets* on January 2, 19   .

3. All of the shareholders' consents to The Corporation election to be taxed under the "S" incorporation provisions of the Internal Revenue Code have not and could not be filed on Form 2553, which is being filed with this letter, for the following reason:

John Doe, the holder of 10 shares out of 100 issued and outstanding, after agreeing to sign a consent, transferred his shares to Robert Greene on January 10, 19   . Mr. Greene has signed the consent. Mr. Doe, believing his signature would not be needed, has embarked on a two-month vacation.

4. Other than John Doe, all other shareholders have consented to the election, and each of those shareholders has consented in writing on Form 2553.

5. The government's interest will not be jeopardized by treating the election to be chaptered under the "S" incorporation provisions of the Internal Revenue Code as valid.

Ace Corporation

By: _Jane Smith_
Jane Smith
Title: President

Or "did business" or "had shareholders"

Director
Internal Revenue Service Center

:

By means of this letter, the   (hereinafter, "The Corporation")
requests an extension of the time for the filing of shareholder consents with respect to The
Corporation's election to be subject to the "S" incorporation provisions of the Internal
Revenue Code. In support of this request, the following information is provided:

1. The Corporation was incorporated under the laws of
on   , 19   .

2. The Corporation first   on   , 19   .

3. All of the shareholders' consents to The Corporation election to be taxed under
the "S" incorporation provisions of the Internal Revenue Code have not and could not be
filed on Form 2553, which is being filed with this letter, for the following reason:

4. Other than   , all other shareholders have consented to the
election, and each of those shareholders has consented in writing on Form 2553.

5. The government's interest will not be jeopardized by treating the election to be
chaptered under the "S" incorporation provisions of the Internal Revenue Code as valid.

By:_____

Title:

6

Four Situations in Which "S" Corporations May Be Taxed

The chief attraction of the "S" corporation is the fact that it is a pass-through entity. Its income, losses, deductions, and credits are passed along—untaxed—to its shareholders, who include each of those items on their personal tax returns. Every rule, however, has its exceptions. Following are the four limited situations in which the "S" corporation itself may be liable for taxes.

Before reviewing those special circumstances, we hasten to give you the good news: If you are starting a new business, none of the four exceptions will affect your "S" corporation. Similarly, if your corporation always operated as an "S" corporation, none of the exceptions will affect your corporation. The occasions on which an "S" corporation does pay a tax all involve businesses that started out as regular "C" corporations.

The four possible occasions when an "S" corporation may pay a tax involve:

- capital gains;
- excess passive investment income;
- the sale or disposition of property on which an investment tax credit was taken when the enterprise was not an "S" corporation; and
- a sale or other disposition of property in a liquidation if there is a gain, the gain arose before the corporation converted from "C" to "S" status, and the sale or other disposition occurred within ten years after the date the corporation converted from "C" to "S" status.

CAPITAL GAINS

A capital gain results when a "capital asset" is sold for more money than it cost to purchase and improve the asset. A "capital asset" is usually an asset used to produce income. So, for example, an office building that produces rental income is a capital asset. The rent it produces is income; if the building is sold at a profit, that profit is a capital gain.

Although many people believe the Tax Reform Act of 1986 did away with capital gains treatment, that is only partially true. Before the 1986 Act, the significance of labeling an asset a "capital asset" stemmed from the fact that capital gains received highly favored tax treatment. This benefit was eliminated by the Tax Reform Act of 1986, which provided that capital gains are to be taxed as if they constitute ordinary income. Nevertheless, the Tax Reform Act left unchanged the format for determining that segment of a taxpayer's income that is capital gain. Most observers believe this was done so that if economic conditions warrant it, a new tax law can reinstitute favorable tax treatment for capital gains without causing disruption and reporting problems for taxpayers.

Given the benefits formerly available through capital gains treatment (up to a 60 percent exclusion of gain for the taxpayer), Congress sought to ensure that taxpayers would not elect to form an "S" corporation solely to take advantage of a one-time capital gain situation. With this concern in mind, Congress determined that an "S" corporation would have to pay a tax on capital gains if four criteria were satisfied:

- The net capital gain was more than $25,000.
- The net capital gain constituted more than half of the corporation's taxable income for the year.
- The corporation had more than $25,000 of taxable income.
- The corporation was not an "S" corporation for each of the three years before the tax year in question or had been in business for less than four years, during which it was not an "S" corporation.

Each of the four criteria must be present if the "S" corporation is to pay a tax on capital gains. The tax is imposed on the amount of net capital gain in excess of $25,000; the tax rate imposed is the lower of 28 percent or the rate that would have been used if the corporation had not been an "S" corporation.

Based on these four criteria, however, it is clear that an "S" corporation will not be subject to a capital gains tax if it has always been an "S" corporation (regardless of how short its period of existence) or it was once a "C" corporation but transferred to "S" status at least three taxable years before the tax year in which the capital gain arose. This means that if you are about to embark on a new business, you need not fear that your "S" corporation will pay a capital gains tax.

If you have an existing corporation and wish to pick up the various advantages of "S" incorporation, you can do so knowing that if you wait for at least three years before selling a capital asset at a gain, the corporation will not pay a capital gains tax. If you opt against waiting three years, your corporation may not pay a capital gains tax if the gain is less than $25,000. Even if the corporation must pay the capital gains tax, the situation will be no different, for capital gains tax purposes, if you had not made the change. Furthermore, you will still have the other benefits of "S" corporation available to minimize the federal government's overall tax bite.

EXCESS PASSIVE INVESTMENT GAINS

An "S" corporation will be required to pay a tax on excess passive investment income earned in a year during which it also had regular corporation earnings and profits. In this situation, the tax clearly affects only those "S" corporations that started life as a "C" corporation. A business that has been only an "S" corporation—for example, a new enterprise—need not concern itself with the tax on excess passive investment income.

There are only a limited number of ways for an "S" corporation to obtain "C" corporation profits and earnings. Shareholders of a "C" corporation may have elected to seek "S" status when the "C" corporation had earnings and profits, or there may have been a merger between a "C" and an "S" corporation. Should either situation arise, the "S" corporation tax can be avoided if, before the end of the tax year, the corporation distributes its accumulated earnings and profits to its shareholders. Although the shareholders will be required to report the distribution as a dividend, the corporation will not be required to pay a tax if the distribution is made before the end of the tax year.

Passive investment income, for purposes of the "S" corporation tax, includes income coming from royalties, rent, dividends, interest, annuities and sale or exchange of stock or other securities.

> *Caution:* Passive investment income for the purposes of a direct tax on an "S" corporation is not the same as passive income that is passed through directly to the shareholder. This latter form of passive income refers to a business activity in which the shareholder does not materially participate.

INVESTMENT TAX CREDITS

Although eliminated by the Tax Reform Act of 1986, the investment tax credit still has some life in it, since it is still being phased out for existing transactions. If an "S" corporation has ITC, that credit is passed through to shareholders. If, on the other hand, an "S" corporation disposes of property on which it took an investment tax credit when it was a "C" corporation, it becomes liable for the recapture of those credits. As was the case with capital gains and excess passive income, this tax only rears its head in situations involving "S" corporations that were formerly "C" corporations.

LIQUIDATIONS

One tax benefit available to shareholders in regular corporations before the enactment of the Tax Reform Act of 1986 involved distribution of appreciated property by the corporation. For example, if under the prior law a corporation sold appreciated property as part of a complete liquidation, it would not be taxed on the gain it made. Instead, that gain would be taxed in the shareholders' hands if the total distribution they received was greater than the investment they made in their stock. The Tax Reform Act repealed this provision.

Today, if a regular corporation disposes of an appreciated asset, it must pay a tax on its gain; the shareholders will pay a second tax if the distribution they receive from the corporation represents a gain to them.

> *Caution:* The Tax Reform Act of 1986 has provided limited relief from this provision for "C" corporations whose assets total $5 million or less. The new provisions do not affect such corporations at all.

Assume a corporation wishes to get around the 1986 changes and converts to "S" status in order to do so. Its efforts will go for naught. The 1986 provisions require the "S" corporation to pay a tax on any appreciation of its property that occurred before the conversion to "S" status—but only if the sale or distribution that is part of the liquidation comes within ten years of the date the election to be treated as an "S" corporation became effective.

Again, this problem exists only for corporations that convert from "C" to "S" status. Furthermore, the tax that can be assessed against the "S" corporation is limited to the appreciation that took place before the conversion; appreciation that occurs after the conversion to "S" status is gain that flows through to the shareholders of the "S" corporation.

7

Maximizing Your Benefits on Corporate Losses

Although an "S" corporation's losses flow through to its shareholders, those losses can be deducted by shareholders on their returns only if they do not exceed the total of the shareholders' bases in their stock and any debt owed to them by the corporation. *Basis* is a tax term that generally refers to the cost of an item.

If an "S" corporation's losses exceed a shareholder's basis in stock and debt, the shareholder cannot deduct his or her pro rata share of the loss but must carry it over until such time as he or she has sufficient basis to cover the loss.

To make maximum use of "S" corporation losses, therefore, a shareholder must know how basis is determined, how it can be increased or decreased and how the carryover rules work.

One other area of interest in this respect involves the unwelcome but always real possibility that the corporation may fail. If that happens and the shareholder's stock becomes worthless, he or she will be required to take a capital loss on the worthless stock. For many investors, however, there is an alternative that permits the loss on the original investment to be treated as an ordinary loss. This tool—Section 1244 stock—is available to most small corporations.

DETERMINING BASIS IN STOCK

As a general rule, a shareholder's basis in "S" corporation stock is the cost of the stock. If, for example the shareholder paid $100 for ten shares of stock, his or her basis per share is $10 and total basis is $100.

If, instead, the shareholder transfers property to the "S" corporation in exchange for shares, the shareholder's basis is determined by reference to whether the transfer is a taxable event. In most situations when a new business is formed, the transfer of property for shares is not a taxable event. In those cases, basis equals: (1) the carryover basis of the property, which is the asset's basis in the shareholder's hands when he or she transferred it to the corporation; (2) minus the amount of any cash paid to the shareholder for the property; (3) plus any gain the shareholder recognizes on the transfer.

> *Example:* Assume Mr. Jones transfers title to a small office building to his newly formed "S" corporation. Assume that when the transfer took place the carryover basis of the building, in Mr. Jones's hands, was $50,000. Now assume that Mr. Jones received 10,000 shares of the "S" corporation stock valued at $4 a share and $15,000 in cash for the building. His basis in his stock would be $40,000 ($50,000 in carryover basis, minus the $15,000 cash payment, plus $5,000 of recognized gain—the $5,000 of recognized gain is determined by adding together the value of the stock and the cash, $55,000, and subtracting the original basis, $50,000).

If the stock was issued for property and the transfer was a taxable event, the basis of the stock would be the fair market value of the property at the time of the transfer.

Two other commonplace transfers of stock in small corporations arise when the owner of the stock dies or makes a gift of the shares. If the stock is inherited because of the original owner's death, the person who receives the stock uses as his or her basis the fair market value of the stock at the time of the decedent's death. If, on the other hand, the stock is given as a gift, the recipient takes the stock with a basis equal to the donor's basis at the time the gift was made.

DETERMINING BASIS IN DEBT

If a shareholder loans money to an "S" corporation, his or her basis in the loan is the amount of money actually loaned. Occasionally, a shareholder will supply services or property in return for an IOU (a note) from the "S" corporation. In that case, the shareholder's basis in the note is equal to the amount of the note the shareholder includes when reporting income for tax purposes.

> **Cautions:** Shareholders should not confuse money they lend to the "S" corporation with loans or other debts the corporation may incur with respect to other persons, but which the shareholder may guarantee. A shareholder has basis only in money he or she lends to the corporation, not money lent to the corporation by other persons.
>
> Second, a shareholder does not obtain a basis in debt merely because he or she guarantees a corporate loan. If, however, the corporation does not meet its obligations under a loan and the shareholder must make good on this guarantee, he or she will have increased his or her basis in corporate debt by the amount actually paid out on the guarantee.

HOW BASIS CHANGES

After it is initially determined, a shareholder's basis changes every year during which the "S" corporation operates at a profit or loss. For example, assume an "S" corporation had a profit of $3,000 in 1992. Now assume the "S" corporation has one shareholder, Ms. Smith, who had a basis of $10,000 in stock when the year began. Her basis at the end of the year would be $13,000. Similarly, if the corporation had lost $3,000, her basis would have been reduced to $7,000 at the end of the year.

When determining annual adjustments in basis, each "S" corporation shareholder increases or decreases his or her basis by the amount of his or her pro rata share of profits or losses.

> **Caution:** If an "S" corporation makes a nontaxable distribution to its shareholders, their bases are reduced by the amount of the distribution each receives. Such distributions can occur when the "S" corporation has assets it no longer needs or if it has accumulated earnings and profits (from its regular "C" corporation days) and distributes the accumulations to its shareholders.
>
> Assume that Joe Jones, an "S" corporation's sole shareholder, believes the corporation will incur losses in the current year and that those losses will exceed his basis in stock or debt. Assume also that Mr. Jones wants to use those losses in the current year rather than carry them forward. He should consider the option of buying more stock in the corporation or lending it additional sums. Either step would increase his basis, and, if projected with care, should be in an amount sufficient to permit him to deduct all of the anticipated "S" corporation loss.

If a shareholder has basis in both stock and debt, there is a formula for determining which of the two bases is increased when the corporation operates at a profit or loss. The general rule is that both accounts are determined separately unless operating losses exceed the shareholder's basis in stock. In that case, the shareholder may deduct the loss only if sufficient basis in debt is owed to him or her by the corporation to cover the loss. If the corporation operates at a profit the next year, the increase in basis would be applied to the debt basis first and the excess, if any, to create basis in stock.

> *Example:* Assume Mr. Jones is the sole shareholder of an "S" corporation. Assume also that he has a basis of $40,000 in stock and that he has loaned the corporation $20,000. In 1992 the corporation operated at a loss of $48,000. Jones can deduct the entire loss, but in doing so he reduces his basis in his stock to zero and reduces his basis in debt to $12,000. If the same corporation operates at a profit of $12,000 in 1993, Mr. Jones's basis in debt would be increased to its original amount, $20,000, and his basis in stock would go from zero to $4,000.

These examples should make clear the following rules for determining how basis can be increased or decreased:

- A shareholder's basis in stock or debt can be reduced to zero but cannot be reduced to a negative amount. If losses exceed the basis in debt and stock, they must be carried forward.
- Decreases in basis caused by operating losses are applied first to the basis in stock and then to the basis in debt.
- If operating losses have been used to decrease the basis in debt and there is a profit in a succeeding year, the debt basis must be increased until it is completely replaced; then remaining profits can increase the basis of stock.

CARRYFORWARD OF LOSSES

As explained above, a shareholder can deduct losses only if the losses do not exceed the total amount of his or her basis in stock and debt. If losses do exceed the combined bases, the shareholder may carry them forward indefinitely, until such time as the shareholder has increased his or her basis through additional investments in stock or loans to the corporation or operating profits supply sufficient basis to cover the losses.

MAKING THE MOST OF A LOSING SITUATION

Although most entrepreneurs embark on a new venture convinced they will succeed, the more realistic businessperson anticipates the possibility of failure and takes measures that will make a possible failure as painless as possible. One technique used by thoughtful businesspeople involves the use of Section 1244 stock. When used, Section 1244 stock enables shareholders to make maximum use of their losses should their business fail and their stock become worthless.

Under existing tax rules, losses suffered by a shareholder when his or her stock becomes worthless are capital losses and can be used only in a restricted manner. If the losses are long-term losses (where the asset is held for more than six months), they can be applied to offset capital gains; then if there are excess capital losses, they can be used to offset ordinary income, but only up to a maximum of $3,000. This means that if a taxpayer has $2,000 of capital gains and $10,000 of long-term capital losses, $5,000 of capital losses cannot be used in the current tax year but must be carried forward. (The loss of $2,000 will offset the $2,000 gain and another $3,000 can be used to offset ordinary income; that leaves a balance of $5,000 of the total $10,000 loss that is unused in the current tax year).

Section 1244 stock addresses just this situation. Created by Congress to assist small businesses, Section 1244 of the Internal Revenue Code provides a special rule for losses incurred when stock of small corporations is sold or transferred at a loss or becomes worthless. The loss suffered by the shareholder is treated as an ordinary loss and can offset up to $50,000 of income ($100,000 if the taxpayers file a joint return).

> ***Example:*** Assume Ms. Taxpayer has ordinary income of $50,000 and that during the current tax year she sold an asset for a long-term capital gain of $2,000. Assume also that Ms. Taxpayer operated a small business as a sideline and that she holds Section 1244 stock in this business. Ms. Taxpayer's basis in her Section 1244 stock is $12,000. Assume next that the sideline business does not work out and that this year Ms. Taxpayer dissolves the business, which has no assets; in other words, her stock is worthless. Ms. Taxpayer's total income of $52,000 ($50,000 of ordinary income plus $2,000 of capital gain) is now reduced to $40,000, since she can deduct all of the $12,000 loss she suffered when her stock became worthless.

To issue Section 1244 stock, the corporation must satisfy five standards, none of which conflict with "S" corporation requirements:

1. The corporation must have been created in the United States.
2. The corporation may not be a holding company.

3. The total amount paid by shareholders for their stock must not be more than $1 million.
4. The stock must have been issued for cash or property and may not have been issued for services or in exchange for other shares of stock.
5. During the five tax years that preceded the year in which the stock became worthless, the corporation must have derived more than half of its income from nonpassive sources. (Passive sources include income from royalties, rents, dividends, interest, annuities and sales or exchanges of stock or other securities.)

Although no one should start a new venture expecting to fail, prudent investors will try to anticipate the possibility of failure. Section 1244 stock, which is quite the same as other forms of common stock, provides a cost-free benefit: In the event the business fails, the losses suffered by the taxpayer will become somewhat less painful when they show up as full deductions on his or her tax return.

8

Compensation and the "S" Corporation

Most individuals who start a new business expect that enterprise to supply them with a form of regular income. Usually, their expectations are realized by a weekly or monthly salary, combined with fringe benefits and, perhaps, some form of retirement plan. If the business is started as an "S" corporation and if it is run profitably, it can satisfy two of those needs without difficulty— salary and retirement plans—but the "S" corporation does not have the capacity to provide the wide range of fringe benefits available when regular "C" incorporation is adopted. As we shall see, however, this weakness is a small price to pay for the other benefits provided by "S" incorporation. Furthermore, there are alternatives that offer the businessperson who forms an "S" corporation the capability of enjoying the same range of fringe benefits he or she would enjoy if a "C" corporation had been formed.

COMPENSATION

Throughout this book, we have stressed that an "S" corporation is a flow-through enterprise that is not taxed on its earnings. More so than in any other area, the flow-through concept takes on added importance when compensation is considered.

Although not apparent to most nonlawyers, one major benefit of the "S" incorporation is that it permits shareholder-employees to pay themselves compensation that reaches the uppermost limits of "reasonableness" without inviting an audit by the IRS. This element of comfort is not so readily available in the regular "C" incorporation. An understanding of this difference in outlook requires a reexamination of just how "C" and "S" corporations are taxed.

A "C" corporation's profits are taxed twice: once as a corporate profit then a second time when those profits are distributed to shareholders as dividends. The shareholder-employees of a "C" corporation will therefore seek to pay themselves as high a salary as possible in order to reduce the amount of tax their corporation will have to pay on its earnings. (Salaries are costs that are deducted from the "C" corporation's gross income in order to determine taxable income.)

The IRS is aware of this technique and monitors the efforts of "C" corporation shareholders to avoid the double tax on corporate profits by paying themselves high salaries. As a result, the IRS regularly challenges executive salaries, claiming they are really dividends. If the IRS is successful, as it often is, the unreasonable segment of the salary is not allowed as a corporate deduction, and the corporation must pay an added tax for the year in question.

This problem does not arise in the "S" corporation, because the goal the "C" corporation shareholder-employee is after—single taxation—is already present in the "S" corporation. Let's assume an "S" corporation pays its sole shareholder-employee an "unreasonably" high salary. If the IRS does not pick it up, the corporation will take a deduction for that salary, but the shareholder must declare it when reporting his or her earnings and will then be taxed on the compensation. If the IRS decides to challenge the unreasonable portion of the salary and wins the point, the payment will be termed a "distribution" and will not be taxed to the shareholder. The "S" corporation, however, will be denied a deduction for the overpayment, or distribution. It will end the year having net profits that are increased by the amount of the unreasonable segment of the compensation. That additional profit, in turn, will flow through to the shareholder and will be taxed as income in his or her hands.

Regardless of the approach taken, the result remains the same: The shareholder has the same amount of taxable income. The IRS, therefore, is less likely to be concerned about "unreasonable" salaries in "S" corporation situations than it would be in "C" corporation operations.

Exceptions

Two situations exist in which the payment of "unreasonable" compensation may cause serious problems for shareholder-employees. One involves "S" corporations that have more than one shareholder-employee; the other involves shareholders who have little or no basis in stock.

Multiple Shareholders. Assume that an "S" corporation has two shareholders, John and Mary, and that they are not related to each other. Both own 50 percent of the shares of the "S" corporation. Although they agree that both will share profits equally, Mary, who had put up most of the money to get the business off the ground, does not work for the corporation nor does she draw a salary. John works for the corporation full-time and is compensated for his services.

Let's now assume that the IRS determines that John's salary was unreasonable and that they conclude it was unreasonable to the extent of $10,000. The result would be that the payment to John would be considered a distribution. He would not have to include the $10,000 when reporting his taxable income.

The story does not end here, however. Since the $10,000 payment to John is a distribution, the corporation cannot claim it as a deduction for salary. That means the corporation will have an additional $10,000 of income that will flow through to its shareholders. John and Mary will each have to report an extra $5,000 of income—in Mary's case, she will be paying tax on money she never received; John, on the other hand, will receive $10,000 and pay tax on $5,000.

Nor do the consequences end there. Mary's basis in her stock will be increased by $5,000—her share of the distribution that was treated as a corporate profit. John, however, will see his basis reduced by $5,000 (the $10,000 decrease because the distribution is partially offset by the $5,000 increase attributable to his share of the $10,000 distribution treated as a corporate profit).

This scenario, particularly its impact on Mary, is not improbable. There is an even more serious danger in this scenario. In recent years, the IRS has proposed new rules under which a salary it determines to be unreasonably high could be viewed as creating a second form of stock. Under this scenario, the corporation would lose its "S" status, since it has more than one class of stock and the two classes possess different economic rights. Although these proposed rules have been withdrawn for reconsideration, they clearly indicate the direction the IRS is taking. Prudent "S" corporation shareholders, therefore, would be well advised to pay heed to the suggestion set out in "Determining Reasonable Compensation," later in this chapter.

Shareholders Without Basis. In the previous example we assumed the shareholders all had sufficient bases in their stock and debt to cover the amount of unreasonable compensation that was treated as a distribution. In this, for instance, John's $10,000 of unreasonable compensation was treated as a tax-free distribution. We assumed John had a basis of at least $10,000 in stock and debt. If John did not have that basis, the distribution would have been treated as taxable income. John, therefore, would have been taxed twice—first on the $10,000 distribution; second, when his half of the $10,000 of added corporate income flowed through to him.

Determining Reasonable Compensation. Although no one fixed guideline establishes precisely what constitutes reasonable compensation, accepted references exist for this purpose. Perhaps the most objective test looks to salaries paid to individuals performing comparable services for comparable businesses. Even this test is subject to other considerations. For example, a new development may have required the executive in question to have offered services far greater in effort or scope than would ordinarily be expected. In such cases, a bonus may very well be in order. Straight salary (or bonuses) can be tied to performance standards, such as gross sales, an approach that may lead to justifiably high or, if performance is poor, low salaries.

Other factors that may be considered when determining reasonable compensation include the following:

- Extensive experience: An employee who has years of experience or special knowledge in a given field generally justifies higher compensation than a less experienced person.
- Business performance: If the business enjoys a meaningful increase in sales volume or net profits, higher compensation can be justified.
- Unusual services: The ability of a shareholder-employee to obtain goods or services in a time of shortages or to successfully introduce operational efficiencies would justify either a raise or bonus in most arm's-length employment relationships and should be valid criteria if the employee is also an owner.

IT PAYS TO MINIMIZE COMPENSATION

All things being equal, it does not matter to a shareholder-employee if his or her income from the "S" corporation takes the form of a salary or a distribution. Either way the shareholder will have the benefit "C" corporation shareholders strive for—single tax on corporate income. This being the case, it is probably wiser for the "S" corporation shareholder-employee to set his or her salary at the lowest end of reasonableness. This observation flows from the following considerations.

Withholding Taxes. Even though an "S" corporation does not pay taxes, it is an entity in the eyes of the law. As an employer, it must withhold a portion of its employees' wages for income tax, Social Security tax and unemployment insurance taxes. Should the "S" corporation seek to avoid withholding for these taxes by not paying its owner-employees a salary, it would do so by making a distribution to those employees. Distributions, since they are not wages, would not be subject to withholding taxes.

The IRS and the Social Security Administration are alert to the possibility just described. Both will be quick to take the position that distributions are disguised wages subject to withholding. Both have been successful in making this argument. Older shareholders, otherwise entitled to Social Security benefits, have another concern: If they do in fact work for their "S" corporation without salary, the Social Security Administration will take the position that distributions they receive are in fact wages and that those wages should be applied to reduce the amount of Social Security benefits the shareholder-employee will be entitled to receive. (This problem, it should be noted, exists for both "C" and "S" corporations.)

One way to minimize the impact of the withholding problem is to minimize the amount of wages received by the shareholder-employee. Wages can be reduced to the lowest reasonable amount that can be justified for the services in question.

Impact on Basis. Earlier, we noted that "S" corporation losses flow through to the corporation shareholders and may be used as deductions against their other income. We also noted a limitation on that rule: Losses can only be used as a deduction if the shareholder has sufficient basis in stock and debt to cover the amount of the loss. If a shareholder-employee draws all of his or her income from the "S" corporation in the form of wages, his or her basis in stock remains unchanged. If, on the other hand, the shareholder draws only a portion of income as wages, the part he or she does not draw will become corporate profit at the end of the year. If the money is removed as a distribution of profits, the amount taken in this form will be added to the shareholder's basis in stock.

> *Example No. 1:* John Taxpayer, the sole shareholder of an "S" corporation, has a basis of $15,000 in the corporate stock. He estimates that if he does not draw any salary in 1992, the corporation will have $40,000 of profits. John determines that a reasonable compensation for his services would be $20,000, and he pays himself that amount over the course of 1992. At the end of the year his projections prove correct, and the corporation has $20,000 left in its coffers. John takes the $20,000 as a distribution.

> *Result:* John's basis in stock is now $35,000.

> *Example No. 2:* Assume all of the facts set out in Example 1. As John plans for 1993, he determines that the business will require additional personnel but that the fruits of their labor will not be seen until 1995. He goes ahead and takes on the new people. As a result, the corporation runs at a $30,000 loss in 1993.

> *Result:* John can apply the entire $30,000 loss against his income from other sources next year. Had he taken this year's income from the corporation entirely as wages, his basis in his stock would have

remained at $15,000, and he would have been able to apply only $15,000 of next year's losses against his other income.

DOVETAILING COMPENSATION AND TAX YEARS

A business may operate on either the cash or accrual method of accounting. If it operates on the cash basis, it deducts its expenses for tax purposes when a payment is actually made. Similarly, a cash-basis taxpayer reports income when it is actually received.

A taxpayer who uses the accrual method of accounting, on the other hand, can deduct expenses when the amount of an expense is positively known and the person who is to receive the payment becomes legally entitled to demand payment. The business using the accrual method of accounting can work out a form of tax deferral at the end of a tax year. By deferring payment to those individuals or businesses whose claim for payment has matured, the taxpayer can take a current year deduction for an expense that is not paid until the following year.

> *Example:* An "S" corporation orders $5,000 of supplies from Ms. Vendor. The supplies are delivered and accepted in late November this year. Ms. Vendor submits her bill when the goods are delivered. "S" corporation, however, does not pay the bill until January 3 of next year.

> *Result:* If "S" corporation is on the accrual method of accounting, it can deduct the $5,000 expense this year. If Ms. Vendor is a cash basis taxpayer, she will not report the $5,000 payment until she files next year's taxes.

Given the fact that most individuals use the cash method of accounting, it would seem possible for most "S" corporations to use the accrual method in order to take a current year deduction for wages owed to shareholder-employees. The cash method shareholder-employee, in theory, would not report the income until the following tax year.

That, however, is not the case. The Internal Revenue Code specifically anticipates this possibility and permits an "S" corporation to deduct the salary it pays to a shareholder-employee only in the year the employee actually receives the salary. The deferral option described previously cannot be used even if the "S" corporation is on the accrual method of accounting and the shareholder-employee uses the cash method.

Further, this approach is taken when wage payments are made to employees who are related to a shareholder. An "S" corporation, therefore, can deduct wage payments made to the following recipients only in the year each of the following receives the payment:

- The husband, wife, brother, sister, parent, grandparent or grandchild of a shareholder, regardless of how small an interest the shareholder has in the "S" corporation
- A partnership in which the people who own 50 percent of the right to profits (or who have invested more than 50 percent of the capital) also own more than 50 percent of the shares of the "S" corporation
- An "S" or "C" corporation in which the people who own more than 50 percent of the shares of stock also own more than 50 percent of the shares of stock of the "S" corporation making the payment

It must be stressed, however, that these rules apply only to "S" corporation payments to shareholder-employees. Payments made to employees who are not shareholders of the corporation (or who do not fit within one of the three related groups described above) may be deferred so that the corporation takes the deduction in the year the payment becomes due even though the employee will not report the payment as income until the following tax year.

Although the focus here has been on the benefits of the accrual method of accounting, there are also benefits to be obtained if a business uses the cash method of accounting. So, for example, a business that bills heavily at the end of the year but does not receive payment until the beginning of the next year may prefer to go on the cash method of accounting. It will be able to include the expenses it incurs producing its products in its current tax year and need not report the payments it receives until the next tax year.

In this respect, the "S" corporation does enjoy an advantage over "C" corporations. All "S" corporations are permitted to use the cash method of accounting. Only those "C" corporations with average gross receipts of $5 million or less that were on the cash method when the Tax Reform Act of 1986 was enacted may use the cash method.

DANGERS OF INCOME SPLITTING

At this time there are five basic tax rates for individuals: 15 percent, 28 percent, 31 percent, 36 percent and 39.6 percent. Given the difference of 24.6 percent between the highest and lowest rates, many taxpayers who form small businesses will be sorely tempted to underpay themselves and maximize the salary they pay to family members—usually children or parents—who are in a lower tax bracket. In the case of parents, the situation ordinarily involves retired persons who receive Social Security. Although they bring a high degree of expertise to the business, they do not want to receive a salary that would jeopardize their Social Security benefits.

Example: Assume Mr. and Mrs. Smith operate an "S" corporation. They anticipate the company will generate about $180,000 in profits at the end of the year. The profits, if nothing is done, will be heavily taxed. For instance, the profits between $89,150 and $140,000 will be taxed at the rate of 31 percent. The profits above $140,000 will be taxed at 36 percent. Their total tax bill will be $45,330.

In order to reduce their tax bill, the Smiths hire each of their four teenage children to work at the office, answering the telephone, doing janitorial work, operating the photocopying machine and typing. Each child is paid $20,000 a year and saves that money towards the day when he or she will go to college. The Smiths then hire their parents, each of whom they pay $5,500, to act as full-time sales representatives. The parents refuse to take a higher salary for three reasons: First, they do not need the money; second, motivated by parental love, they refuse to take money they view as belonging to their children and grandchildren; and third, they do not want to reduce their Social Security retirement income. The Smiths then pay themselves $44,500 each.

Result: The "S" corporation will have no profits for the year and will supply no flow-through income to the Smiths. The Smiths, with $89,000 of income, will not have any portion of their income taxed at more than 28 percent. Their tax bill will be $15,124. Each child will be in the 15 percent bracket and will pay $3,000 in taxes. The likelihood is that the Smith's parents have enough deductions to avoid paying any tax on their combined earnings of $11,000. Instead of paying $45,330, the entire Smith family will pay only $27,124 in income taxes—a savings of $18,206. The savings came about because the Smiths removed $91,000 from the 31 percent and 36 percent tax brackets and put that money into 15 percent and 0 percent brackets.

The machinations of the Smith family, however, point out how overly aggressive people can get in trouble with the Internal Revenue Service. Because of the possibilities raised in the example, the Internal Revenue Code allows the IRS to reallocate income in situations where a family member draws an unreasonably high or low salary for his or her efforts.

The family member in question does not have to be a shareholder in the "S" corporation but may be a spouse, parent, grandparent, child or grandchild of a shareholder. A parent, for example, may be willing to work full-time to assist a child and may prefer not to draw a salary either as an act of parental generosity or to avoid reducing Social Security benefits.

What factors does the IRS look at when determining whether a person has received an unreasonably low salary? It is safe to assume they look at the same factors they rely on when determining wither an individual has received an unreasonably high salary (see the "Determining Reasonable Compensation" section, under "Exceptions," earlier in this chapter).

The fact that the IRS can reallocate "S" corporation income should not dissuade entrepreneurs from utilizing the services of family members who are in a lower or higher tax bracket. What must be done is simply to act within reason. In the example involving the Smiths, that family made two mistakes. First, they underpaid their parents as full-time employees. Their parents should have been employed as part-time sales representatives, and the $5,500 payment probably would have passed muster. Second, they paid their children almost as much for janitorial and ministerial services (a total of $80,000) as they paid themselves ($89,000) for running the business. The Smiths, therefore, were virtually inviting the Internal Revenue Service to reallocate income. Had they paid their children a more realistic amount, perhaps as much as $10,00 a year per child, for services honestly rendered, then they might not have had a problem. If they had taken this approach, Mr. and Mrs. Smith would have had combined earnings of $129,000 and would have paid $27,518 in taxes. Each child would have paid at most $1,500 in taxes, and the grandparents probably would have paid nothing. The entire Smith family would have paid $33,518 in taxes—a savings of $11,812. Although this savings is less than the savings in the example set out above, it would not have been reallocated and completely lost.

THE DANGER OF INTEREST-FREE LOANS

It is not unusual for a financially comfortable family member to lend money to another member of the family at low or modest interest rates. For example, a parent may provide a child with an interest-free loan to enable the child to start a business or get over a temporary cash crunch. If a loan to an "S" corporation is set below market rate, the Internal Revenue Code authorizes the IRS to reallocate "S" corporation income so that the lender (the parent) is attributed the amount of interest the loan would have received had it been made in an arm's-length transaction. This rule, which undercuts the most basic and honorable of parental feelings, love for a child, can put a parent between a rock and a hard place if he or she cannot afford to make a gift of the sum involved but does not want to charge a child's "S" corporation interest.

One way out of this morass might be for the parents to make a loan at an interest rate keyed to the rate on short-term Treasury bills. Upon receipt of the interest the parents could make a gift to the child (not to the "S" corporation) of the interest they received (perhaps net of any income tax they paid on the interest). This gift would be tax-free income to the child. Note that if this approach is taken, the "S" corporation will have a deduction for the interest paid, a deduction that flows through to the benefit of the child.

9

Fringe Benefits and Retirement Plans

FRINGE BENEFITS

In 1982, when it thoroughly revamped the laws governing "S" corporations, Congress sought to provide the "S" corporation with as many partnership tax attributes as possible. Most of the changes worked to assist entrepreneurs who sought the benefits of limited liability associated with incorporation and the single tax on earnings available in a sole proprietorship or partnership. Not everything worked to the favor of the "S" corporation, however.

Prior to the 1982 changes an "S" corporation could provide the same fringe benefits—medical, accident, disability, life insurance plans and so on—on the same terms as a "C" corporation. Premiums paid by the corporation were deductible as a business expense; benefits received by the employee were excluded from taxable income.

Partnerships, on the other hand, were not accorded the same treatment. If a partnership provided a fringe benefit to a partner, the cost of the benefit, whether in the form of a premium or a direct payment to the partner, was not eligible for treatment as a business deduction. The partner who received the benefit, furthermore, had to declare it as income.

When it put "S" corporations on a par with partnerships in 1982, Congress applied the rule on partnerships and fringe benefits to "S" corporations. This means that the "S" corporation cannot deduct as a business expense the cost of fringe benefits provided to most shareholder-employees. As is the case with partnerships, the shareholder-employee who receives a benefit must include that benefit when he or she reports taxable income.

Applying the Rules

There are four factors to consider when applying the rules just stated.

1. Fringe benefits may be provided for nonshareholder-employees. The cost of those benefits is deductible from the "S" corporation income, and the employee is not required to report any benefits he or she may receive when calculating taxable income.
2. The rules apply to all shareholder-employees who own more than 2 percent of the "S" corporation stock or, if the corporation has both voting and nonvoting stock, more than 2 percent of the corporation's total combined voting stock. If either of these ownership requirements is satisfied for just one day of the corporation's tax year, the rule applies.

   Example: On January 1, 1993, John Taxpayer owned 2.25 percent of "S" corporation stock. At 9:00 A.M. that same day, he sold his shares to the other shareholders and agreed to continue to work for the corporation. On January 2, 1993, the other shareholder-employees voted to provide Mr. Taxpayer with the same fringe benefit package available to their other employees, including medical, life and disability insurance coverage.

   Result: The "S" corporation cannot deduct the cost of the premiums paid on the policies covering Taxpayer. He, in turn, cannot exclude the benefits when he reports his taxable income. If Taxpayer remains with the corporation in 1994, the deduction will be available to the business, and he need not include the benefits in his taxable income.

3. The rules applicable to "S" corporations and fringe benefits encompass within their scope the shareholder-employee who satisfies the "more than 2 percent" test and members of that shareholder's family who are employed by the "S" corporation: husbands, wives, brothers and sisters (including half-brothers and half-sisters), parents, grandparents, children and grandchildren. Furthermore, the rule also reaches a relative who owns no stock but is related to a shareholder who passes the "more than 2 percent" test, even if the shareholder is not an employee of the "S" corporation.
4. The partnership rule would seem to apply to any fringe benefit offered by an "S" corporation to its shareholder-employees. The statute in question, Section 1372 of the Internal Revenue Code, states simply and directly that "For purposes of applying the provisions . . . which relate to employee fringe benefits—the 'S' corporation shall be treated as a partnership. . ." This would seem to include such traditional benefits as the following:

- Premiums paid by the "S" corporation for medical and disability plans and payments received under the coverage of the plans
- Premiums paid for $50,000 group life insurance policies
- Meals and lodging furnished by the "S" corporation to the shareholder-employee for the corporation's convenience
- The $5,000 death benefit exclusion available to the estate of an employee whose employer provides this benefit

Three Approaches to the Problem

If the endeavor for which an "S" corporation is to be formed will require the full-time efforts of its shareholder-employees, some consideration must be given to their need for the forms of insurance protection provided by most employers. Three possible approaches to these problems follow:

1. Adjust compensation levels so that the shareholder-employee can purchase a comparable package of benefits tailored to his or her specific needs. The drawback to this is that the shareholder-employee must include the compensation received for this purpose when determining taxable income and will not receive a deduction for the amounts expended to purchase insurance coverage.
2. Assume the business to be formed can be divided into separate parts. There is nothing to prevent the entrepreneur from forming two corporations, a "C" and an "S" corporation. The "C" corporation may provide a service or product for the "S" corporation and, given its limited market, should break even or make a slight profit. The "C" corporation, however, can provide all of its employees (including shareholder-employees) with fringe benefits and deduct the cost of those expenses as business expenses. The recipient will not be required to include the benefit when determining taxable income.

   This approach is available in a host of situations. So, for example, a retail business may be served by a buying corporation that supplies it with all of its product needs. The fact that the same individual or individuals own the stock of both corporations should not defeat the goal of providing deductible fringe benefits through one of the corporations.
3. Use qualified retirement plans that may fund life insurance plans for shareholder-employees and take a deduction. If this is done the employee may not have to report the benefits when determining taxable income.

RETIREMENT PLANS

In 1982 when the Tax Equity and Fiscal Responsibility Act was passed, Congress put "S" corporations, "C" corporations and partnerships on a level playing field with respect to qualified retirement plans. In large measure, there are few significant differences in the treatment accorded the three types of business forms.

A qualified retirement plan provides the following benefits: The corporation is permitted to take a deduction for the full amount of its contribution to the plan, and the shareholder-employee does not include as income either the contribution made on his or her behalf by the corporation or the earnings on the contribution until he or she receives a distribution from the qualified plan.

There are limits on the amount an employer may contribute on behalf of the employee. Those limits are similar to the requirements concerning compensation—only a reasonable salary will be treated as compensation when paid to a shareholder-employee. Similarly, the contribution made on behalf of a shareholder-employee must be reasonable when considered along with other compensation paid to the shareholder-employee.

The use of a qualified retirement plan may answer one of the problems posed in the previous section, supplying certain fringe benefits to the shareholder-employee of an "S" corporation. If the corporation has an HR 10 plan, it may deduct that portion of contributions it uses to purchase life insurance for shareholder-employees.

There are two drawbacks if "S" incorporation is chosen over "C" incorporation:

1. Should shareholder-employees intend to form an Employee Stock Ownership Plan (ESOP), they will have to form a trust, which is not eligible to hold stock in an "S" corporation. An ESOP, therefore, would cause the corporation to lose its "S" status. Since a growing number of entrepreneurs are forming ESOPs with the thought that the ESOP may be a potential buyer should they decide to sell the business at some future date, this weakness in the "S" corporation should be kept in mind. It is not fatal, however, since it is always possible to switch from "S" to "C" status if the success of the business justifies the creation of an ESOP.
2. Shareholder-owners of "S" corporations, unlike their "C" corporation counterparts, may not receive loans from a qualified plan if they hold 5 percent or more of the corporation stock.

Finally, it should be kept in mind that if an "S" corporation intends to set up a qualified retirement plan, its owners must consider getting professional advice before doing so. This advice—available without charge from most financial institutions—is necessary, because the average small business, whether it opts for "S" or "C" status, is likely to have a "top-heavy" plan. Such plans are subject to highly technical and complicated tax rules.

A "top-heavy" plan exists if 60 percent of the plan's benefits or contributions are for the benefit of key employees. A key employee is someone who satisfies one of the following standards. He or she:

- is an officer of the corporation.
- is one of the ten employees who owns the greatest interest in the corporation.
- owns at least 5 percent of the "S" corporation stock.
- receives more than $150,000 in compensation from the "S" corporation and owns 1 percent of the corporation stock.

In determining the percentages of stock ownership listed above, the employee is deemed the owner of shares held by a spouse, children, parents, grandparents and grandchildren.

10

Transferring Shares Back to the Corporation

A shareholder may transfer shares back to the corporation for a variety of reasons and under a host of different circumstances. The following are among the more commonplace reasons:

- The selling shareholder, wishing to obtain a tax-free distribution from the "S" corporation, offers to sell a portion of his or her shareholdings back to the business.
- The shareholder's basis has been reduced, and he or she intends to take a long-term capital loss by selling a portion of shares in a year when he or she will realize long-term gains on other holdings.
- Given reduced participation in the business, a majority shareholder is willing to sell a portion of shares back to the corporation in order to equalize his or her holdings with those of the minority shareholder.
- An existing shareholder, because of differences with other shareholders or the desire to retire from active business, wishes to sell all shareholdings back to the corporation.

Depending on the circumstances, the transfer of shares back to the corporation may be treated as a distribution or a sale or exchange. The consequences for the transferring shareholder, however, may be meaningfully different if the transfer is held to be a distribution rather than a sale or exchange, or vice versa.

If the transfer of stock is treated as a distribution, the shareholder may receive a tax-free payment of money from the corporation. If a transfer is found to be a sale or exchange, the shareholder will end up with a capital gain or loss, depending on the basis he or she had in the stock before the transfer.

WHEN IS A TRANSFER A SALE OR EXCHANGE?

A transfer of shares by a shareholder to the "S" corporation is treated as a sale or exchange if upon completion of the transfer there will be a meaningful change at the corporate or shareholder levels. A sale or exchange, therefore, can be found in the following circumstances:

- The shareholder transfers all of his or her stock.
- The transfer is viewed as a redemption that is not equivalent to a dividend.
- There is a substantially disproportionate redemption of stock.
- The redemption takes place as part of a partial liquidation of the "S" corporation.
- The shareholder's stock in the "S" corporation exceeds 35 percent of his estate and the shares are sold back to the corporation in order to provide the estate with money to pay death taxes.

Sale of All Shares

Obviously, if a shareholder sells all shareholdings back to the corporation, there has been a meaningful change at both the shareholder and corporate levels. Such a transfer will constitute a sale or exchange only if the selling shareholder completely severs his or her relationship with the "S" corporation. To satisfy this requirement, the selling shareholder may not continue on as an officer, employee or director of the "S" corporation. The selling shareholder may, however, offer his or her services to the corporation as an independent contractor.

The selling shareholder will not be viewed as having completely terminated his or her interest if the shareholder's spouse (other than a legally separated spouse), children, grandchildren or parents will continue to own stock in the corporation. In that case, the sale to the corporation will be viewed as a distribution. The same result is obtained if the selling shareholder retains an option to purchase shares in the "S" corporation.

The fact that the corporation may owe the selling shareholder money based on an earlier loan should not cause the IRS to complain that the sale or exchange is a distribution. The debt in question, however, should carry the same terms as a loan to the corporation would bear if it were made by a stranger: Interest rates should be comparable to market rates, there must be a fixed obligation to pay interest and return the principal and, if the debt is subordinated to other debts, this fact should be reflected in a higher interest rate.

Transfer Is Not a Dividend

If the selling shareholder can show that a transfer of fewer than all of his or her shares is not a dividend, the transfer will be viewed as a sale or exchange. Essentially, this test is satisfied if the shareholder can show that as a result of the transfer there has been a meaningful reduction in the shareholder's pro rata interest in the "S" corporation. This test, therefore, applies only to corporations that have more than one shareholder.

In determining whether there has been a meaningful reduction in the shareholder's proportionate interest, the IRS appears to focus on voting power. As a result of this approach, for example, if a shareholder who owns 75 percent of the corporation stock sells 24 percent back to the corporation, the IRS will view the transfer as a distribution rather than a sale. The logic here is that the transferring shareholder will end up with 51 percent of the stock and will retain voting control.

If that shareholder had instead sold 25 percent of the outstanding stock so that he or she retained exactly half the voting stock, the transfer would be viewed as a sale or exchange. Such a determination would be made in this case because the selling shareholder would no longer have voting control, retaining only the right to veto proposed action, since a 50-50 split results in less than the majority needed for most matters determined by shareholder vote.

According to the IRS, most other partial share redemptions, even those involving a minority shareholder, may qualify as sales or exchanges. Of course, if there is a pro rata transfer by all shareholders, there will not be a meaningful change, and the transfers will be treated as distributions.

Disproportionate Reductions

A transfer of shares back to the "S" corporation will be treated as a sale or exchange if the selling shareholder can show three things following the transfer:

1. The selling shareholder owns less than 50 percent of the total voting power of the corporation after the transfer.
2. The selling shareholder owns not more than 79 percent of the percentage of voting stock he or she had before the transfer.
3. If the "S" corporation has nonvoting common stock, the selling shareholder may not be left with more than 79 percent of the total amount of stock he or she held before the transfer. In this test, the percentages are based on the fair market value of the shares.

CONSEQUENCES OF SALE OR EXCHANGE VERSUS DISTRIBUTION

Assuming that an "S" corporation has always been such—or that, if it was once a regular "C" corporation, it has distributed any earnings or profits from its "C" operations—the consequences to the corporation itself are no different regardless of whether the transfer of shares back to the corporation is treated as a sale or a distribution. The transferring shareholder, however, may not realize his or her goals if the intention is to treat the transfer as a distribution and it is found to be a sale or exchange.

If a transfer is treated as a sale or exchange, the following consequences will result:

- If the shareholder receives more for transferred stock than his or her basis in the shares, he or she will have capital gain. If the shareholder receives less than basis, he or she will have a capital loss. If the shareholder sells fewer than all of his or her shares and remains with an ownership interest of more than 50 percent of the corporation's value, the capital loss will not be allowed by the IRS.
- If the selling shareholder transfers all shares back to the corporation, he or she loses the benefit of all unused carryover losses the shareholder was unable to use in previous years because of an insufficient basis in stock. Should there be unused losses, the selling shareholder might be better served in selling fewer than all shares and holding the remainder until such time that his or her basis can allow for use of the losses.
- If the "S" corporation holds property on which it took an investment tax credit, the selling shareholder may be liable for the recapture of the credit.

If the shareholder is viewed as receiving a distribution when returning shares to the corporation, the following results are obtained:

- The amount received from the corporation is tax-free to the extent of the shareholder's basis in shares.
- If the distribution exceeds the shareholder's basis in shares, the excess is treated as a capital gain—the shareholder may not apply the excess against any basis in corporate debt.
- To the extent the distribution is tax-free, the shareholder's basis in stock is reduced.

Based on these factors, the primary difference between a distribution and a sale or exchange occurs when a shareholder is prepared to transfer fewer than all of his or her shares to the corporation. In such a case the shareholder will receive an immediate benefit (tax-free receipt of money) if the transfer is viewed as a distribution; the cost, however, will be a reduced basis in stock.

This means the shareholder may not be able to use operating losses of the "S" corporation in subsequent years. Should the shareholder be viewed as having sold or exchanged shares, he or she may have a capital gain or loss on the shares transferred; the shareholder's basis in remaining shares will be unchanged and he or she will be in a position to use subsequent losses, if they occur, to the extent of that basis.

> *Example No. 1:* An "S" corporation has two shareholders, John and Mary. John owns 70 shares and has a $7,000 basis in the shares. Mary owns 30 shares. The "S" corporation acquires 30 of John's shares for $6,000. Since the transfer does not fit within any of the sale or exchange categories, it will be treated as a distribution.

> *Result:* John will have a $6,000 tax-free distribution; his basis in remaining stock will be $1,000 ($7,000 minus $6,000). Before the transfer, each of John's 70 shares had a basis of $100; after the transfer, each of John's remaining 40 shares will have a basis of $25 ($1,000 divided by 40).

> *Example No. 2:* Assume the same facts as in Example 1, except that John transfers 40 shares and receives $6,500. John's transfer will be treated as a sale or exchange, since he has given up voting control (John and Mary now own 30 shares each).

> *Result:* John will have a capital gain of $2,500 ($6,500 minus the $4,000 John had as a basis in the 40 shares). John's basis in his remaining 30 shares will remain unchanged at $100 per share for a total of $3,000.

CLOSING THE BOOKS IF ALL SHARES ARE SOLD

If the selling shareholder transfers all stock to the corporation, the transaction will be treated as a sale or exchange. In that situation, the selling shareholder and the remaining shareholders may opt to close the books of the corporation as of the date of the sale or continue to keep them open. If the books are kept open for the remainder of the tax year, the selling shareholder will report income, losses, deductions and credits from the corporation on a pro rata basis.

If all of the shareholders agree, the corporation is permitted to close its books as of the date the shareholder transfers all shares to the "S" corporation. In this event, the corporation will have two short tax years, and the selling shareholder will report only his or her share of flow-through items for that portion of the year during which he or she owned stock.

Example No. 1: "S" corporation has two shareholders, each of whom owns 30 shares of stock in which they have a basis of $10 per share. On July 1 one shareholder, John Taxpayer, sells all of his shares to the corporation for $500. As of that date, the corporation had $300 of net income; due to losses incurred over the next six months, the corporation had a net loss for the year of $1,200.

When John Taxpayer transferred his stock on July 1, both shareholders agreed the corporation books would be closed.

Result: John Taxpayer reports on only events that occur through July 1. Therefore, he has $150 of income (his half of the $300 of net income), which raises his basis in his stock to $450. Since he received $500 on shares that have a new basis of $450, his capital gain is $50, which he reports in addition to the $150 of income.

Example No. 2: Assume the same facts as in Example No. 1, except that the shareholders do not agree to close the books on July 1.

Result: John Taxpayer now reports a loss of $600 (his half of the $1,200 loss). The loss, in turn, reduces his basis in stock to zero. The $500 he receives for his shares will be all be capital gain, which is negated by the $600 loss. John's bottom line will be a $100 loss.

The foregoing examples are designed for illustrative purposes only. Since there is no way to predict what will happen after a shareholder leaves the corporation, it is impossible to determine which approach will work best in a given situation. If, however, the "S" corporation is running in the red when the shareholder sells shares back to the business, a prudent approach might be to close the books as of the date of the sale. That way the shareholder gets the benefit of those losses. This approach makes even more sense if the corporation business is seasonal and its high season will follow the sale.

SALES TO A THIRD PERSON

Until this point, we have focused on transfers of shares from a shareholder to the corporation. An "S" corporation shareholder, however, may choose to sell shares to an individual, either another shareholder or a person previously unassociated with the corporation.

If the sale is to an individual, the result for the selling shareholder is exactly what it would have been had there been a sale or exchange with the corporation. The amount received by the shareholder will be capital gain or loss; and the books of the corporation can be closed (if all shareholders consent) or kept open for the purpose of accounting for the seller's share of income, losses, deductions and credits during the portion of the year in which he or she owned shares.

The shareholder who purchases the stock is entitled to participate in the decision to close the books, since he or she will have to report a pro rata share of income and loss that flows through to him or her during the period in which he or she owns the shares.

ELECTION TO CLOSE CORPORATE BOOKS

The form that appears on the next page must be used if a shareholder sells all shares and ends the relationship with the "S" corporation, and the shareholders agree to create two short tax years.

When completed, the form must be attached to the corporation income tax form (Form 1120S). Every shareholder who owned the "S" corporation stock at any time during the course of the tax year, even if only for one day, must consent to the closing of the corporation books upon the transfer of all of a shareholder's shares.

Note also that the following form may be used when the shareholder sells his or her shares to the "S" corporation or to an individual.

ELECTION TO CLOSE CORPORATE BOOKS

Acme Corporation
100 Main Street
Anywhere, USA 00000

Employer Identification Number:

    This Election is hereby made as Attachment to Form 1120S for Acme Corporation's Tax Year which ends December 31, 19   .

    Acme Corporation hereby elects to have the provisions of Internal Revenue Code Section 1377(a)(1) enforced as if Acme Corporation's taxable year consisted of two taxable years, the first of which shall end on July 1, 19   .

    The reason for this election is that John Taxpayer, a shareholder of Acme Corporation, sold all of his shares in the Corporation, and terminated his interest in the Corporation, on July 1, 19   .

    Pursuant to this election, Acme Corporation's tax year, which runs from January 1 through December 1, i.e., a calendar year, will consist of the following two parts: (1) January 1, 19   , through June 30, 19   , and (2) July 1, 19   , through December 31, 19   .

Dated: July 5, 19

Acme Corporation

By: _Philip Brown_
    Philip Brown
    President

SHAREHOLDERS' CONSENT

    The undersigned who include every person who was a shareholder of Acme Corporation at any time during calendar year 19   all consent to the election described above.

Name of Shareholder

Signature of Shareholder

_____

_____

_____

_____

_____

_____

ELECTION TO CLOSE CORPORATE BOOKS

Employer Identification Number:

    This Election is hereby made as Attachment to Form 1120S for Tax Year which ends   , 19   .

    Acme Corporation hereby elects to have the provisions of Internal Revenue Code Section 1377(a)(1) enforced as if   taxable year consisted of two taxable years, the first of which shall end on   , 19   .

    The reason for this election is that   , a shareholder of   , sold all of his shares in the Corporation, and terminated his interest in the Corporation, on   , 19   .

    Pursuant to this election,   tax year, which runs from January 1 through December 1, i.e., a calendar year, will consist of the following two parts: (1)   , 19   , through   , 19   , and (2)   , 19   , through   , 19   .

Dated: , 19

                                        By:_____

SHAREHOLDERS' CONSENT

    The undersigned who include every person who was a shareholder of   at any time during calendar year 19   all consent to the election described above.

Name of Shareholder   Signature of Shareholder

_____   _____

_____   _____

_____   _____

11

Revoking or Terminating the "S" Corporation Election

One of the key attributes of a corporation is that it has perpetual existence unless its shareholders decide to end its existence or it is run in a manner that causes the state to step in and terminate its existence. Just as "C" corporations enjoy the right to perpetual existence, so do "S" corporations.

The shareholders of any "S" or "C" corporation have the right to determine the tax status the corporation will occupy. Having made that decision, the shareholders are not locked in—a corporation's shareholders may opt to switch from "C" status to "S" status or vice versa. If the decision is made to switch from "S" to "C" status, it is termed a revocation of "S" status.

The "S" corporation status will also come to an end if the corporation fails to continue to satisfy the Internal Revenue Code requirements for a valid election to be taxed as an "S" corporation. The involuntary ending of the "S" corporation election is referred to as a termination of the election.

REVOCATION

Shareholders who own more than 50 percent of all outstanding shares, voting and nonvoting shares, can revoke the "S" corporation election at any time by filing a notice with the IRS district director.

Example No. 1: John owns 50 shares of voting stock in an "S" corporation; Mary owns 51 shares of stock in the corporation. Mary controls the decision to revoke the "S" election, since she owns more than one-half of the outstanding stock.

Example No. 2: Assume the same facts as in Example 1 and that Mary votes to revoke the election and John votes not to. Assume also that Mary does not hold an office with the corporation, and that John is its only officer.

Result: John may be able to block Mary's decision, since the Internal Revenue Code requires that the notice of revocation be signed by an authorized corporate officer and filed with the district director. Mary might have to bring a lawsuit to compel John to follow the dictates of the majority.

When It Becomes Effective

If shareholders decide to revoke the election to be treated as an "S" corporation, the revocation can become effective on three possible dates:

1. The year before the tax year during which the notice of revocation is filed. If the notice is filed on or before the fifteenth day of the third month of the corporation tax year, the corporation "S" status ends with the close of the previous tax year.

   Example No. 1: An "S" corporation, which is a calendar year corporation, files its notice of revocation on March 15, 1992.

   Result: The corporation's last year as an "S" corporation will be 1991; it will be taxed as a "C" corporation in 1992.

2. The tax year during which the notice of revocation is filed. If the notice of revocation is filed at any time after the fifteenth day of the third month of the corporation tax year, the election will remain in place for the balance of the tax year.

   Example No. 2: An "S" corporation, which is a calendar year corporation, files its notice of revocation on March 16, 1992.

   Result: When "S" corporation files its return for 1992, it must do so as an "S" corporation. It will not be a "C" corporation for tax purposes until the tax year starting January 1, 1993.

3. A date chosen by the shareholders. The shareholders can choose any effective date for their revocation just as long as the date chosen falls on or after the date of the revocation.

> *Example No. 3:* An "S" corporation, which is a calendar year corporation, files its notice of revocation on March 15, 1992. The notice specifies that the effective date will be July 1, 1992.

> *Result:* Unlike the result in Example 1, the "S" election will end on July 1, 1992, not with the end of 1991.

If the third option is chosen, the corporation will have two short tax years—one for "S" corporation treatment, a second for "C" corporation treatment. This means that the corporation books will be closed as of the day the first short year ends and reopened on the day the second year starts.

> *Example No. 4:* Assume the same facts as those stated in Example 3.

> *Result:* The corporation would have a short "S" corporation tax year that runs from January 1, 1991, through June 30, 1992, and a short "C" corporation tax year that starts July 1, 1992, and ends December 31, 1992.

TERMINATION

To qualify as an "S" corporation, the corporation must be a small business corporation (see Chapter 4). To remain qualified for "S" status, the corporation must continue to be a small business corporation. If the "S" corporation fails to continue to satisfy any one of the requirements needed to qualify it as a small business corporation, its "S" status comes to an end as of the day the terminating or disqualifying event occurs. The disqualifying events (treated more fully in Chapter 4) include:

- share ownership by more than 35 persons. For example, if a husband and wife, who count as one shareholder, divorce and each keeps one half the stock they jointly owned, the corporation will now have two shareholders instead of one. If the corporation already had 35 shareholders when the divorce took place, it would go over the limit and its election would terminate.
- the transfer of shares to an entity or to a person who is not eligible to be an "S" corporation shareholder. Ineligible shareholders include any corporation or partnership, certain trusts or nonresident aliens.

- issuance of a second class of stock. An "S" corporation is permitted to issue only one class of stock. The exception to this rule allows an "S" corporation to create a second class of common stock that differs from the first class only with respect to voting rights.
- acquisition of a subsidiary in which the "S" corporation owns more than 80 percent of the outstanding stock.
- engaging in ineligible business activities. This includes a banking or other type of financial institution, a DISC or an insurance company.
- using an improper tax year. Although not a violation of the requirements concerning a small business corporation, an "S" corporation may lose its status if it does not use a proper tax year. In most instances, "S" corporations are required to use a calendar year, since they are obliged to use the year as their owner's tax year.
- excessive passive income. Although not a factor that goes to the question of whether a business is a small business corporation, an "S" corporation that has excessive passive income will have its "S" status terminated. This cause of termination can only affect "S" corporations that started out in life as a "C" corporation. The test for excessive passive income applies to an "S" corporation that has accumulated earnings and profits from its "C" corporation operations and those earnings and profits remain in the "S" corporation for three consecutive "S" corporation tax years; and passive income for three consecutive tax years, which exceeds 25 percent of the "S" corporation gross receipts for each of those years.

Passive income includes royalties of all kinds—rents from real or personal property, interest from virtually any source, dividends, annuities and gain on the sales of securities.

Termination Procedure

If a corporation's "S" status is terminated, this event must be reported to the IRS in a statement that includes the date the event occurred and the nature of the termination. If the event involved an ineligible purchaser of shares, the purchaser must be identified and the number of shares purchased must be stated.

If the termination was inadvertent or accidental, it is possible to get the IRS to reinstate the corporation's "S" status. Waivers may be granted for any of the seven disqualifying events described in the previous section, other than the use of an improper tax year. Although there are no guidelines as to what will convince the IRS that a disqualifying event was caused by inadvertence, it is clear the IRS will not accede to a request if the event was caused by an intentional act.

> *Example No. 1:* Assume that an "S" corporation, acting on the advice of its certified public accountant, believed, incorrectly, that it did not

have accumulated earnings and profits from its previous history as a "C" corporation. Based on this error, it violates the passive investment income rules.

Result: The IRS will probably go along with a request to waive the termination.

Effective Date

A corporation's "S" status ends on the day before a terminating event occurs. In other words, it is a "C" corporation on the day of the terminating event. As a result, the corporation will have two tax years for the year during which the terminating event took place: a short tax year for its "S" corporation period of operations, followed by a second, short tax year for its "C" operations.

IMPACT OF TERMINATION OR REVOCATION

If a corporation's election to be taxed as an "S" corporation is revoked or terminated, it automatically becomes a "C" corporation. As a general rule, it cannot elect to return to "S" status until the fifth year after the year in which the revocation or termination occurred. For example, if an "S" corporation revoked its "S" election on May 15, 1992, and it was a calendar year corporation, it cannot become an "S" corporation again until January 1, 1997.

Although the IRS can waive the five-year rule, it rarely, if ever, does so where there was a revocation or an intentional termination unless there has been a change of more than 50 percent of the corporation's stock ownership.

REVOCATION OF "S" CORPORATION ELECTION

Each of the two forms that follow can be used to revoke an "S" election. The first form should be used when the shareholders do not wish to have an effective date different than the date supplied by the Internal Revenue Code. The second form should be used when the shareholders wish to set an effective date on or after the date of the filing of the form.

When completing the form, the preparer should be careful to include the combined total of both voting and nonvoting shares outstanding on the date of the filing.

REVOCATION NOTICE

Acme Corporation
100 Main Street
Anywhere, USA   00000

March 15, 19

District Director of Internal Revenue
Upper Taxbite Street
Greedy City, DC   00000

Dear sir:

Acme Corporation hereby revokes its election to be taxed as an "S" corporation under the provisions of Section 1362 of the Internal Revenue Code. Acme Corporation has a total of one thousand shares of stock issued and outstanding as of this date. This revocation shall be effective as of July 1, 19   .

Sincerely,
Acme Corporation

By John Taxpayer
John Taxpayer,
President

SHAREHOLDERS' CONSENT

The undersigned, owners of more than fifty percent of the outstanding stock of Acme Corporation as of the date of this notice, have consented to the revocation of Acme Corporation's election to be treated as an "S" corporation under Section 1362 of the Internal Revenue Code.

Name	Signature	Number of Shares Owned
_____	_____	_____
_____	_____	_____
_____	_____	_____

REVOCATION NOTICE

, 19

District Director of Internal Revenue

Dear sir:

hereby revokes its election to be taxed as an "S" corporation under the provisions of Section 1362 of the Internal Revenue Code. has a total of shares of stock issued and outstanding as of this date. This revocation shall be effective as of 19 .

Sincerely,

By _____

SHAREHOLDERS' CONSENT

The undersigned, owners of more than fifty percent of the outstanding stock of as of the date of this notice, have consented to the revocation of election to be treated as an "S" corporation under Section 1362 of the Internal Revenue Code.

Name	Signature	Number of Shares Owned
_____	_____	_____
_____	_____	_____
_____	_____	_____

A

Suggested Readings

A list of some of the author's other books as well as favorite readings are included. Some titles have little to do with incorporating but are included as aids to thinking. Others are oriented toward business. Still others are philosophical or psychological in nature. All are suggested aids to thinking, self-improvement or formulating business ideas.

Bangs, David H., Jr. *The Business Planning Guide.* Portsmouth, New Hampshire: Upstart Publishing, 1989.

Branden, Nathaniel. *The Disowned Self.* New York: Bantam, 1973.

Caples, John. *Making Ads Pay.* New York: Dover Press, 1957.

Dawson, George M. *Borrowing for Your Business.* Portsmouth, New Hampshire: Upstart Publishing, 1991.

Dible, Donald M. *Up Your Own Organization.* Santa Clara, California: Entrepreneur Press, n.d.

Friedman, Robert. *The Complete Small Business Guide.* Chicago: Enterprise • Dearborn, 1993.

Hopkins, Claude. *My Life in Advertising.* Lincolnwood, Illinois: National Textbook Company, 1986.

Joffee, Gerardo. *How You Too Can Make at Least $1 Million in the Mail Order Business.* Costa Mesa, California: ISC Publications, 1983.

Joseph, Richard A., Anna M. Nekoranec and Carl H. Steffens. *How To Buy a Business.* Chicago: Enterprise • Dearborn, 1993.

Nicholas, Ted. *The Executive's Business Letter Book.* Chicago: Enterprise • Dearborn, 1992.

―――. *The Complete Guide to Business Agreements*. Chicago: Enterprise • Dearborn, 1992.

―――. *The Complete Guide to Nonprofit Corporations*. Chicago: Enterprise • Dearborn, 1993.

―――. *The Complete Book of Corporate Forms*. Chicago: Enterprise • Dearborn, 1992.

―――. *How To Form Your Own Corporation Without a Lawyer for under $75*. Chicago: Enterprise • Dearborn, 1992.

―――. *How To Get Your Own Trademark*. Chicago: Enterprise • Dearborn, 1993.

―――. *Secrets of Entrepreneurial Leadership*. Chicago: Enterprise • Dearborn, 1993.

Pinson, Linda and Jerry Jinnett. *Anatomy of a Business Plan*. Chicago: Enterprise • Dearborn, 1993.

Rand, Ayn. *Atlas Shrugged*. New York: NAL-Dutton, 1992.

Rand, Ayn. *Capitalism: The Unknown Ideal*. New York: NAL-Dutton, 1988.

Shenson, Howard and Ted Nicholas. *The Complete Guide to Consulting Success*. Chicago: Enterprise • Dearborn, 1993.

Westhem, Andrew D. and Donald Jay Korn. *Winning the Wealth Game: How To Keep Your Money In Your Family*. Chicago: Dearborn Financial Publishing, Inc., 1992.

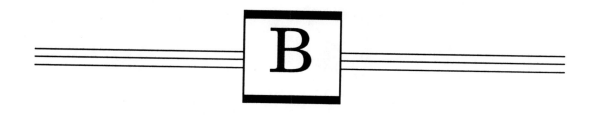

IRS Form 1120S: U.S. Income Tax Return for an "S" Corporation

1991

**Department of the Treasury
Internal Revenue Service**

Instructions for Form 1120S

U.S. Income Tax Return for an S Corporation

(Section references are to the Internal Revenue Code unless otherwise noted.)

Paperwork Reduction Act Notice

We ask for the information on these forms to carry out the Internal Revenue laws of the United States. You are required to give us the information. We need it to ensure that you are complying with these laws and to allow us to figure and collect the right amount of tax.

The time needed to complete and file the following forms will vary depending on individual circumstances. The estimated average times are:

Form	Recordkeeping	Learning about the law or the form	Preparing the form	Copying, assembling, and sending the form to the IRS
1120S	62 hr., 40 min.	18 hr., 38 min.	34 hr., 26 min.	4 hr., 1 min.
Sch. D (1120S)	7 hr., 53 min.	4 hr., 31 min.	9 hr., 31 min.	1 hr., 20 min.
Sch. K-1 (1120S)	13 hr., 39 min.	9 hr., 43 min.	14 hr., 5 min.	1 hr., 4 min.

If you have comments concerning the accuracy of these time estimates or suggestions for making these forms more simple, we would be happy to hear from you. You can write to both the **Internal Revenue Service,** Washington, DC 20224, Attention: IRS Reports Clearance Officer, T:FP; and the **Office of Management and Budget,** Paperwork Reduction Project (1545-0130), Washington, DC 20503. **DO NOT** send the tax forms to either of these offices. Instead, see the instructions on page 2 for information on where to file.

Contents

Voluntary Contributions To Reduce the Public Debt

Quite often, inquiries are received about how to make voluntary contributions to reduce the public debt. A corporation may contribute by enclosing with the tax return a check made payable to "Bureau of the Public Debt."

A Change You Should Note

Corporations may claim a credit on **Form 8830,** Enhanced Oil Recovery Credit, for 15% of qualified enhanced oil recovery costs paid or incurred in tax years beginning after 1990. These costs generally include amounts paid or incurred in connection with a qualified enhanced oil recovery project for:

1. Certain tangible property for which the corporation can claim a deduction for depreciation or amortization,

2. Intangible drilling and development costs eligible for the election under section 263(c) or required to be capitalized under section 291(b)(1), and

3. Qualified tertiary injectant expenses for which a deduction is allowed under section 193.

If a corporation claims this credit, the amounts otherwise deductible (or required to be capitalized and recovered through depreciation, depletion, or amortization), for costs that were used in figuring the credit must be reduced by the amount of the credit attributable to such costs.

For more information, see section 43 and Form 8830.

General Instructions

Note: *In addition to the publications listed throughout these instructions, you may wish to get:* **Pub. 334,** *Tax Guide for Small Business;* **Pub. 535,** *Business Expenses;* **Pub. 550,** *Investment Income and Expenses;* **Pub. 556,** *Examination of Returns, Appeal Rights, and Claims for Refund; and* **Pub. 589,** *Tax Information on S Corporations.*

The above publications and other publications referenced throughout these instructions may be obtained at most IRS offices. To order publications and forms, call our toll-free number 1-800-TAX-FORM (829-3676).

Purpose of Form

Form 1120S is used to report the income, deductions, gains, losses, etc., of a domestic corporation that has filed **Form 2553,** Election by a Small Business Corporation, to be treated as an S corporation, and whose election is in effect for the tax year.

Who Must File

A corporation must file Form 1120S if **(a)** it elected by filing Form 2553 to be treated as an S corporation, **(b)** IRS accepted the election, and **(c)** the election remains in effect. Do not file Form 1120S until the corporation has been notified by the IRS that the election has been accepted.

Termination of Election

Once the election is made, it stays in effect until it is terminated. During the 5 years after the tax year the election has been terminated, the corporation may make another election on Form 2553 only with IRS consent. See section 1362(g).

The election terminates **automatically** in any of the following cases:

1. The corporation is no longer a small business corporation as defined in section 1361(b). The termination of an election in this manner is effective as of the day on which the corporation ceases to be a small business corporation. See sections 1362(d)(2) and 1362(e) for more information.

2. If, for each of three consecutive tax years, the corporation has both subchapter C earnings and profits and gross receipts more than 25% of which are derived from passive investment income as defined in section 1362(d)(3)(D), the election terminates on the first day of the first tax year beginning after the third consecutive tax year. The corporation must pay a tax for each year it has excess net passive income. See specific instructions for line 22a for details on how to figure the tax.

3. The election may be revoked if shareholders who collectively own a majority of the stock in the corporation on the day on which the revocation is made consent to the revocation. If the revocation specifies a date for revocation that is on or after the date that the revocation is made, the revocation is effective as of the specified date. If no date is specified, the revocation is effective as of the beginning of a tax year if it is made during the tax year and on or before the 15th day of the 3rd month of such tax year. If no date is specified and the revocation is made during the tax year but after the 15th day of the 3rd month, it is not effective until the beginning of the following tax year. See section 1362(d)(1) for more information.

When To File

In general, file Form 1120S by the 15th day of the 3rd month after the end of the tax year.

Extension

Use **Form 7004,** Application for Automatic Extension of Time To File Corporation Income Tax Return, to request an automatic 6-month extension of time to file Form 1120S.

Period Covered

File the 1991 return for calendar year 1991 and fiscal years beginning in 1991 and ending in 1992. If the return is for a fiscal year, fill in the tax year space at the top of the form.

Note: *The 1991 Form 1120S may also be used if **(a)** the corporation has a tax year of less than 12 months that begins and ends*

*in 1992 and **(b)** the 1992 Form 1120S is not available by the time the corporation is required to file its return. However, the corporation must show its 1992 tax year on the 1991 Form 1120S and incorporate any tax law changes that are effective for tax years beginning after December 31, 1991.*

Where To File

Use the preaddressed envelope. If you do not use the envelope, file your return at the applicable IRS address listed below.

If the corporation's principal business, office, or agency is located in	Use the following Internal Revenue Service Center address
New Jersey, New York (New York City and counties of Nassau, Rockland, Suffolk, and Westchester)	Holtsville, NY 00501
Connecticut, Maine, Massachusetts, New Hampshire, New York (all other counties), Rhode Island, Vermont	Andover, MA 05501
Florida, Georgia, South Carolina	Atlanta, GA 39901
Indiana, Kentucky, Michigan, Ohio, West Virginia	Cincinnati, OH 45999
Kansas, New Mexico, Oklahoma, Texas	Austin, TX 73301
Alaska, Arizona, California (counties of Alpine, Amador, Butte, Calaveras, Colusa, Contra Costa, Del Norte, El Dorado, Glenn, Humboldt, Lake, Lassen, Marin, Mendocino, Modoc, Napa, Nevada, Placer, Plumas, Sacramento, San Joaquin, Shasta, Sierra, Siskiyou, Solano, Sonoma, Sutter, Tehama, Trinity, Yolo, and Yuba), Colorado, Idaho, Montana, Nebraska, Nevada, North Dakota, Oregon, South Dakota, Utah, Washington, Wyoming	Ogden, UT 84201
California (all other counties), Hawaii	Fresno, CA 93888
Illinois, Iowa, Minnesota, Missouri, Wisconsin	Kansas City, MO 64999
Alabama, Arkansas, Louisiana, Mississippi, North Carolina, Tennessee	Memphis, TN 37501
Delaware, District of Columbia, Maryland, Pennsylvania, Virginia	Philadelphia, PA 19255

Who Must Sign

The return must be signed and dated by the president, vice president, treasurer, assistant treasurer, chief accounting officer, or any other corporate officer (such as a tax officer) authorized to sign. A receiver, trustee, or assignee must sign and date any return he or she is required to file on behalf of a corporation.

If a corporate officer filled in Form 1120S, the Paid Preparer's space under

"Signature of Officer" should remain blank. If someone prepares Form 1120S and does not charge the corporation, that person should not sign the return. Certain others who prepare Form 1120S should not sign. For example, a regular, full-time employee of the corporation such as a clerk, secretary, etc., should not sign.

Generally, anyone paid to prepare Form 1120S must sign the return and fill in the other blanks in the Paid Preparer's Use Only area of the return.

The preparer required to sign the return MUST complete the required preparer information and:

● Sign it, by hand, in the space provided for the preparer's signature. (Signature stamps or labels are not acceptable.)

● Give a copy of Form 1120S to the taxpayer in addition to the copy filed with the IRS.

Accounting Information

Accounting Methods

Figure ordinary income using the method of accounting regularly used in keeping the corporation's books and records. Generally, permissible methods include the cash receipts and disbursements method, the accrual method, or any other method permitted by the Internal Revenue Code. In all cases, the method adopted must clearly reflect income. (See section 446.)

Generally, an S corporation may not use the cash method of accounting if the corporation is a tax shelter (as defined in section 448(d)(3)). See section 448 for details.

Generally, an accrual basis taxpayer can deduct accrued expenses in the tax year that all events have occurred that determine the liability, the amount of the liability can be determined with reasonable accuracy, and economic performance takes place with respect to the expense. There are exceptions for recurring items.

For long-term contracts (except certain real property construction contracts), taxpayers must generally use the percentage of completion method described in section 460. However, for purposes of the percentage of completion method, the corporation may elect to postpone recognition of income and expense under a long-term contract entered into after July 10, 1989, until the first tax year as of the end of which at least 10% of the estimated total contract costs have been incurred.

Unless otherwise allowed by law, a corporation may change the method of accounting used to report income in earlier years (for income as a whole or for any material item) only by first getting consent on **Form 3115,** Application for Change in Accounting Method. See **Pub. 538,** Accounting Periods and Methods, for more information.

Change in Accounting Period

Generally, an S corporation may not change its accounting period to a tax year that is not a permitted year. A "permitted year" is a calendar year or any other accounting period for which the corporation can establish to the satisfaction of the IRS that there is a business purpose for the tax year.

To change an accounting period, see Regulations section 1.442-1 and **Form 1128,** Application to Adopt, Change, or Retain a Tax Year. Also see Pub. 538.

Election of a tax year other than a required year.—Under the provisions of section 444, an S corporation may elect to have a tax year other than a permitted year, but only if the deferral period of the tax year is not longer than 3 months. This election is made by filing **Form 8716,** Election To Have a Tax Year Other Than a Required Tax Year.

An S corporation may not make or continue an election under section 444 if it is a member of a tiered structure, other than a tiered structure that consists entirely of partnerships and S corporations all of which have the same tax year. For the S corporation to have a section 444 election in effect, it must make the payments required by section 7519 and file **Form 8752,** Required Payment or Refund Under Section 7519.

Rounding Off to Whole-Dollar Amounts

You may show the money items on the return and accompanying schedules as whole-dollar amounts. To do so, drop any amount less than 50 cents, and increase any amount from 50 cents through 99 cents to the next higher dollar.

Depositary Method of Tax Payment

The corporation must pay the tax due (line 25, page 1) in full, no later than the 15th day of the 3rd month after the end of the tax year.

Deposit corporation income tax payments (and estimated tax payments) with **Form 8109,** Federal Tax Deposit Coupon. Be sure to darken the "1120" box on the coupon. Make these tax deposits with either a financial institution qualified as a depositary for Federal taxes or the Federal Reserve bank or branch servicing the geographic area where the corporation is located. Do not submit deposits directly to an IRS office; otherwise, the corporation may be subject to a penalty. Records of deposits will be sent to the IRS for crediting to the corporation's account. See the instructions contained in the coupon book (Form 8109) for more information.

To help ensure proper crediting to your account, write the corporation's employer identification number, "Form 1120S," and the tax year to which the deposit applies on the corporation's check or money order.

To get more deposit forms, use the reorder form (**Form 8109A**) provided in the coupon book.

For additional information concerning deposits, see **Pub. 583,** Taxpayers Starting a Business.

Estimated Tax

Generally, the corporation must make estimated tax payments for the following taxes, if the total of these taxes is $500 or more: (a) the tax on certain capital gains, (b) the tax on built-in gains, (c) the excess net passive income tax, and (d) the investment credit recapture tax.

The amount of estimated tax required to be paid annually is the lesser of (a) 90% of the above taxes shown on the return for the tax year (or if no return is filed, 90% of these taxes for the year); or (b) the sum of (i) 90% of the sum of the investment credit recapture tax and the built-in gains tax (or the tax on certain capital gains) shown on the return for the tax year (or if no return is filed, 90% of these taxes for the year), and (ii) 100% of any excess net passive income tax shown on the corporation's return for the preceding tax year. If the preceding tax year was less than 12 months, the estimated tax must be determined under (a).

The estimated tax is generally payable in four equal installments. However, the corporation may be able to lower the amount of one or more installments by using the annualized income installment method or adjusted seasonal installment method under section 6655(e).

For a calendar year corporation, the installments are due by April 15, June 15, September 15, and December 15. For a fiscal year corporation, they are due by the 15th day of the 4th, 6th, 9th, and 12th months of the fiscal year.

The installments are made using the depositary method of tax payment.

Interest and Penalties

Interest

Interest is charged on taxes not paid by the due date, even if an extension of time to file is granted. Interest is also charged from the due date (including extensions) to the date of payment on the failure to file penalty, the accuracy-related penalty, and the fraud penalty. The interest charge is figured at a rate determined under section 6621.

Late Filing of Return

Form 1120S is required to be filed under sections 6037(a) and 6012. A corporation that does not file its tax return by the due date, including extensions, generally may have to pay a penalty of 5% a month, or fraction of a month, up to a maximum of 25%, for each month the return is not filed. The penalty is imposed on the net amount due. See section 6651(a)(1). The minimum penalty for not filing a tax return within 60 days of the due date for filing (including extensions) is the lesser of the underpayment of tax or $100.

The penalty will not be imposed if the corporation can show that failure to file a timely return was due to reasonable cause

and not due to willful neglect. If the failure was due to reasonable cause, attach an explanation to the return.

Late Payment of Tax

A corporation that does not pay the tax when due generally may have to pay a penalty of ½ of 1% a month or fraction of a month, up to a maximum of 25%, for each month the tax is not paid. The penalty is imposed on the net amount due. See section 6651(a)(2).

The penalty will not be imposed if the corporation can show that failure to pay on time was due to reasonable cause and not due to willful neglect.

Underpayment of Estimated Tax

A corporation that fails to make estimated tax payments when due may be subject to an underpayment penalty for the period of underpayment. Use **Form 2220,** Underpayment of Estimated Tax by Corporations, to see if the corporation owes a penalty and to figure the amount of the penalty. If you attach Form 2220 to Form 1120S, be sure to check the box on line 24, page 1, and enter the amount of any penalty on this line.

Failure To Furnish Information Timely

Section 6037(b) requires an S corporation to furnish to each shareholder a copy of such information shown on Schedule K-1 (Form 1120S) that is attached to Form 1120S. The Schedule K-1 must be furnished to each shareholder on or before the day on which the Form 1120S was filed.

For each failure to furnish Schedule K-1 to a shareholder when due and each failure to include on Schedule K-1 all of the information required to be shown (or the inclusion of incorrect information), a penalty of $50 may be imposed with respect to each Schedule K-1 for which a failure occurs. If the requirement to report correct information is intentionally disregarded, each $50 penalty is increased to $100 or, if greater, 10% of the aggregate amount of items required to be reported. See sections 6722 and 6724 for more information.

The penalty will not be imposed if the corporation can show that not furnishing information timely was due to reasonable cause and not due to willful neglect.

Unresolved Tax Problems

The IRS has a Problem Resolution Program for taxpayers who have been unable to resolve their problems with the IRS. If the corporation has a tax problem it has been unable to resolve through normal channels, write to the corporation's local IRS district director or call the corporation's local IRS office and ask for Problem Resolution Assistance. Hearing-impaired persons who have access to TDD equipment may call 1-800-829-4059 to ask for help. The Problem Resolution office will take responsibility for your problem and ensure

Page 3

that it receives proper attention. Although the office cannot change the tax law or make technical decisions, it can frequently clear up misunderstandings that may have resulted from previous contacts.

Other Forms, Returns, Schedules, and Statements That May Be Required

Forms W-2 and W-3, Wage and Tax Statement; and Transmittal of Income and Tax Statements.

Form 720, Quarterly Federal Excise Tax Return. Use Form 720 to report the 10% excise tax on the first retail sale of the following items sold to the extent the sales price exceeds the amounts shown: **(a)** passenger vehicles, $30,000; **(b)** boats and yachts, $100,000; **(c)** aircraft, $250,000; and **(d)** jewelry and furs, $10,000. Form 720 is also used to report environmental excise taxes, communications and air transportation taxes, fuel taxes, manufacturers taxes, ship passenger tax, and certain other excise taxes.

Form 966, Corporate Dissolution or Liquidation.

Forms 1042 and 1042S, Annual Withholding Tax Return for U.S. Source Income of Foreign Persons; and Foreign Person's U.S. Source Income Subject to Withholding. Use these forms to report and transmit withheld tax on payments made to nonresident alien individuals, foreign partnerships, or foreign corporations to the extent such payments constitute gross income from sources within the United States (see sections 861 through 865). For more information, see sections 1441 and 1442, and **Pub. 515,** Withholding of Tax on Nonresident Aliens and Foreign Corporations.

Form 1096, Annual Summary and Transmittal of U.S. Information Returns.

Form 1098, Mortgage Interest Statement. This form is used to report the receipt from any individual of $600 or more of mortgage interest and points in the course of the corporation's trade or business.

Forms 1099-A, B, DIV, INT, MISC, OID, PATR, S, and R. You may have to file these information returns to report abandonments, acquisitions through foreclosure, proceeds from broker and barter exchange transactions, certain dividends, interest payments, medical and dental health care payments, miscellaneous income payments, original issue discount, patronage dividends, distributions from pensions, annuities, retirement or profit-sharing plans, IRAs, insurance contracts, etc., and proceeds from real estate transactions. Also use certain of these returns to report amounts that were received as a nominee on behalf of another person.

Use Form 1099-DIV to report actual dividends paid by the corporation. Only distributions from accumulated earnings and profits are classified as dividends. Do not issue Form 1099-DIV for dividends received by the corporation that are allocated to shareholders on line 4b of Schedule K-1.

For more information, see the separate **Instructions for Forms 1099, 1098, 5498, and W-2G.**

Note: *Every corporation must file Forms 1099-MISC if it makes payments of rents, commissions, or other fixed or determinable income (see section 6041) totaling $600 or more to any one person in the course of its trade or business during the calendar year.*

Form 5713, International Boycott Report. Every corporation that had operations in, or related to, a "boycotting" country, company, or national of a country must file Form 5713. In addition, persons who participate in or cooperate with an international boycott may have to complete Schedule A or Schedule B and Schedule C of Form 5713 to compute their loss of the foreign tax credit, the deferral of earnings of a controlled foreign corporation, IC-DISC benefits, and FSC benefits.

Form 8264, Application for Registration of a Tax Shelter, is used by tax shelter organizers to register tax shelters with the IRS for the purpose of receiving a tax shelter registration number.

Form 8271, Investor Reporting of Tax Shelter Registration Number, is used by corporations that have acquired an interest in a tax shelter that is required to be registered to report the tax shelter's registration number. Form 8271 must be attached to any return on which a deduction, credit, loss, or other tax benefit attributable to a tax shelter is taken or any income attributable to a tax shelter is reported.

Form 8281, Information Return for Publicly Offered Original Issue Discount Instruments. This form is used by issuers of publicly offered debt instruments having OID to provide the information required by section 1275(c).

Forms 8288 and 8288-A, U.S. Withholding Tax Return for Dispositions by Foreign Persons of U.S. Real Property Interests; and Statement of Withholding on Dispositions by Foreign Persons of U.S. Real Property Interests. Use these forms to report and transmit withheld tax on the sale of U.S. real property by a foreign person. See section 1445 and the related regulations for additional information.

Form 8300, Report of Cash Payments Over $10,000 Received in a Trade or Business. This form is used to report the receipt of more than $10,000 in cash or foreign currency in one transaction (or a series of related transactions).

Form 8594, Asset Acquisition Statement, is to be filed by both the purchaser and seller of a group of assets constituting a trade or business if goodwill or a going concern value attaches, or could attach, to such assets and if the purchaser's basis in the assets is determined only by the amount paid for the assets.

Form 8697, Interest Computation Under the Look-Back Method for Completed Long-Term Contracts. Certain S corporations that are not closely held may have to file Form 8697. Form 8697 is used to figure the interest due or to be refunded under the look-back method of section 460(b)(3) on certain long-term contracts entered into after February 28, 1986, that are accounted for under either the percentage of completion-capitalized cost method or the percentage of completion method. Closely held corporations should see the instructions for line 20, item 13, of Schedule K-1 for details on the Form 8697 information they must provide to their shareholders.

Stock ownership in foreign corporations.—If the corporation owned at least 5% in value of the outstanding stock of a foreign personal holding company, attach the statement required by section 551(c).

A corporation that (a) controls a foreign corporation; (b) is a 10%-or-more shareholder of a controlled foreign corporation; or (c) acquires, disposes of, or owns 5% or more in value of the outstanding stock of a foreign corporation, may have to file **Form 5471,** Information Return of U.S. Persons With Respect to Certain Foreign Corporations.

Transfers to corporation controlled by transferor.—If a person acquires stock of a corporation in exchange for property, and no gain or loss is recognized under section 351, the transferor and transferee must attach to their respective tax returns the information required by Regulations section 1.351-3.

Attachments

Attach **Form 4136,** Credit for Federal Tax on Fuels, after page 4, Form 1120S. Attach schedules in alphabetical order and other forms in numerical order after Form 4136.

To assist us in processing the return, please complete every applicable entry space on Form 1120S and Schedule K-1. Do not attach statements and write "See attached" in lieu of completing the entry spaces on Form 1120S and Schedule K-1.

If you need more space on the forms or schedules, attach separate sheets and show the same information in the same order as on the printed forms. **But show your totals on the printed forms.** Please use sheets that are the same size as the forms and schedules. Attach these separate sheets after all the schedules and forms. Be sure to put the corporation's name and employer identification number (EIN) on each sheet.

Amended Return

To correct an error in a Form 1120S already filed, file an amended Form 1120S and check box F(4). If the amended return results in a change to income, or a change in the distribution of any income or other information provided to shareholders, an amended Schedule K-1 (Form 1120S) must also be filed with the amended Form 1120S and given to each shareholder. Be sure to check box D(2) on each Schedule K-1 to indicate that it is an amended Schedule K-1.

Page 4

Note: *If an S corporation does not meet the small S corporation exception under Temporary Regulations section 301.6241-1T or if it is a small S corporation that has made the election described in Temporary Regulations section 301.6241-1T(c)(2)(v), and such corporation files an amended return, the amended return will be a request for administrative adjustment and Form 8082, Notice of Inconsistent Treatment or Amended Return (Administrative Adjustment Request (AAR)), must be filed by the tax matters person. See the Temporary Regulations under section 6241 for more information.*

Passive Activity Limitations

In general, section 469 limits the amount of losses, deductions, and credits that shareholders may claim from "passive activities." The passive activity limitations do not apply to the corporation. Instead, they apply to each shareholder's share of any income or loss and credit attributable to a passive activity. Because the treatment of each shareholder's share of corporation income or loss and credit depends upon the nature of the activity that generated it, the corporation must report income or loss and credits separately for each activity.

The instructions below (pages 5 through 8) and the instructions for Schedules K and K-1 (pages 13 through 20) explain the applicable passive activity limitation rules and specify the type of information the corporation must provide to its shareholders for each activity. If the corporation had more than one activity, it must report information for each activity on an attachment to Schedules K and K-1.

Generally, passive activities include **(a)** activities that involve the conduct of a trade or business in which the shareholder does not materially participate, and **(b)** any rental activity (see definition on page 6) even if the shareholder materially participates. The level of each shareholder's participation in an activity must be determined by the shareholder.

The passive activity rules provide that losses and credits from passive activities can generally be applied only against income and tax from passive activities. Thus, passive losses and credits cannot be applied against income from salaries, wages, professional fees, or a business in which the shareholder materially participates; against "portfolio income" (see definition on page 7); or against the tax related to any of these types of income.

Special transitional rules apply to losses incurred by investors in qualified low-income housing projects. In addition, special rules require that net income from certain activities that would otherwise be treated as passive income must be recharacterized as nonpassive income for purposes of the passive activity limitations.

To allow each shareholder to apply the passive activity limitations at the individual level, the corporation must report income or loss and credits separately for each of the following: trade or business activities, rental real estate activities, rental activities other than rental real estate, and portfolio income. For definitions of each type of activity or income, see **Types of Activities and Income,** below. For details on the special reporting requirements for passive activities, see **Passive Activity Reporting Requirements** on page 7.

Identifying Activities

Generally, each undertaking the corporation owns is a separate activity.

An undertaking includes all the business or rental operations owned at the same location. Operations not actually conducted at the same location are treated as conducted at the location with which they are most closely associated under all the facts and circumstances. For example, if a business sends employees from a central office to perform services at the customer's home, the operations are treated as conducted at the central office. If the corporation conducts all its business or rental operations at the same location directly or through one entity, the corporation has only one undertaking and one activity.

Rental undertakings.—If the corporation owns an undertaking that conducts both rental and nonrental operations, it must treat the two types of operations as two separate undertakings unless **(a)** the rental operations, if treated as a separate activity, would not be a rental activity (see **Rental activities** on page 6) or **(b)** one type of operation produces more than 80% of the combined undertaking's gross income.

Combining corporate undertakings into activities.—Once corporate undertakings are identified, treat each undertaking as a separate activity unless one of the following rules requires or permits the corporation to combine undertakings into a larger activity:

Trade or business undertakings.— Generally, the corporation must combine trade or business undertakings into a larger activity if the undertakings are similar and commonly controlled. For details, see Temporary Regulations sections 1.469-4T(f) and (j). Trade or business undertakings include all nonrental undertakings except professional service undertakings (described in the next paragraph) and oil or gas wells treated as separate undertakings under Temporary Regulations section 1.469-4T(e). Trade or business activities that constitute an integrated business may have to be combined into an even larger activity under Temporary Regulations section 1.469-4T(g).

Professional service undertakings.— Professional service undertakings principally provide services in the fields of health, law, engineering, architecture, accounting, actuarial science, the performing arts, or consulting. Generally, the corporation must combine its interests in professional service undertakings into a single activity if the undertakings provide services in the same field or earn more than 20% of their gross income from serving the same customers, or if the undertakings are controlled by the same interests. For details, see Temporary Regulations section 1.469-4T(h).

The corporation can elect to treat combined nonrental undertakings acquired in 1991 as separate activities for purposes other than determining participation in activities. To make this election, the corporation must attach to Form 1120S a statement that **(a)** gives the corporation name, address, and employer identification number; **(b)** declares that the election is being made under Temporary Regulations section 1.469-4T(o); **(c)** identifies the undertaking that is treated as a separate activity; and **(d)** identifies the rest of the activity from which the undertaking was separated.

If the corporation wants to treat as separate activities any undertakings it acquired in 1991 that these rules would otherwise combine into a larger activity, it must attach this statement to its 1991 return or it will not be able to treat the undertakings as separate activities for 1991 or any later year. For details, see Temporary Regulations section 1.469-4T(o).

If undertakings the corporation acquired in a previous year were combined into a larger activity on a prior return, those undertakings cannot be divided into separate activities in 1991 or any later year.

Rental real estate undertakings.—A rental real estate undertaking is a rental undertaking in which at least 85% of the unadjusted basis of the property made available for use by customers is real property. The corporation may treat a single rental real estate undertaking as a single activity, or it may treat any combination of rental real estate undertakings as a single activity. Under certain circumstances, the corporation may also elect to divide a single rental real estate undertaking into separate undertakings. For details, see Temporary Regulations section 1.469-4T(k)(2)(iii).

Generally, the corporation must attach a statement to Form 1120S if it combines separate rental real estate undertakings or portions of undertakings into the same activity or divides a single rental real estate undertaking into separate undertakings. If the corporation wants to divide a single rental real estate undertaking it acquired in 1991 into separate undertakings, it must attach this statement to its 1991 Form 1120S or it will not be able to treat the undertaking as separate undertakings for 1991 or any later year.

If the corporation divided a single rental real estate undertaking it acquired in a previous year into separate undertakings on a prior year return, it must treat the undertakings as separate undertakings in 1991 and any later year.

Futhermore, if the corporation combined rental real estate undertakings it acquired in a previous year into a larger activity on a prior year return, the larger activity cannot be divided into separate activities in 1991 or any later year.

Page 5

Types of Activities and Income

Trade or business activities.—A trade or business activity involves the conduct of a trade or business within the meaning of section 162.

If the shareholder does not materially participate in the activity, a trade or business activity of the corporation is a passive activity for the shareholder.

Note: *The section 469(c)(3) exception for a working interest in oil and gas properties is not applicable to an S corporation because state law generally limits the liability of corporate shareholders, including shareholders of an S corporation.*

Accordingly, an activity of holding a working interest in oil or gas properties is a trade or business activity and the material participation rules apply to determine if the activity is a passive activity. See Temporary Regulations section 1.469-1T(e)(4).

The determination whether a shareholder materially participated in an activity must be made by each shareholder. As a result, while the corporation's overall trade or business income (loss) is reported on page 1 of Form 1120S, the specific income and deductions from each separate trade or business activity must be reported on attachments to Form 1120S. Similarly, while each shareholder's allocable share of the corporation's overall trade or business income (loss) is reported on line 1 of Schedule K-1, each shareholder's allocable share of the income and deductions from each trade or business activity must be reported on attachments to each Schedule K-1. See **Passive Activity Reporting Requirements** on page 7 for more information.

Rental activities.—Generally, except as noted below, if the gross income from an activity consists of amounts paid principally for the use of real or personal tangible property held by the corporation, the activity is a rental activity. There are several exceptions to this general rule. Under these exceptions, an activity involving the use of real or personal tangible property is not a rental activity if **(a)** the average period of customer use (see definition below) for such property is 7 days or less; **(b)** the average period of customer use for such property is 30 days or less and significant personal services (see definition below) are provided by or on behalf of the corporation; **(c)** extraordinary personal services (see definition below) are provided by or on behalf of the corporation; **(d)** the rental of such property is treated as incidental to a nonrental activity of the corporation under Temporary Regulations section 1.469-1T(e)(3)(vi); or **(e)** the corporation customarily makes the property available during defined business hours for nonexclusive use by various customers. In addition, if a corporation owns an interest in a partnership that conducts a nonrental activity, and the corporation provides property for use in that activity in the corporation's capacity as an owner of an interest in the partnership, the provision of the property is not a rental activity. Consequently, the corporation's distributive share of income

Page 6

from the activity is not income from a rental activity. A guaranteed payment described in section 707(c) is not income from a rental activity under any circumstances.

Whether the corporation provides property used in an activity of a partnership in the corporation's capacity as an owner of an interest in the partnership is based on all the facts and circumstances.

Average period of customer use.—The average period of customer use of property is computed by dividing the total number of days in all rental periods by the number of rentals during the tax year. If the activity involves renting more than one class of property, multiply the average period of customer use of each class by the ratio of the gross rental income from that class to the activity's total gross rental income. The activity's average period of customer use equals the sum of these class-by-class average periods weighted by gross income. See Temporary Regulations section 1.469-1T(e)(3)(iii).

Significant personal services.—Personal services include only services performed by individuals. In determining whether personal services are significant personal services, all of the relevant facts and circumstances are considered. Relevant facts and circumstances include the frequency that the services are provided, the type and amount of labor required to perform the services, and the value of the services in relation to the amount charged for the use of the property. The following services are excluded from consideration in determining whether personal services are significant: **(a)** services necessary to permit the lawful use of the rental property; **(b)** services performed in connection with improvements or repairs to the rental property that extend the useful life of the property substantially beyond the average rental period; and **(c)** services provided in connection with the use of any improved real property that are similar to those commonly provided in connection with long-term rentals of high-grade commercial or residential property (e.g., cleaning and maintenance of common areas, routine repairs, trash collection, elevator service, and security at entrances).

Extraordinary personal services.—Services provided in connection with making rental property available for customer use are extraordinary personal services only if the services are performed by individuals and the customers' use of the rental property is incidental to their receipt of the services. For example, a patient's use of a hospital room generally is incidental to the care that the patient receives from the hospital's medical staff. Similarly, a student's use of a dormitory room in a boarding school is incidental to the personal services provided by the school's teaching staff.

Rental property incidental to a nonrental activity.—An activity is not a rental activity if the rental of the property is incidental to a nonrental activity, such as the activity of holding property for

investment, a trade or business activity, or the activity of dealing in property.

Rental property is incidental to an activity of holding property for investment if the main purpose for holding the property is to realize a gain from the appreciation of the property and the gross rental income from such property for the tax year is less than 2% of the smaller of the unadjusted basis of the property or the fair market value of the property.

Rental property is incidental to a trade or business activity if **(a)** the corporation owns an interest in the trade or business at all times during the year; **(b)** the rental property was mainly used in the trade or business activity during the tax year or during at least two of the five preceding tax years; and **(c)** the gross rental income from the property is less than 2% of the smaller of the unadjusted basis of the property or the fair market value of the property.

The sale or exchange of property that is also rented during the tax year (where the gain or loss is recognized) is treated as incidental to the activity of dealing in property if, at the time of the sale or exchange, the property was held primarily for sale to customers in the ordinary course of the corporation's trade or business.

See Temporary Regulations section 1.469-1T(e)(3) for more information on the definition of rental activities for purposes of the passive activity limitations.

Reporting of rental activities.—In reporting the corporation's income or losses and credits from rental activities, the corporation must separately report **(a)** rental real estate activities and **(b)** rental activities other than rental real estate activities.

Shareholders who actively participate in a rental real estate activity may be able to deduct part or all of their rental real estate losses (and the deduction equivalent of rental real estate credits) against income (or tax) from nonpassive activities. Generally, the combined amount of rental real estate losses and the deduction equivalent of rental real estate credits from all sources (including rental real estate activities not held through the corporation) that may be claimed is limited to $25,000.

Special transitional rules apply to investors in qualified low-income housing projects. See section 502 of the Tax Reform Act of 1986 and **Pub. 925,** Passive Activity and At-Risk Rules, for more information.

Rental real estate activity income (loss) is reported on **Form 8825,** Rental Real Estate Income and Expenses of a Partnership or an S Corporation, and on line 2 of Schedules K and K-1 rather than on page 1 of Form 1120S.

Credits related to rental real estate activities are reported on lines 12c and 12d of Schedules K and K-1. Low-income housing credits are reported on line 12b of Schedules K and K-1.

Income (loss) from rental activities other than rental real estate is reported on line 3 of Schedules K and K-1. Credits related to rental activities other than rental real estate are reported on line 12e of Schedules K and K-1.

Portfolio income.—Generally, portfolio income includes all gross income, other than income derived in the ordinary course of a trade or business, that is attributable to interest; dividends; royalties; income from a real estate investment trust, a regulated investment company, a real estate mortgage investment conduit, a common trust fund, a controlled foreign corporation, a qualified electing fund, or a cooperative; income from the disposition of property that produces income of a type defined as portfolio income; and income from the disposition of property held for investment.

Solely for purposes of the preceding paragraph, gross income derived in the ordinary course of a trade or business includes **(and portfolio income, therefore, does not include)** only the following types of income: **(a)** interest income on loans and investments made in the ordinary course of a trade or business of lending money; **(b)** interest on accounts receivable arising from the performance of services or the sale of property in the ordinary course of a trade or business of performing such services or selling such property, but only if credit is customarily offered to customers of the business; **(c)** income from investments made in the ordinary course of a trade or business of furnishing insurance or annuity contracts or reinsuring risks underwritten by insurance companies; **(d)** income or gain derived in the ordinary course of an activity of trading or dealing in any property if such activity constitutes a trade or business (unless the dealer held the property for investment at any time before such income or gain is recognized); **(e)** royalties derived by the taxpayer in the ordinary course of a trade or business of licensing intangible property; **(f)** amounts included in the gross income of a patron of a cooperative by reason of any payment or allocation to the patron based on patronage occurring with respect to a trade or business of the patron; and **(g)** other income identified by the IRS as income derived by the taxpayer in the ordinary course of a trade or business.

See Temporary Regulations section 1.469-2T(c)(3) for more information on portfolio income.

Portfolio income is reported on line 4 of Schedules K and K-1, rather than on page 1 of Form 1120S.

Expenses related to portfolio income are reported on line 9 of Schedules K and K-1.

Recharacterization of Passive Income

Under the provisions of Temporary Regulations section 1.469-2T(f), net passive income from certain passive activities must be treated as nonpassive income. Income from the six sources listed below is subject to recharacterization. In addition, any net passive income from an activity of renting substantially nondepreciable property from an equity-financed lending activity, or from an activity related to an interest in a pass-through entity that licenses intangible property that is recharacterized as nonpassive income, is treated as investment income for purposes of computing investment interest expense limitations. "Net passive income" means the excess of passive activity gross income from the activity over passive activity deductions (current year deductions and prior year unallowed losses) from the activity.

1. Significant participation passive activities.—A significant participation passive activity is any trade or business activity in which the shareholder both participates for more than 100 hours during the tax year and does not materially participate. Because each shareholder must determine his or her level of participation, the corporation will not be able to identify significant participation passive activities.

2. Certain nondepreciable rental property activities.—Net passive income from a rental activity is nonpassive income if less than 30% of the unadjusted basis of the property used or held for use by customers in the activity is subject to depreciation under section 167.

3. Passive equity-financed lending activities.—If the corporation has net income from a passive equity-financed lending activity, the lesser of the net passive income or equity-financed interest income from the activity is nonpassive income.

Note: *The amount of income from the activities in items 1 through 3, above, that any shareholder will be required to recharacterize as nonpassive income may be limited under Temporary Regulations section 1.469-2T(f)(8). Because the corporation will not have information regarding all of a shareholder's activities, it must identify all corporate activities meeting the definitions in items 1 through 3 as activities that may be subject to recharacterization.*

4. Rental activities incidental to a development activity.—Net rental activity income is nonpassive income for a shareholder if all of the following apply: **(a)** the corporation recognizes gain from the sale, exchange, or other disposition of the rental property during the tax year; **(b)** the use of the item of property in the rental activity started less than 12 months before the date of disposition (the use of an item of rental property begins on the first day on which (i) the corporation owns an interest in the property; (ii) substantially all of the property is either rented or held out for rent and ready to be rented; and (iii) no significant value-enhancing services remain to be performed), and **(c)** the shareholder materially participated or significantly participated for any tax year in an activity that involved the performance of services for the purpose of enhancing the value of the property (or any other item of property, if the basis of the property disposed of is determined in whole or in part by reference to the basis of that item of property). "Net rental activity income" means the excess of passive activity gross income from renting or disposing of property over passive activity deductions (current year deductions and prior year unallowed losses) that are reasonably allocable to the rented property.

Because the corporation cannot determine a shareholder's level of participation, the corporation must identify net income from property described in items (a) and (b) above as income that may be subject to recharacterization.

5. Activities involving property rented to a nonpassive activity.—If a taxpayer rents property to a trade or business activity in which the taxpayer materially participates, the taxpayer's net rental activity income from the property is nonpassive income. "Net rental activity income" means the excess of passive activity gross income from renting or disposing of property over passive activity deductions (current year deductions and prior year unallowed losses) that are reasonably allocable to the rented property.

6. Acquisition of an interest in a pass-through entity that licenses intangible property.—Generally, net royalty income from intangible property is nonpassive income if the taxpayer acquired an interest in the pass-through entity after the pass-through entity created the intangible property or performed substantial services or incurred substantial costs in developing or marketing the intangible property. "Net royalty income" means the excess of passive activity gross income from licensing or transferring any right in intangible property over passive activity deductions (current year deductions and prior year unallowed losses) that are reasonably allocable to the intangible property.

See Temporary Regulations section 1.469-2T(f)(7)(iii) for exceptions to this rule.

Passive Activity Reporting Requirements

To allow shareholders to correctly apply the passive activity loss and credit limitation rules, any corporation that carries on more than one activity must:

1. Provide an attachment for each activity conducted through the corporation that identifies the type of activity conducted (trade or business, rental real estate, rental activity other than rental real estate, or investment).

2. On the attachment for each activity, provide a schedule, using the same line numbers as shown on Schedule K-1, detailing the net income (loss), credits, and all items required to be separately stated under section 1366(a)(1) from each trade or business activity, from each rental real estate activity, from each rental activity other than a rental real estate activity, and from investments.

3. Identify the net income (loss) and the shareholder's share of corporation interest expense from each activity of renting a dwelling unit that the shareholder also uses for personal purposes during the year for

Page 7

more than the greater of 14 days or 10% of the number of days that the residence is rented at fair rental value.

4. Identify the net income (loss) and the shareholder's share of interest expense from each activity of trading personal property conducted through the corporation.

5. With respect to any gain (loss) from the disposition of an interest in an activity or of an interest in property used in an activity (including dispositions before 1987 from which gain is being recognized after 1986):

a. Identify the activity in which the property was used at the time of disposition;

b. If the property was used in more than one activity during the 12 months preceding the disposition, identify the activities in which the property was used and the adjusted basis allocated to each activity; and

c. For gains only, if the property was substantially appreciated at the time of the disposition and the applicable holding period specified in Temporary Regulations section 1.469-2T(c)(2)(iii)(A) was not satisfied, identify the amount of the nonpassive gain and indicate whether or not the gain is investment income under the provisions of Temporary Regulations section 1.469-2T(c)(2)(iii)(E).

6. Specify the amount of gross portfolio income, the interest expense properly allocable to portfolio income, and expenses other than interest expense that are clearly and directly allocable to portfolio income.

7. Identify the ratable portion of any section 481 adjustment (whether a net positive or a net negative adjustment) allocable to each corporate activity.

8. Identify any gross income from sources that are specifically excluded from passive activity gross income, including income from intangible property if the shareholder is an individual and the shareholder's personal efforts significantly contributed to the creation of the property; income from a qualified low-income housing project (as defined in section 502 of the Tax Reform Act of 1986) conducted through the corporation; income from state, local, or foreign income tax refunds; and income from a covenant not to compete (in the case of a shareholder who is an individual and who contributed the covenant to the corporation).

9. Identify any deductions that are not passive activity deductions.

10. If the corporation makes a full or partial disposition of its interest in another entity, identify the gain (loss) allocable to each activity conducted through the entity, and the gain allocable to a passive activity that would have been recharacterized as nonpassive had the corporation disposed of its interest in property used in the activity (because the property was substantially appreciated at the time of the disposition, and the gain represented more than 10% of the shareholder's total gain from the disposition).

11. Identify the following items with respect to activities which may be subject to the recharacterization rules under Temporary Regulations section 1.469-2T(f):

a. Net income from an activity of renting substantially nondepreciable property;

b. The lesser of equity-financed interest income or net passive income from an equity-financed lending activity;

c. Net rental activity income from property that was developed (by the shareholder or the corporation), rented, and sold within 12 months after the rental of the property commenced;

d. Net rental activity income from the rental of property by the corporation to a trade or business activity in which the shareholder had an interest (either directly or indirectly); and

e. Net royalty income from intangible property if the shareholder acquired the shareholder's interest in the corporation after the corporation created the intangible property or performed substantial services or incurred substantial costs in developing or marketing the intangible property.

12. With respect to credits, identify separately the credits from the corporation that are associated with each activity conducted by or through the corporation.

Specific Instructions

General Information

Name, Address, and Employer Identification Number

Use the label on the package that was mailed to the corporation. If the corporation's name, address, or employer identification number is wrong on the label, mark through it and write the correct information on the label.

If the corporation does not have a package with a label, print or type the corporation's true name (as set forth in the corporate charter or other legal document creating it), address, and employer identification number on the appropriate lines.

Include the suite, room, or other unit number after the street address. If a preaddressed label is used, please include the information on the label. If the Post Office does not deliver to the street address and the corporation has a P.O. box, show the P.O. box number instead of the street address.

Item B—Business Code No.

See **Codes for Principal Business Activity** on page 22 of these instructions.

Item E—Total Assets

Enter the total assets, as determined by the accounting method regularly used in maintaining the corporation's books and records, at the end of the corporation's tax year. If there are no assets at the end of the tax year, enter the total assets as of the beginning of the tax year.

Item F—Initial Return, Final Return, Change in Address, and Amended Return

If this is the corporation's first return, check box F(1). If the corporation has ceased to exist, check box F(2). Also check box D(1) on each Schedule K-1 to indicate that it is a final Schedule K-1. Indicate a change in address by checking box F(3). If the corporation has a change of mailing address after filing its return, it can notify the IRS by filing **Form 8822,** Change of Address. If this amends a previously filed return, check box F(4).

Item G—Consolidated Audit Procedures

With certain exceptions, the tax treatment of S corporation items is determined at the S corporation level in a consolidated audit proceeding, rather than in separate proceedings with individual shareholders. Check the box for item G if any of the following apply.

● The S corporation had more than five shareholders at any time during the tax year (for this purpose a husband and wife, and their estates, are treated as one shareholder).

● Any shareholder was other than a natural person or estate.

● The small S corporation (five or fewer shareholders) has elected as provided in Temporary Regulations section 301.6241-1T(c)(2)(v) to be subject to the rules for consolidated proceedings.

Note: *The S corporation does not make the section 301.6241-1T(c)(2)(v) election when it checks the box for item G. This election must be made separately.*

For more information on the consolidated audit procedures for S corporations, see sections 6241 through 6245, Temporary Regulations section 301.6241-1T, and **Pub. 556,** Examination of Returns, Appeal Rights, and Claims for Refund.

Income

Caution: *Report only trade or business activity income or loss on lines 1a through 6. **Do not report rental activity income or portfolio income or loss on these lines.** (See the instructions on **Passive Activity Limitations** beginning on page 5 for definitions of rental income and portfolio income.) Rental activity income and portfolio income are reported on Schedules K and K-1 (rental real estate activities are also reported on Form 8825).*

Note: *Do not include any tax exempt income on lines 1 through 5, or any nondeductible expenses on lines 7 through 19. However, these income and expense items are used in figuring the accumulated adjustments account and the other adjustments account in Schedule M-2. Also, see instructions for line 18 of Schedule K and line 20 of Schedule K-1.*

A corporation that receives any exempt income other than interest, or holds any property or engages in an activity that

Page 8

produces exempt income, must attach to its return an itemized statement showing the amount of each type of exempt income and the expenses allocated to each type.

Line 1—Gross Receipts or Sales

Enter gross receipts or sales from all trade or business operations except those you report on lines 4 and 5. For reporting advance payments, see Regulations section 1.451-5. To report income from long-term contracts, see section 460.

Generally, the installment method cannot be used for dealer dispositions of property. A "dealer disposition" means any disposition of personal property by a person who regularly sells or otherwise disposes of personal property of the same type on the installment plan or any disposition of real property held for sale to customers in the ordinary course of the taxpayer's trade or business. The disposition of property used or produced in a farming business is not included as a dealer disposition. See section 453(l) for details and exceptions. For dealer dispositions of property before March 1, 1986, dispositions of property used or produced in the trade or business of farming, and certain dispositions of timeshares and residential lots reported under the installment method, enter on line 1a the gross profit on collections from installment sales and carry the same amount to line 3. Attach a schedule showing the following for the current year and the 3 preceding years: (a) gross sales, (b) cost of goods sold, (c) gross profits, (d) percentage of gross profits to gross sales, (e) amount collected, and (f) gross profit on amount collected.

Line 2—Cost of Goods Sold

See the instructions for Schedule A.

Line 4—Net Gain (Loss) From Form 4797

Caution: *Include only ordinary gains or losses from the sale, exchange, or involuntary conversion of assets used in a trade or business activity. Ordinary gains or losses from the sale, exchange, or involuntary conversions of assets of rental activities must be reported separately on Schedule K as part of the net income (loss) from the rental activity in which the property was used.*

In addition to the ordinary gains or losses reported on line 4 from the corporation's attached **Form 4797**, Sales of Business Property, a corporation that is a partner in a partnership must include its partnership share of ordinary gains (losses) from sales, exchanges, or involuntary or compulsory conversions (other than casualties or thefts) of the partnership's trade or business assets.

Do not include any recapture of the section 179 expense deduction. See the instructions for Schedule K-1, line 20, item 6, and for Form 4797 for more information.

Line 5—Other Income

Enter on line 5 trade or business income (loss) that is not included on lines 1a through 4. Examples of such income include: **(a)** interest income derived in the ordinary course of the corporation's trade or business, such as interest charged on receivable balances; **(b)** recoveries of bad debts deducted in earlier years under the specific charge-off method; **(c)** taxable income from insurance proceeds; and **(d)** the amount of credit figured on **Form 6478**, Credit for Alcohol Used as Fuel.

Also include on line 5 all section 481 income adjustments resulting from changes in accounting methods. Show the computation of the section 481 adjustment on an attached schedule. Do not include items requiring separate computations by shareholders that must be reported on Schedule K. (See the instructions for Schedules K and K-1.) Do not offset current year's taxes with tax refunds.

The corporation must include as other income the recapture amount for section 280F if the business use of listed property drops to 50% or less. See section 280F(b)(2). To figure the recapture amount, the corporation must complete Part V of Form 4797.

If "other income" consists of only one item, identify it by showing the account caption in parentheses on line 5. A separate schedule need not be attached to the return in this case.

Do not net any expense item (such as interest) with a similar income item. Report all trade or business expenses on lines 7 through 19.

Deductions

Caution: *Report only trade or business activity expenses on lines 7 through 19.* **Do not report rental activity expenses or deductions allocable to portfolio income on these lines.** *Rental activity expenses are separately reported on Form 8825 or line 3 of Schedules K and K-1. Deductions allocable to portfolio income are separately reported on line 9 of Schedules K and K-1. See the instructions on* **Passive Activity Limitations** *beginning on page 5 for more information on rental activities and portfolio income.*

Limitations on Deductions

Section 263A uniform capitalization rules.—The uniform capitalization rules of section 263A require corporations to capitalize or include in inventory certain costs incurred in connection with the production of real and personal tangible property held in inventory or held for sale in the ordinary course of business. Tangible personal property produced by a corporation includes a film, sound recording, video tape, book, or similar property. The rules also apply to personal property (tangible and intangible) acquired for resale. Corporations subject to the rules are required to capitalize not only direct costs but an allocable portion of most indirect costs (including taxes) that benefit the assets produced or acquired for resale.

Interest expense paid or incurred during the production period of certain property must be capitalized and is governed by special rules. For more information, see Notice 88-99, 1988-2 C.B. 422. The uniform capitalization rules also apply to the production of property constructed or improved by a corporation for use in its trade or business or in an activity engaged in for profit.

Section 263A does not apply to personal property acquired for resale if the taxpayer's annual average gross receipts are $10 million or less. It does not apply to timber or to most property produced under a long-term contract. Special rules apply to certain corporations engaged in farming (see below). The rules do not apply to property that is produced for use by the taxpayer if substantial construction occurred before March 1, 1986.

In the case of inventory, some of the indirect costs that must be capitalized are: administration expenses; taxes; depreciation; insurance; compensation paid to officers attributable to services; rework labor; and contributions to pension, stock bonus, and certain profit-sharing, annuity, or deferred compensation plans.

The costs required to be capitalized under section 263A are not deductible until the property to which the costs relate is sold, used, or otherwise disposed of by the corporation.

Research and experimental costs under section 174, intangible drilling costs for oil and gas and geothermal property, and mining exploration and development costs are separately reported to shareholders for purposes of determinations under section 59(e). Temporary Regulations section 1.263A-1T specifies other indirect costs that may be currently deducted and those that must be capitalized with respect to production or resale activities. For more information, see Temporary Regulations section 1.263A-1T; Notice 88-86, 1988-2 C.B. 401; and Notice 89-67, 1989-1 C.B. 723.

Special rules for certain corporations engaged in farming.—For S corporations not required to use the accrual method of accounting, the rules of section 263A do **not** apply to expenses of raising **(a)** any animal or **(b)** any plant that has a preproductive period of 2 years or less. Shareholders of S corporations not required to use the accrual method of accounting may elect to currently deduct the preproductive period expenses of certain plants that have a preproductive period of more than 2 years. Because the election to deduct these expenses is made by the shareholder, the farming corporation should not capitalize such preproductive expenses but should separately report these expenses on line 18 of Schedule K, and each shareholder's share on line 20 of Schedule K-1. See sections 263A(d) and (e) and Temporary Regulations section 1.263A-1T(c) for definitions and other details. Also see Notice 88-24, 1988-1 C.B. 491 and Notice 89-67.

Transactions between related taxpayers.—Generally, an accrual basis S

Page 9

corporation may deduct business expenses and interest owed to a related party (including any shareholder) **only** in the tax year of the corporation that includes the day on which the payment is includible in the income of the related party. See section 267 for details.

Section 291 limitations.—If the S corporation was a C corporation for any of the 3 immediately preceding years, the corporation may be required to adjust deductions allowed to the corporation for depletion of iron ore and coal, and the amortizable basis of pollution control facilities. See section 291 to determine the amount of the adjustment.

Business start-up expenses.—Business start-up expenses must be capitalized. An election may be made to amortize them over a period of not less than 60 months. See section 195.

Line 7—Compensation of Officers

Enter on line 7 the total compensation of all officers paid or incurred in the trade or business activities of the corporation, including fringe benefit expenditures made on behalf of officers owning more than 2% of the corporation's stock. Also report these fringe benefits as wages in Box 10 of Form W-2. Do not include on line 7 amounts paid or incurred for fringe benefits of officers owning 2% or less of the corporation's stock. These amounts are reported on line 18, page 1, of Form 1120S. See the instructions for that line for information on the types of expenditures that are treated as fringe benefits and for the stock ownership rules.

If you report amounts on line 7 that were paid for insurance that constitutes medical care for a more than 2% shareholder, that shareholder's spouse, and that shareholder's dependents, the shareholder may be allowed a deduction of up to 25% of such amounts on Form 1040, line 26. Report the amount paid for medical insurance for that shareholder as an information item in Box 18 of his or her Form W-2.

Do not include on line 7 compensation reported elsewhere on the return, such as amounts included in cost of goods sold, elective contributions to a section 401(k) cash or deferred arrangement, or amounts contributed under a salary reduction SEP agreement.

Line 8—Salaries and Wages

Enter on line 8a the amount of salaries and wages paid or incurred for the tax year, including fringe benefit expenditures made on behalf of employees (other than officers) owning more than 2% of the corporation's stock. Also report these fringe benefits as wages in Box 10 of Form W-2. Do not include on line 8a amounts paid or incurred for fringe benefits of employees owning 2% or less of the corporation's stock. These amounts are reported on line 18, page 1, of Form 1120S. See the instructions for that line for information on the types of expenditures that are treated as fringe benefits and for the stock ownership rules.

If you report amounts on line 8a that were paid for insurance that constitutes medical care for a more than 2% shareholder, that shareholder's spouse, and that shareholder's dependents, the shareholder may be allowed a deduction of up to 25% of such amounts on Form 1040, line 26. Report the amount paid for medical insurance for that shareholder as an information item in Box 18 of his or her Form W-2.

Do not include on line 8a salaries and wages reported elsewhere on the return, such as amounts included in cost of goods sold, elective contributions to a section 401(k) cash or deferred arrangement, or amounts contributed under a salary reduction SEP agreement.

Enter on line 8b the applicable jobs credit from **Form 5884,** Jobs Credit. See the instructions for Form 5884 for more information.

If a shareholder or a member of the family of one or more shareholders of the corporation renders services or furnishes capital to the corporation for which reasonable compensation is not paid, the IRS may make adjustments in the items taken into account by such individuals and the value of such services or capital. See section 1366(e).

Line 9—Repairs

Enter the cost of incidental repairs, such as labor and supplies, that do not add to the value of the property or appreciably prolong its life, but only to the extent that such repairs relate to a trade or business activity and are not claimed elsewhere on the return. New buildings, machinery, or permanent improvements that increase the value of the property are not deductible. They are chargeable to capital accounts and may be depreciated or amortized.

Do not include any section 179 expense deduction on this line. See the instructions for line 8 of Schedules K and K-1 for details on reporting these items to shareholders.

Line 10—Bad Debts

Enter the total debts that became worthless in whole or in part during the year, but only to the extent such debts relate to a trade or business activity.

Caution: *Cash method taxpayers cannot take a bad debt deduction unless the amount was previously included in income.*

Line 11—Rents

If the corporation rented or leased a vehicle, enter the total annual rent or lease expense paid or incurred in the trade or business activities of the corporation. Also complete Part V of **Form 4562,** Depreciation and Amortization. If the corporation leased a vehicle for a term of 30 days or more, the deduction for vehicle lease expense may have to be reduced by an amount called the **inclusion amount.** You may have an inclusion amount if—

The lease term began:	And the vehicle's fair market value on the first day of the lease exceeded:
After 12/31/86	$12,800
After 4/2/85 but before 1/1/87 .	$28,000
After 6/18/84 but before 4/3/85 .	$40,500

See **Pub. 917,** Business Use of a Car, for instructions on how to figure the inclusion amount.

Line 12—Taxes

Enter taxes paid or incurred in the trade or business activities of the corporation, if not reflected in cost of goods sold. Federal import duties and Federal excise and stamp taxes are deductible only if paid or incurred in carrying on the trade or business of the corporation. Taxes incurred in the production or collection of income, or for the management, conservation, or maintenance of property held for the production of income are not deductible on line 12. Report these taxes separately on Schedules K and K-1, line 10.

Do not deduct taxes, including state and local sales taxes, paid or accrued in connection with the acquisition or disposition of business property. These taxes must be added to the cost of the property, or in the case of a disposition, subtracted from the amount realized. See section 164.

Do not deduct taxes assessed against local benefits that increase the value of the property assessed (such as for paving, etc.); Federal income taxes; estate, inheritance, legacy, succession, and gift taxes; or taxes reported elsewhere on the return.

Do not deduct section 901 foreign taxes. These taxes are reported separately on line 15e, Schedule K.

See section 263A(a) for information on capitalization of allocable costs (including taxes) for any property.

Line 13—Interest

Include on line 13 only interest incurred in the trade or business activities of the corporation that is not claimed elsewhere on the return.

Do not include interest expense on debt used to purchase rental property or debt used in a rental activity. Interest allocable to a rental real estate activity is reported on Form 8825 and is used in arriving at net income (loss) from rental real estate activities on line 2 of Schedules K and K-1. Interest allocable to a rental activity other than a rental real estate activity is included on line 3b of Schedule K and is used in arriving at net income (loss) from a rental activity (other than a rental real estate activity). This net amount is reported on line 3c of Schedule K and line 3 of Schedule K-1.

Do not include interest expense that is clearly and directly allocable to portfolio or investment income. This interest expense is reported separately on line 11a of Schedule K.

Page 10

Do not include interest on debt proceeds allocated to distributions made to shareholders during the tax year. Instead, report such interest on line 10 of Schedules K and K-1. To determine the amount to allocate to distributions to shareholders, see Notice 89-35, 1989-1 C.B. 675.

Do not include interest expense on debt required to be allocated to the production of qualified property. Interest that is allocable to certain property produced by an S corporation for its own use or for sale must be capitalized. The corporation must also capitalize any interest on debt that is allocable to an asset used to produce the above property. A shareholder may have to capitalize interest that the shareholder incurs during the tax year for the production expenditures of the S corporation. Similarly, interest incurred by an S corporation may have to be capitalized by a shareholder for the shareholder's own production expenditures. The information required by the shareholder to properly capitalize interest for this purpose must be provided by the corporation in an attachment for line 20 of Schedule K-1 (see the instructions for Schedule K-1, line 20, item 12). See section 263A(f) and Notice 88-99 for additional information.

Temporary Regulations section 1.163-8T gives rules for allocating interest expense among activities so that the limitations on passive activity losses, investment interest, and personal interest can be properly figured. Generally, interest expense is allocated in the same manner as debt is allocated. Debt is allocated by tracing disbursements of the debt proceeds to specific expenditures. These regulations give rules for tracing debt proceeds to expenditures.

Generally, prepaid interest can only be deducted over the period to which the prepayment applies. See section 461(g) for details.

Line 14—Depreciation

Enter on line 14a only the depreciation claimed on assets used in a trade or business activity. See the Instructions for Form 4562 or **Pub. 534**, Depreciation, to figure the amount of depreciation to enter on this line. For depreciation, you must complete and attach Form 4562 only if the corporation placed property in service during 1991 or claims depreciation on any car or other listed property.

Do not include any section 179 expense deduction on this line. This amount is not deductible by the corporation. Instead, it is passed through to the shareholders on line 8 of Schedule K-1.

Line 15—Depletion

If the corporation claims a deduction for timber depletion, complete and attach **Form T**, Forest Industries Schedules.

Caution: *Do not report depletion deductions for oil and gas properties on this line. Each shareholder figures depletion on these properties under section 613A(c)(11). See the instructions for line 20*

of Schedule K-1 for information on oil and gas depletion that must be supplied to the shareholders by the corporation.

Line 17—Pension, Profit-Sharing, etc., Plans

Enter the deductible contributions not claimed elsewhere on the return made by the corporation for its employees under a qualified pension, profit-sharing, annuity, or simplified employee pension (SEP) plan, and under any other deferred compensation plan.

If the corporation contributes to an individual retirement arrangement (IRA) for employees, include the contribution in salaries and wages on page 1, line 8a, or Schedule A, line 3, and not on line 17.

Employers who maintain a pension, profit-sharing, or other funded deferred compensation plan, whether or not qualified under the Internal Revenue Code and whether or not a deduction is claimed for the current tax year, generally are required to file one of the forms listed below:

Form 5500, Annual Return/Report of Employee Benefit Plan (with 100 or more participants).

Form 5500-C/R, Return/Report of Employee Benefit Plan (with fewer than 100 participants).

Form 5500EZ, Annual Return of One-Participant (Owners and Their Spouses) Pension Benefit Plan. Complete this form for a one-participant plan.

There are penalties for failure to file these forms on time and for overstating the pension plan deduction.

Line 18—Employee Benefit Programs

Enter amounts for fringe benefits paid or incurred on behalf of employees owning 2% or less of the corporation's stock. These fringe benefits include **(a)** up to $5,000 paid by reason of an employee's death to his estate or beneficiary, **(b)** employer contributions to certain accident and health plans, **(c)** the cost of up to $50,000 of group-term life insurance on an employee's life, and **(d)** meals and lodging furnished for the employer's convenience.

Do not deduct amounts that are an incidental part of a pension, profit-sharing, etc., plan included on line 17 or amounts reported elsewhere on the return.

Report amounts paid on behalf of more than 2% shareholders on line 7 or 8 of Form 1120S, whichever applies. A shareholder is considered to own more than 2% of the corporation's stock if that person owns on any day during the tax year more than 2% of the outstanding stock of the corporation or stock possessing more than 2% of the combined voting power of all stock of the corporation. See section 318 for attribution rules.

Line 19—Other Deductions

Attach a separate sheet listing all allowable deductions related to any trade or business activity for which there is no line on page 1 of the return. Enter the total on this line. Do not include those items that must be reported separately on Schedules K and K-1.

An S corporation may not take the deduction for net operating losses provided by section 172 or the special deductions in sections 241 through 249 (except the election to amortize organizational expenditures under section 248). Subject to limitations, the corporation's net operating loss is allowed as a deduction from the shareholders' gross income. See section 1366.

Do not include qualified expenditures to which an election under section 59(e) may apply. See instructions for lines 16a and 16b of Schedule K-1 for details on treatment of these items.

Include on line 19 the deduction taken for amortization. See instructions for Form 4562 for more information. You must complete and attach Form 4562 if the corporation is claiming amortization of costs that begin during its 1991 tax year.

In most cases, you may not take a deduction for any part of any item allocable to a class of exempt income. (See section 265 for exceptions.) Items directly attributable to wholly exempt income must be allocated to that income. Items directly attributable to any class of taxable income must be allocated to that taxable income.

If an item is indirectly attributable both to taxable income and to exempt income, allocate a reasonable proportion of the item to each, based on all the facts in each case.

Attach a statement showing **(a)** the amount of each class of exempt income and **(b)** the amount of expense items allocated to each such class. Show the amount allocated by apportionment separately.

Section 464(f) limits the deduction for certain expenditures of S corporations engaged in farming that use the cash method of accounting, and whose prepaid expenses for feed, seed, fertilizer, and other farm supplies, and the cost of poultry are more than 50% of other deductible farming expenses. Generally, any excess (amount over 50%) may be deducted only in the tax year the items are actually used or consumed. See section 464(f) for more information.

Generally, the corporation can deduct only 80% of the amount otherwise allowable for meals and entertainment expenses paid or incurred in its trade or business. In addition, meals must not be lavish or extravagant; a bona fide business discussion must occur during, immediately before, or immediately after the meal; and an employee of the corporation must be present at the meal. See section 274(k)(2) for exceptions.

Additional limitations apply to deductions for gifts, skybox rentals, luxury water

Page 11

travel, convention expenses, and entertainment tickets. See section 274 and **Pub. 463,** Travel, Entertainment, and Gift Expenses, for details.

Generally, a corporation can deduct all other ordinary and necessary travel and entertainment expenses paid or incurred in its trade or business. However, it cannot deduct an expense paid or incurred for a facility (such as a yacht or hunting lodge) that is used for an activity that is usually considered entertainment, amusement, or recreation.

Note: *The corporation may be able to deduct the expense if the amount is treated as compensation and reported on Form W-2 for an employee or on Form 1099-MISC for an independent contractor.*

Do not deduct penalties imposed on the corporation such as those included in the General Instruction on **Interest and Penalties.**

Line 21—Ordinary Income (Loss)

This is nonseparately computed income or loss as defined in section 1366(a)(2) attributable to trade or business activities of the corporation. This income or loss is entered on line 1 of Schedule K.

Line 21 income is not used in figuring the tax on line 22a or 22b. See the instructions for line 22a for figuring taxable income for purposes of line 22a or 22b tax.

Line 22a—Excess Net Passive Income Tax

If the corporation has always been an S corporation, the excess net passive income tax does not apply to the corporation. If the corporation has subchapter C earnings and profits (defined in section 1362(d)(3)(B)) at the close of its tax year, has passive investment income for the tax year that is in excess of 25% of gross receipts, and has taxable income at year end, the corporation must pay a tax on the excess net passive income. Complete lines 1 through 3 and line 9 of the worksheet below to make this determination. If line 2 is greater than line 3 and the corporation has taxable income (see instructions for line 9 of worksheet), it must pay the tax. Complete a separate schedule using the format of lines 1 through 11 of the worksheet below to figure the tax. Enter the tax on line 22a, page 1, Form 1120S, and attach the computation schedule to Form 1120S.

Reduce each item of passive income passed through to shareholders by its portion of tax on line 22a. See section 1366(f)(3).

Worksheet for Line 22a

1. Enter gross receipts for the tax year (see section 1362(d)(3)(C) for gross receipts from the sale of capital assets)* . . . . _____
2. Enter passive investment income as defined in section 1362(d)(3)(D)* . _____
3. Enter 25% of line 1 (If line 2 is less than line 3, stop here. You are not liable for this tax.) . . . . _____

4. Excess passive investment income—Subtract line 3 from line 2 . . . _____
5. Enter deductions directly connected with the production of income on line 2 (see section 1375(b)(2))* . . . _____
6. Net passive income—Subtract line 5 from line 2 . . . . . . _____
7. Divide amount on line 4 by amount on line 2 . . . . _____ %

8. Excess net passive income—Multiply line 6 by line 7 . . . . . . _____
9. Enter taxable income (see instructions for taxable income below) . . _____
10. Enter smaller of line 8 or line 9 . . _____
11. Excess net passive income tax—Enter 34% of line 10. Enter here and on line 22a, page 1, Form 1120S . . . _____

*Income and deductions on lines 1, 2, and 5 are from total operations for the tax year. This includes applicable income and expenses from page 1, Form 1120S, as well as those reported separately on Schedule K. See sections 1362(d)(3)(D) and 1375(b)(4) for exceptions regarding lines 2 and 5.

Line 9 of Worksheet.—Taxable income.—

Line 9 taxable income is defined in Regulations section 1.1374-1A(d). Figure this income by completing lines 1 through 28 of **Form 1120,** U.S. Corporation Income Tax Return. Include the Form 1120 computation with the worksheet computation you attach to Form 1120S. You do not have to attach the schedules, etc., called for on Form 1120. However, you may want to complete certain Form 1120 schedules, such as Schedule D (Form 1120), if you have capital gains or losses.

Line 22b—Tax From Schedule D (Form 1120S)

If the corporation elected to be an S corporation before 1987 (or elected to be an S corporation during 1987 or 1988 and qualifies for transitional relief from the built-in gains tax), see instructions for Part III of Schedule D (Form 1120S) to determine if the corporation is liable for the capital gains tax.

If the corporation made its election to be an S corporation after 1986, see the instructions for Part IV of Schedule D to determine if the corporation is liable for the built-in gains tax.

Note: *For purposes of line 13 of Part III and line 17 of Part IV of Schedule D, taxable income is defined in section 1375(b)(1)(B) and is generally figured in the same manner as taxable income for line 9 of the worksheet above for line 22a of Form 1120S.*

Line 22c

Include in the total for line 22c the following:

Investment credit recapture tax.— Section 1371(d) provides that an S corporation is liable for investment credit recapture attributable to credits allowed for tax years for which the corporation was not an S corporation.

Figure the corporation's investment credit recapture tax by completing **Form 4255,** Recapture of Investment Credit. Include the tax in the total amount to be entered on line 22c. Write to the left of the line 22c total the amount of recapture tax and the words "Tax From Form 4255," and attach Form 4255 to Form 1120S.

LIFO recapture tax.—If the corporation used the LIFO inventory pricing method for its last tax year as a C corporation, the corporation may be liable for the additional tax due to LIFO recapture under section 1363(d).

The LIFO recapture tax is figured for the last tax year the corporation was a C corporation. See the Instructions for Forms 1120 and 1120-A for details. The LIFO tax is paid in four equal installments. The first installment is due with the corporation's Form 1120 (or 1120-A) for the corporation's last tax year as a C corporation, and each of the remaining installments is paid with the corporation's Form 1120S for the 3 succeeding tax years. Include this year's installment in the total amount to be entered on line 22c, page 1, Form 1120S. Write to the left of the total on line 22c the installment amount and the words "LIFO tax."

Interest due under the look-back method for completed long-term contracts.—If the corporation completed **Form 8697,** Interest Computation Under the Look-Back Method for Completed Long-Term Contracts, and owes interest, write to the left of the line 22c total the amount of interest and "From Form 8697." Attach the completed form to Form 1120S.

Line 23d

If the S corporation is a beneficiary of a trust and the trust makes a section 643(g) election to credit its estimated tax overpayments to its beneficiaries, include the corporation's share of the overpayment (reported to the corporation on Schedule K-1 (Form 1041)) in the total amount entered on line 23d. Also, to the left of line 23d, write "T" and the amount of the overpayment.

Schedule A—Cost of Goods Sold

Section 263A Uniform Capitalization Rules

The uniform capitalization rules of section 263A are discussed under **Limitations on Deductions** on page 9. See those instructions before completing Schedule A.

Page 12

Line 4—Additional Section 263A Costs

An entry is required on this line only for corporations that have elected a simplified method of accounting. For corporations that have elected the simplified production method, additional section 263A costs are generally those costs, other than interest, that were not capitalized or included in inventory costs under the corporation's method of accounting immediately prior to the effective date in Temporary Regulations section 1.263A-1T that are now required to be capitalized under section 263A. For corporations that have elected a simplified resale method, additional section 263A costs are generally those costs incurred with respect to the following categories: off-site storage or warehousing; purchasing; handling, processing, assembly, and repackaging; and general and administrative costs (mixed service costs). Enter on line 4 the balance of section 263A costs paid or incurred during the tax year not included on lines 2 and 3. See Temporary Regulations section 1.263A-1T for more information.

Line 5—Other Costs

Enter on line 5 any other inventoriable costs paid or incurred during the tax year not entered on lines 2 through 4.

Line 7—Inventory At End of Year

See Temporary Regulations section 1.263A-1T for details on figuring the amount of additional section 263A costs to be capitalized and added to ending inventory.

Lines 9a through 9e—Inventory Valuation Methods

Inventories can be valued at (a) cost, (b) cost or market value (whichever is lower), or (c) any other method approved by the IRS that conforms to the provisions of the applicable regulations cited below.

Taxpayers using erroneous valuation methods must change to a method permitted for Federal income tax purposes. To make this change, file Form 3115. For more information, see Regulations section 1.446-1(e)(3) and Rev. Proc. 84-74, 1984-2 C.B. 736; Notice 88-78, 1988-2 C.B. 394; and Notice 89-67.

On line 9a, check the method(s) used for valuing inventories. Under "lower of cost or market," *market* generally applies to normal market conditions when there is a current bid price prevailing at the date the inventory is valued. When no regular open market exists or quotations are nominal because of inactive market conditions, use fair market prices from the most reliable sales or purchase transactions that occurred near the date the inventory is valued. For additional requirements, see Regulations section 1.471-4 and Notice 88-86, 1988-2 C.B. 401 (section IV(N)).

Inventory may be valued below cost when the merchandise is unsalable at normal prices or unusable in the normal way because the goods are "subnormal" (i.e., because of damage, imperfections, shop wear, etc.) within the meaning of Regulations section 1.471-2(c). Such goods may be valued at a current bona fide selling price less direct cost of disposition (but not less than scrap value) when the taxpayer can establish such a price. See Regulations section 1.471-2(c) for additional requirements.

If this is the first year the "last-in-first-out" (LIFO) inventory method was either adopted or extended to inventory goods not previously valued under the LIFO method, as provided in section 472, attach **Form 970**, Application To Use LIFO Inventory Method, or a statement showing the information required by Form 970, with Form 1120S and check the LIFO box in line 9b. On line 9c, enter the amount or percent (estimates may be used) of total closing inventories covered under section 472.

If you have changed or extended your inventory method to LIFO and have had to "write up" your opening inventory to cost in the year of election, report the effect of this writeup as income (line 5, page 1) proportionately over a 3-year period that begins in the tax year you made this election. (See section 472(d).)

Schedule B—Other Information

Be sure to answer the questions and provide other information in items 1 through 10.

Line 5—Foreign Financial Accounts

Check the "Yes" box if either **1** or **2** below applies to the corporation. Otherwise, check the "No" box.

1. At any time during the year, the corporation had an interest in or signature or other authority over a financial account in a foreign country (such as a bank account, securities account, or other financial account); AND

● The combined value of the accounts was more than $10,000 during the year; AND

● The account was NOT with a U.S. military banking facility operated by a U.S. financial institution.

2. The corporation owns more than 50% of the stock in any corporation that would answer "Yes" to item **1** above.

Get form **TD F 90-22.1**, Report of Foreign Bank and Financial Accounts, to see if the corporation is considered to have an interest in or signature or other authority over a financial account in a foreign country (such as a bank account, securities account, or other financial account).

If "Yes" is checked for this question, file form TD F 90-22.1 by June 30, 1992, with the Department of the Treasury at the address shown on the form. Form TD F 90-22.1 is not a tax return, so do not file it with Form 1120S. Form TD F 90-22.1 may be ordered by calling our toll-free number, 1-800-829-3676.

Also, if "Yes" is checked for this question, enter the name of the foreign country or countries. Attach a separate sheet if you need more space.

Line 9

Complete line 9 if the corporation: (a) filed its election to be an S corporation after 1986; (b) was a C corporation before it elected to be an S corporation or the corporation acquired an asset with a basis determined by reference to its basis (or the basis of any other property) in the hands of a C corporation; and (c) has net unrealized built-in gain (defined below) in excess of the net recognized built-in gain from prior years.

The corporation is liable for section 1374 tax if (a), (b), and (c) above apply and it has a net recognized built-in gain (section 1374(d)(2)) for its tax year.

Section 633(d)(8) of the Tax Reform Act of 1986 provides transitional relief from the built-in gains for certain corporations that elected to be S corporations in 1987 or 1988. However, the relief rule does **not** apply to ordinary gains or losses (determined without regard to section 1239), gains or losses from the disposition of capital assets held 6 months or less, and gains from the disposition of any asset acquired by the corporation with a substituted basis if a principal purpose for acquiring the asset was to secure transitional relief from the built-in gains tax. See the instructions for Part IV of Schedule D (Form 1120S) for more information.

The corporation's "net unrealized built-in gain" is the amount, if any, by which the fair market value of the assets of the corporation at the beginning of its first S corporation year (or as of the date the assets were acquired, for any asset with a basis determined by reference to its basis (or the basis of any other property) in the hands of a C corporation) exceeds the aggregate adjusted basis of such assets at that time.

Enter on line 9 the corporation's net unrealized built-in gain reduced by the net recognized built-in gain for prior years. See sections 1374(c)(2) and (d)(1).

Line 10

Check the box on line 10 if the corporation was a C corporation in a prior year and has subchapter C earnings and profits (E&P) at the close of its 1991 tax year. For this purpose, "subchapter C E&P" means E&P of any corporation for any tax year when it was not an S corporation. See sections 1362(d)(3)(B) and 312 for other details. If the corporation has subchapter C E&P, it may be liable for tax imposed on excess net passive income. See the instructions for line 22a, page 1, of Form 1120S for details on this tax.

Designation of Tax Matters Person (TMP)

If the S corporation is subject to sections 6241 through 6245 (consolidated audit

Page 13

procedures), it may designate a shareholder as the TMP for the tax year for which the return is filed by completing the **Designation of Tax Matters Person** section at the bottom of page 2 of Form 1120S. Temporary Regulations section 301.6241-1T provides an exception to the consolidated provisions for small S corporations with 5 or fewer shareholders each of whom is a natural person or an estate. See the instructions for **Item G, Consolidated Audit Procedures,** on page 8, sections 6241 through 6245, and Temporary Regulations section 301.6241-1T for other details.

General Instructions For Schedules K and K-1— Shareholders' Shares of Income, Credits, Deductions, Etc.

Purpose of Schedules

The corporation is liable for taxes on lines 22a, b, and c, page 1, Form 1120S. Shareholders are liable for income tax on their shares of the corporation's income (reduced by any taxes paid by the corporation on income) and must include their share of the income on their tax return whether or not it is distributed to them. Unlike most partnership income, S corporation income is **not** self-employment income and is not subject to self-employment tax.

Schedule K is a summary schedule of all the shareholders' shares of the corporation's income, deductions, credits, etc. Schedule K-1 shows each shareholder's separate share. A copy of each shareholder's Schedule K-1 must be attached to the Form 1120S filed with the IRS. A copy is kept as a part of the corporation's records, and the corporation must give each shareholder a separate copy.

The total pro rata share items (column (b)) of all Schedules K-1 should equal the amount reported on the same line of Schedule K. Lines 1 through 17 of Schedule K correspond to lines 1 through 17 of Schedule K-1. Other lines do not correspond, but instructions will explain the differences.

Be sure to give each shareholder a copy of the Shareholder's Instructions for Schedule K-1 (Form 1120S). These instructions are available, separately from Schedule K-1, at most IRS offices.

Note: *Instructions that apply only to line items reported on Schedule K-1 may be prepared and given to each shareholder in lieu of the instructions printed by the IRS.*

Substitute Forms

You **do not** need IRS approval to use a substitute Schedule K-1 if it is an exact facsimile of the IRS schedule, **or** if it contains only those lines the taxpayer is required to use, and the lines have the same numbers and titles and are in the

Page 14

same order as on the comparable IRS Schedule K-1. In either case, your substitute schedule must include the OMB number, and either **(a)** the Shareholder's Instructions for Schedule K-1 (Form 1120S), or **(b)** instructions that apply to the items reported on Schedule K-1 (Form 1120S).

Other substitute Schedules K-1 require approval. You may apply for approval of a substitute form by writing to: Internal Revenue Service, Attention: Substitute Forms Program Coordinator, R:R:R, 1111 Constitution Avenue, NW, Washington, DC 20224.

You may be subject to a penalty if you file a substitute Schedule K-1 that does not conform to the specifications of Rev. Proc. 91-16, 1991-1 C.B. 487.

Shareholder's Pro Rata Share Items

Items of income, loss, deductions, etc., are allocated to a shareholder on a daily basis, according to the number of shares of stock held by the shareholder on each day during the tax year of the corporation. See **Item A** below.

A transferee shareholder (rather than the transferor) is considered to be the owner of stock on the day it is transferred.

Special rule.—If a shareholder terminates his or her interest in a corporation during the tax year, the corporation, with the consent of all shareholders (including the one whose interest is terminated), may elect to allocate income and expenses, etc., as if the corporation's tax year consisted of 2 tax years, the first of which ends on the date of the shareholder's termination. To make the election, the corporation must file a statement of election with the return for the tax year of election and attach a statement of consent signed by all shareholders. If the election is made, write "Section 1377(a)(2) Election Made" at the top of each Schedule K-1. See section 1377(a)(2) and Temporary Regulations section 18.1377-1 for details.

Specific Instructions (Schedule K Only)

Enter the total pro rata share amount for each applicable line item on Schedule K.

Specific Instructions (Schedule K-1 Only)

General Information

On each Schedule K-1, complete the date spaces at the top; enter the names, addresses, and identifying numbers of the shareholder and corporation; complete items A through D; and enter the shareholder's pro rata share of each item. **Schedule K-1 must be prepared and given to each shareholder on or before the day on which Form 1120S is filed.**

Note: *Space has been provided on line 20 (Supplemental Information) of Schedule*

K-1 for the corporation to provide additional information to shareholders. This space, if sufficient, should be used in place of any attached schedules required for any lines on Schedule K-1, or other amounts not shown on lines 1 through 19 of Schedule K-1. Please be sure to identify the applicable line number next to the information entered below line 20.

Specific Items

Item A

If there was no change in shareholders or in the relative interest in stock the shareholders owned during the tax year, enter the percentage of total stock owned by each shareholder during the tax year. For example, if shareholders X and Y each owned 50% for the entire tax year, enter 50% in item A for each shareholder. Each shareholder's pro rata share items (lines 1 through 17 of Schedule K-1) are figured by multiplying the Schedule K amount on the corresponding line of Schedule K by the percentage in item A.

If there was a change in shareholders or in the relative interest in stock the shareholders owned during the tax year, each shareholder's percentage of ownership is weighted for the number of days in the tax year that stock was owned. For example, A and B each held 50% for half the tax year and A, B, and C held 40%, 40%, and 20%, respectively, for the remaining half of the tax year. The percentage of ownership for the year for A, B, and C is figured as follows and is then entered in item A.

	a	b	c (a × b)	
	% of total stock owned	% of tax year held	% of ownership for the year	
A	50 40	50 50	25 +20	45
B	50 40	50 50	25 +20	45
C	20	50	10	10
Total 100%

If there was a change in shareholders or in the relative interest in stock the shareholders owned during the tax year, each shareholder's pro rata share items can also be figured on a daily basis, based on the percentage of stock held by the shareholder on each day. See sections 1377(a)(1) and (2) for details.

Item B

Enter the Internal Revenue service center address where the Form 1120S, to which a copy of this K-1 was attached, was or will be filed.

Item C

If the corporation is a registration-required tax shelter, it must enter its tax shelter registration number in item C(1) and identify the type of shelter in C(2). If the corporation invested in a registration-required shelter, the corporation must also attach a copy of its Form 8271 to Schedule K-1. See Form

8271 for a list of the types of tax shelters and for more information.

Special Reporting Requirements for Corporations With Multiple Activities

If items of income, loss, deduction, or credit from more than one activity (determined for purposes of the passive activity loss and credit limitations) are reported on lines 1, 2, or 3 of Schedule K-1, the corporation must provide information for each activity to its shareholders. See **Passive Activity Reporting Requirements** on page 7 for details on the reporting requirements.

Special Reporting Requirements for At-Risk Activities

If the corporation is involved in one or more at-risk activities for which a loss is reported on Schedule K-1, the corporation must report information separately for each at-risk activity. See section 465(c) for a definition of at-risk activities.

For each at-risk activity, the following information must be provided on an attachment to Schedule K-1:

1. A statement that the information is a breakdown of at-risk activity loss amounts.

2. The identity of the at-risk activity; the loss amount for the activity; other income, deductions; and other information that relates to the activity.

Specific Instructions (Schedules K and K-1, Except as Noted)

Income (Loss)

Reminder: Before entering income items on Schedule K or K-1, be sure to reduce the items of income for the following:

1. Built-in gains tax (Schedule D, Part IV, line 23).—Each recognized built-in gain item (within the meaning of section 1374(d)(3)) is reduced by its proportionate share of the built-in gains tax.

2. Capital gains tax (Schedule D, Part III, line 15).—The net long-term capital gain on line 6 of Schedule D or the section 1231 gain included on line 5 or 6 of Schedule K is reduced by this tax.

3. Excess net passive income tax (line 22a, page 1, Form 1120S).—Each item of passive investment income (within the meaning of section 1362(d)(3)(D)) is reduced by its proportionate share of the net passive income tax.

Line 1—Ordinary Income (Loss) From Trade or Business Activities

Enter the amount from line 21, page 1. Enter the income or loss without reference to **(a)** shareholders' basis in the stock of the corporation and in any indebtedness of the corporation to the shareholders (section 1366(d)), **(b)** shareholders' at-risk limitations, and **(c)** shareholders' passive activity limitations. These limitations, if applicable, are determined at the shareholder level.

If the corporation is involved in more than one trade or business activity, see **Passive Activity Reporting Requirements** on page 7 for details on the information to be reported for each activity. If an at-risk activity loss is reported on line 1, see **Special Reporting Requirements for At-Risk Activities** on this page.

Line 2—Net Income (Loss) From Rental Real Estate Activities

Enter the net income or loss from rental real estate activities of the corporation from **Form 8825,** Rental Real Estate Income and Expenses of a Partnership or an S Corporation. Each Form 8825 has space for reporting the income and expenses of up to 8 properties.

If the corporation has income or loss from more than one rental real estate activity reported on line 2, see **Passive Activity Reporting Requirements** on page 7 for details on the information to be reported for each activity. If an at-risk activity loss is reported on line 2, see **Special Reporting Requirements for At-Risk Activities** on this page.

If a loss from a qualified low-income housing project is reported on line 2, identify this loss on a statement attached to the Schedule K-1 of each shareholder who is a qualified investor in the project. Any loss sustained by a qualified investor in a qualified low-income housing project for any tax year in the relief period is not subject to the passive activity loss limitations under section 502 of the Tax Reform Act of 1986. See Act section 502 for definitions and other information on qualified low-income housing projects.

Line 3—Income and Expenses of Other Rental Activities

Enter on lines 3a and 3b of Schedule K (line 3 of Schedule K-1) the income and expenses of rental activities other than the income and expenses reported on Form 8825. If the corporation has more than one rental activity reported on line 3, see **Passive Activity Reporting Requirements** on page 7 for details on the information to be reported for each activity. If an at-risk activity loss is reported on line 3, see **Special Reporting Requirements for At-Risk Activities** on this page. Also see **Rental activities** on page 6 for a definition and other details on other rental activities.

Lines 4a Through 4f—Portfolio Income (Loss)

Enter portfolio income (loss) on lines 4a through 4f. See **Portfolio income** on page 6 for a definition of portfolio income. Do not reduce portfolio income by expenses allocated to it. Such expenses (other than interest expense) are reported on line 9 of Schedules K and K-1. Interest expense allocable to portfolio income is generally investment interest expense and is reported on line 11a of Schedules K and K-1.

Lines 4a and 4b.—Enter only taxable interest and dividends that are portfolio income. Interest income derived in the ordinary course of the corporation's trade or business, such as interest charged on receivable balances, is reported on line 5, page 1, Form 1120S. See Temporary Regulations section 1.469-2T(c)(3).

Lines 4d and 4e.—Enter on line 4d the net short-term capital gain or loss (reduced by any applicable taxes) from line 3 of Schedule D (Form 1120S) that is portfolio income. Enter on line 4e the net long-term capital gain or loss (reduced by any applicable taxes) from line 6 of Schedule D (Form 1120S) that is portfolio income. If any gain or loss from lines 3 and 6 of Schedule D is not portfolio income (e.g., gain or loss from the disposition of nondepreciable personal property used in a trade or business), do not report this income or loss on lines 4d and 4e. Instead, report it on line 6 of Schedules K and K-1. If the income or loss is attributable to more than one activity, report the income or loss amount separately for each activity on an attachment to Schedule K-1 and identify the activity to which the income or loss relates.

Line 4f.—Enter any other portfolio income not reported on lines 4a through 4e.

If the corporation holds a residual interest in a REMIC, report on an attachment for line 4f each shareholder's share of taxable income (net loss) from the REMIC (line 1b of Schedule Q (Form 1066)); excess inclusion (line 2c of Schedule Q (Form 1066)); and section 212 expenses (line 3b of Schedule Q (Form 1066)). Because Schedule Q (Form 1066) is a quarterly statement, the corporation must follow the Schedule Q (Form 1066) Instructions for Residual Holder to figure the amounts to report to shareholders for the corporation's tax year.

Line 5—Net Gain (Loss) Under Section 1231 (Other Than Due to Casualty or Theft)

Enter the gain (loss) under section 1231 shown on line 7 of Form 4797. Do not include net gains or losses from involuntary conversions due to casualties or thefts on this line. Instead, report them on line 6.

Line 6—Other Income (Loss)

Enter any other item of income or loss not included on lines 1 through 5, such as:

1. Recoveries of tax benefit items (section 111).

2. Gambling gains and losses (section 165(d)).

3. Net gain (loss) from involuntary conversions due to casualty or theft. The amount for this item is shown on **Form 4684,** Casualties and Thefts, Section B, line 20a or 20b.

4. Any net gain or loss from section 1256 contracts from **Form 6781,** Gains and Losses From Section 1256 Contracts and Straddles.

Page 15

Deductions

Line 7—Charitable Contributions

Enter the amount of charitable contributions paid by the corporation during its tax year. Attach an itemized list that separately shows the corporation's charitable contributions subject to the 50%, 30%, and 20% limitations.

If the corporation contributes property other than cash and the deduction claimed for such property exceeds $500, **Form 8283**, Noncash Charitable Contributions, must be completed and attached to Form 1120S. The corporation must give a copy of its Form 8283 to every shareholder if the deduction for any item or group of similar items of contributed property exceeds $5,000, even if the amount allocated to any shareholder is $5,000 or less. If this requirement is not met, the corporation does not have to furnish the shareholders with a copy of its Form 8283. However, the corporation must report each shareholder's pro rata share of the amount of noncash contributions to enable individual shareholders to complete their own Forms 8283. See the Instructions for Form 8283 for more information.

If the corporation made a qualified conservation contribution under section 170(h), also include the fair market value of the underlying property before and after the donation, as well as the type of legal interest contributed, and describe the conservation purpose furthered by the donation. Give a copy of this information to each shareholder.

Line 8—Section 179 Expense Deduction

An S corporation may elect to expense part of the cost of certain tangible property that the corporation purchased during the tax year for use in its trade or business or certain rental activities. See the instructions for Form 4562 for more information.

Complete Part I of Form 4562 to figure the corporation's section 179 expense deduction. The corporation does not deduct the expense itself but passes the expense through to its shareholders. Attach Form 4562 to Form 1120S and show the total section 179 expense deduction on Schedule K, line 8. Report each individual shareholder's pro rata share on Schedule K-1, line 8. Do not complete line 8 of Schedule K-1 for any shareholder that is an estate or trust.

See the instructions for line 20 of Schedule K-1, item 6, for any recapture of a section 179 amount.

Line 9—Deductions Related to Portfolio Income (Loss)

Enter on line 9 the deductions clearly and directly allocable to portfolio income (other than interest expense). Interest expense related to portfolio income is investment interest expense and is reported on line 11a of Schedules K and K-1. Generally, the line 9 expenses are section 212

expenses and are subject to section 212 limitations at the shareholder level.

Note: *No deduction is allowed under section 212 for expenses allocable to a convention, seminar, or similar meeting. Because these expenses are not deductible by shareholders, the corporation does not report these expenses on line 9 or line 10. The expenses are nondeductible and are reported as such on line 18 of Schedule K and line 20 of Schedule K-1.*

Line 10—Other Deductions

Enter any other deductions not included on lines 7, 8, 9, and 15e, such as:

● Amounts (other than investment interest required to be reported on line 11a of Schedules K and K-1) paid by the corporation that would be allowed as itemized deductions on a shareholder's income tax return if they were paid directly by a shareholder for the same purpose. These amounts include, but are not limited to, expenses under section 212 for the production of income other than from the corporation's trade or business.

● Any penalty on early withdrawal of savings not reported on line 9 because the corporation withdrew funds from its time savings deposit before its maturity.

● Soil and water conservation expenditures (section 175).

● Expenditures paid or incurred for the removal of architectural and transportation barriers to the elderly and disabled that the corporation has elected to treat as a current expense. See section 190.

● Interest expense allocated to debt-financed distributions. See Notice 89-35 for more information.

● If there was a gain (loss) from a casualty or theft to property not used in a trade or business or for income producing purposes, provide each shareholder with the needed information to complete Form 4684.

Investment Interest

Lines 11a and 11b must be completed for all shareholders.

Line 11a—Investment Interest Expense

Include on this line the interest properly allocable to debt on property held for investment purposes. Property held for investment includes property that produces investment income (interest, dividends, annuities, royalties, etc.).

Investment interest expense **does not** include interest expense allocable to a passive activity.

Report investment interest expense only on line 11a of Schedules K and K-1.

The amount on line 11a will be deducted by individual shareholders on Form 1040 after applying the investment interest expense limitations of section 163(d). The section 163(d) limitations are figured on **Form 4952**, Investment Interest Expense Deduction.

Lines 11b(1) and 11b(2)—Investment Income and Expenses

Enter on line 11b(1) only the investment income included on line 4 of Schedule K-1. Enter on line 11b(2) only the investment expense included on line 9 of Schedule K-1.

If there are items of investment income or expense included in the amounts that are required to be passed through separately to the shareholders on Schedule K-1 (items other than the amounts included on lines 4 and 9 of Schedule K-1), give each shareholder a schedule identifying these amounts.

Investment income includes gross income from property held for investment, gain attributable to the disposition of property held for investment, and other amounts that are gross portfolio income. Generally, investment income and investment expenses do not include any income or expenses from a passive activity. See Temporary Regulations section 1.469-2T(f)(10) for exceptions.

Property subject to a net lease is not treated as investment property because it is subject to the passive loss rules. Do not reduce investment income by losses from passive activities.

Investment expenses are deductible expenses (other than interest) directly connected with the production of investment income. See the Instructions for Form 4952 for more information on investment income and expenses.

Credits

Note: *If the corporation has credits from more than one trade or business activity on line 12a or 13, or from more than one rental activity on line 12b, 12c, 12d, or 12e, it must report separately on an attachment to Schedule K-1, the amount of each credit and provide any other applicable activity information listed in **Passive Activity Reporting Requirements** on page 7.*

Line 12a—Credit for Alcohol Used as Fuel

Enter on line 12a of Schedule K the credit for alcohol used as fuel computed by the corporation that is attributable to a trade or business activity. Enter on line 12d or 12e, the credit for alcohol used as fuel attributable to rental activities. The credit for alcohol used as fuel is figured on **Form 6478**, Credit for Alcohol Used as Fuel, and the form is attached to Form 1120S. The credit must be included as income on page 1, line 5, of Form 1120S. See section 40(f) for an election the corporation can make to have the credit not apply.

Enter each shareholder's share of the credit for alcohol used as fuel on line 12a, 12d, or 12e of Schedule K-1.

Line 12b—Low-Income Housing Credit

Section 42 provides for a low-income housing credit that may be claimed by owners of low-income residential rental

Page 16

buildings. If shareholders are eligible to claim the low-income housing credit, complete the applicable parts of **Form 8586,** Low-Income Housing Credit, and attach it to Form 1120S. Enter the credit figured by the corporation on Form 8586, and any low-income housing credit received from other entities in which the corporation is allowed to invest on the applicable line as explained below. The corporation must also complete and attach **Form 8609,** Low-Income Housing Credit Allocation Certification, and **Schedule A (Form 8609),** Annual Statement, to Form 1120S. See the Instructions for Form 8586 and Form 8609 for information on completing these forms.

Note: *No credit may be claimed for any building in a qualified low-income housing project for which any person was allowed to claim a loss from the project by reason of not being subject to the passive activity limitations (see section 502 of the Tax Reform Act of 1986 for details).*

Line 12b(1).—If the corporation invested in a partnership to which the provisions of section 42(j)(5) apply, report on line 12b(1) the credit the partnership reported to the corporation on line 13b(1) of Schedule K-1 (Form 1065). If the corporation invested **before 1990** in a section 42(j)(5) partnership, also include on this line any credit the partnership reported to the corporation on line 13b(3) of Schedule K-1 (Form 1065).

Line 12b(2).—Report on line 12b(2) any low-income housing credit for property placed in service before 1990 and not reported on line 12b(1). This includes any credit from a building placed in service before 1990 in a project owned by the corporation and any credit from a partnership reported to the corporation on line 13b(2) of Schedule K-1 (Form 1065). Also include on this line any credit from a partnership reported to the corporation on line 13b(4) of Schedule K-1 (Form 1065), if the corporation invested in that partnership **before 1990.**

Line 12b(3).—If the corporation invested **after 1989** in a partnership to which the provisions of section 42(j)(5) apply, report on line 12b(3) the credit the partnership reported to the corporation on line 13b(3) of Schedule K-1 (Form 1065).

Line 12b(4).—Report on line 12b(4) any low-income housing credit for property placed in service after 1989 and not reported on any other line. This includes any credit from a building placed in service after 1989 in a project owned by the corporation and any credit from a partnership reported to the corporation on line 13b(4) of Schedule K-1 (Form 1065), if the corporation invested in that partnership **after 1989.**

Line 12c—Qualified Rehabilitation Expenditures Related to Rental Real Estate Activities

Enter total qualified rehabilitation expenditures related to rental real estate activities of the corporation, and for line 12c of Schedule K, complete the applicable lines of **Form 3468,** Investment Credit, that apply to qualified rehabilitation expenditures for property related to rental real estate activities of the corporation for which income or loss is reported on line 2 of Schedule K. See Form 3468 for details on qualified rehabilitation expenditures. Attach Form 3468 to Form 1120S.

For line 12c of Schedule K-1, enter each shareholder's pro rata share of the expenditures. On the dotted line to the left of the entry space for line 12c, enter the line number of Form 3468 on which the shareholder should report the expenditures. If there is more than one type of expenditure, or the expenditures are from more than one line 2 activity, report this information separately for each expenditure or activity on an attachment to Schedules K and K-1.

Note: *Qualified rehabilitation expenditures not related to rental real estate activities must be listed separately on line 20 of Schedule K-1.*

Line 12d—Credits (Other Than Credits Shown on Lines 12b and 12c) Related to Rental Real Estate Activities

Enter on line 12d any other credit (other than credits on lines 12b and 12c) related to rental real estate activities. On the dotted line to the left of the entry space for line 12d, identify the type of credit. If there is more than one type of credit or the credit is from more than one line 2 activity, report this information separately for each credit or activity on an attachment to Schedules K and K-1. These credits may include any type of credit listed in the instructions for line 13.

Line 12e—Credits Related to Other Rental Activities

Enter on line 12e any credit related to other rental activities for which income or loss is reported on line 3 of Schedules K and K-1. On the dotted line to the left of the entry space for line 12e, identify the type of credit. If there is more than one type of credit or the credit is from more than one line 3 activity, report this information separately for each credit or activity on an attachment to Schedules K and K-1. These credits may include any type of credit listed in the instructions for line 13.

Line 13—Other Credits

Enter on line 13 any other credit (other than credits or expenditures shown or listed for lines 12a through 12e of Schedules K and K-1). On the dotted line to the left of the entry space for line 13, identify the type of credit. If there is more than one type of credit or the credit is from more than one activity, report this information separately for each credit or activity on an attachment to Schedules K and K-1.

The credits to be reported on line 13 and other required attachments follow:

● Nonconventional source fuel credit. This credit is figured by the corporation on a separate schedule prepared by the corporation. This computation schedule must also be attached to Form 1120S. See section 29 for computation provisions and other special rules for figuring this credit.

● Unused investment credit from cooperatives. If the corporation is a member of a cooperative that passes an unused investment credit through to its members, the credit is in turn passed through to the corporation's shareholders.

● Credit for backup withholding on dividends, interest, or patronage dividends.

● Credit for increasing research activities and orphan drug credit. Complete and attach **Form 6765,** Credit for Increasing Research Activities (or for claiming the orphan drug credit), to Form 1120S.

● Jobs credit. Complete and attach **Form 5884,** Jobs Credit, to Form 1120S.

● Disabled access credit. Complete and attach **Form 8826,** Disabled Access Credit, to Form 1120S.

● Enhanced oil recovery credit. Complete and attach **Form 8830,** Enhanced Oil Recovery Credit, to Form 1120S. This credit applies to costs paid or incurred in connection with qualified enhanced oil recovery projects located in the United States for which the first injection of liquids, gases, or other matter began after 1990.

See the instructions for line 18 (Schedule K) and line 20 (Schedule K-1) to report expenditures qualifying for the **(a)** rehabilitation credit not related to rental real estate activities, **(b)** energy credit, or **(c)** reforestation credit.

Adjustments and Tax Preference Items

Lines 14a through 14f must be completed for all shareholders.

Enter items of income and deductions that are adjustments or tax preference items. See **Form 6251,** Alternative Minimum Tax—Individuals, and **Pub. 909,** Alternative Minimum Tax for Individuals, to determine the amounts to enter and for other information.

Do not include as a tax preference item any qualified expenditures to which an election under section 59(e) may apply. Because these expenditures are subject to an election by each shareholder, the corporation cannot compute the amount of any tax preference related to them. Instead, the corporation must pass through to each shareholder on lines 16a and 16b of Schedule K-1 the information needed to compute the deduction. Each shareholder computes both the deduction he or she will claim and the resulting tax preference item, if any.

Line 14c—Depreciation Adjustment on Property Placed in Service After 1986

Figure the adjustment for line 14c based only on tangible property placed in service after 1986 (and tangible property placed in service after July 31, 1986 and before

Page 17

1987 for which the corporation elected to use the General Depreciation System).

Refigure depreciation as follows: For property other than real property and property on which the straight line method was used, use the 150% declining balance method, switching to straight line method for the first tax year when that method gives a better result. (For property on which the straight line method was used, use the straight line method.) Use the class life (instead of the recovery period) and the same conventions as the corporation used on Form 4562. For personal property having no class life, use 12 years. For residential rental and nonresidential real property, use the straight line method over 40 years. Determine the depreciation adjustment by subtracting the recomputed depreciation from the depreciation claimed on Form 4562. If the recomputed depreciation exceeds the depreciation claimed on Form 4562, enter the difference as a negative amount. See the instructions for Form 6251 and Form 4562 for more information.

Line 14d—Depletion (Other Than Oil and Gas)

Do not include any depletion on oil and gas wells. The shareholders must compute their depletion deductions separately under section 613A.

In the case of mines, wells, and other natural deposits, other than oil and gas wells, enter the amount by which the deduction for depletion under section 611 (including percentage depletion for geothermal deposits) is more than the adjusted basis of such property at the end of the tax year. Figure the adjusted basis without regard to the depletion deduction and figure the excess separately for each property.

Lines 14e(1) and 14e(2)

Generally, the amounts to be entered on these lines are only the income and deductions for oil, gas, and geothermal properties that are used to figure the amount on line 21, page 1, Form 1120S.

If there are any items of income or deductions for oil, gas, and geothermal properties included in the amounts that are required to be passed through separately to the shareholders on Schedule K-1, give each shareholder a schedule for the line on which the income or deduction is included and which shows the amount of income or deductions included in the total amount for that line. Do not include any of these direct passthrough amounts on line 14e(1) or 14e(2). The shareholder is told in the Shareholder's Instructions for Schedule K-1 (Form 1120S) to adjust the amounts on lines 14e(1) and 14e(2) for any other income or deductions from oil, gas, or geothermal properties included on lines 2 through 10 and 20 of Schedule K-1 in order to determine the total income and deductions from oil, gas, and geothermal properties for the corporation.

Figure the amounts for lines 14e(1) and 14e(2) separately for oil and gas properties which are not geothermal deposits and for

all properties which are geothermal deposits.

Give the shareholders a schedule that shows the separate amounts that are included in the computation of the amounts on lines 14e(1) and 14e(2).

Line 14e(1). Gross income from oil, gas, and geothermal properties.— Enter the aggregate amount of gross income (within the meaning of section 613(a)) from all oil, gas, and geothermal properties received or accrued during the tax year and included on page 1, Form 1120S.

Line 14e(2). Deductions allocable to oil, gas, and geothermal properties.— Enter the amount of any deductions allocable to oil, gas, and geothermal properties reduced by the excess intangible drilling costs that were included on page 1, Form 1120S, on properties for which the corporation made an election to expense intangible drilling costs in tax years beginning before 1983. Do not include nonproductive well costs included on page 1.

Figure excess intangible drilling costs as follows: From the allowable intangible drilling and development costs (except for costs in drilling a nonproductive well), subtract the amount that would have been allowable if the corporation had capitalized these costs and either amortized them over the 120 months that started when production began, or treated them according to any election the corporation made under section 57(b)(2).

See section 57(a)(2) for more information.

Line 14f—Other Adjustments and Tax Preference Items

Attach a schedule that shows each shareholder's share of other items not shown on lines 14a through 14e(2) that are adjustments or tax preference items or that the shareholder needs to complete Form 6251 or Form 8656. See these forms and their instructions to determine the amount to enter. Other adjustments or tax preference items include the following:

● Amortization of certified pollution control facilities.—The deduction allowable under section 169 for any facility placed in service after 1986 must be refigured using the alternative depreciation system under section 168(g).

● Long-term contracts entered into after February 28, 1986.—Except for certain home construction contracts, the taxable income from these contracts must be figured using the percentage of completion method of accounting for alternative minimum tax purposes.

● Installment sales of inventory or stock in trade after March 1, 1986.—Generally, the installment method may not be used for these sales in computing alternative minimum taxable income.

● Charitable contributions of appreciated property.—Generally, the deduction for charitable contributions claimed on line 7 of Schedules K and K-1 is reduced by the difference between the fair market value and the adjusted basis of the capital gain

and section 1231 property donated to a charitable organization. For tax years beginning in 1991, no reduction is made for any contribution of tangible personal property.

● Losses from tax shelter farm activities.— No loss from any tax shelter farm activity is allowed for alternative minimum tax purposes.

Foreign Taxes

Lines 15a through 15g must be completed whether or not a shareholder is eligible for the foreign tax credit, if the corporation has foreign income, deductions, or losses, or has paid or accrued foreign taxes.

In addition to the instructions below, see **Form 1116,** Foreign Tax Credit (Individual, Fiduciary, or Nonresident Alien Individual), and the related instructions.

Line 15a—Type of Income

Enter the type of income from outside the United States as follows:

● Passive income.

● High withholding tax interest.

● Financial services income.

● Shipping income.

● Dividends from a DISC or former DISC.

● Certain distributions from a foreign sales corporation (FSC) or former FSC.

● Dividends from each noncontrolled section 902 corporation.

● Taxable income attributable to foreign trade income (within the meaning of section 923(b)).

● General limitation income (all other income from sources outside the United States, including income from sources within U.S. possessions).

If, for the country or U.S. possession shown on line 15b, the corporation had more than one type of income, enter "See attached" and attach a schedule for each type of income for lines 15b through 15g.

Line 15b—Foreign Country or U.S. Possession

Enter the name of the foreign country or U.S. possession. If, for the type of income shown on line 15a, the corporation had income from, or paid taxes to, more than one foreign country or U.S. possession, enter "See attached" and attach a schedule for each country for lines 15a and 15c through 15g.

Line 15c—Total Gross Income From Sources Outside the U.S.

Enter in U.S. dollars the total gross income from sources outside the United States. Attach a schedule that shows each type of income listed in the instructions for line 15a.

Line 15d—Total Applicable Deductions and Losses

Enter in U.S. dollars the total applicable deductions and losses attributable to income on line 15c. Attach a schedule that shows each type of deduction or loss as follows:

- Expenses directly allocable to each type of income listed above.
- Pro rata share of all other deductions not directly allocable to specific items of income.
- Pro rata share of losses from other separate limitation categories.

Line 15e—Total Foreign Taxes

Enter in U.S. dollars the total foreign taxes (described in section 901) that were paid or accrued by the corporation to foreign countries or U.S. possessions. Attach a schedule that shows the dates the taxes were paid or accrued, and the amount in both foreign currency and in U.S. dollars, as follows:

- Taxes withheld at source on dividends.
- Taxes withheld at source on rents and royalties.
- Other foreign taxes paid or accrued.

Line 15f—Reduction in Taxes Available for Credit

Enter in U.S. dollars the total reduction in taxes available for credit. Attach a schedule that shows separately the:
- Reduction for foreign mineral income.
- Reduction for failure to furnish returns required under section 6038.
- Reduction for taxes attributable to boycott operations (section 908).
- Reduction for foreign oil and gas extraction income (section 907(a)).
- Reduction for any other items (specify).

Line 15g—Other Foreign Tax Information

Enter in U.S. dollars any items not covered on lines 15c through 15f.

Other

Lines 16a and 16b

Generally, section 59(e) allows each shareholder to make an election to deduct the shareholder's pro rata share of the corporation's otherwise deductible qualified expenditures ratably over 10 years (3 years for circulation expenditures), beginning with the tax year in which the expenditures were made (or for intangible drilling and development costs, over the 60-month period beginning with the month in which such costs were paid or incurred). The term "qualified expenditures" includes only the following types of expenditures paid or incurred during the tax year: circulation expenditures, research and experimental expenditures, intangible drilling and development costs, and mining exploration and development costs. If a shareholder makes this election, these items are not treated as tax preference items.

Because the shareholders are generally allowed to make this election, the corporation cannot deduct these amounts or include them as adjustments or tax

preference items on Schedule K-1. Instead, on lines 16a and 16b of Schedule K-1, the corporation passes through the information the shareholders need to compute their separate deductions.

Enter on line 16a the qualified expenditures paid or incurred during the tax year to which an election under section 59(e) may apply. Enter this amount for all shareholders whether or not any shareholder makes an election under section 59(e). On line 16b, enter the type of expenditure claimed on line 16a. If the expenditure is for intangible drilling and development costs, enter the month in which the expenditure was paid or incurred (after the type of expenditure on line 16b). If there is more than one type of expenditure included in the total shown on line 16a (or intangible drilling and development costs were paid or incurred for more than one month), report this information separately for each type of expenditure (or month) on an attachment to Schedules K and K-1.

Line 17

Enter total distributions made to each shareholder other than dividends reported on line 19 of Schedule K. Noncash distributions of appreciated property are valued at fair market value. See Schedule M-2 instructions for ordering rules on distributions.

Line 18 (Schedule K Only)

Attach a statement to Schedule K to report the corporation's total income, expenditures, or other information for items 1 through 16 of the line 20 (Schedule K-1 Only) instruction below.

Line 19 (Schedule K Only)

Enter total dividends paid to shareholders from accumulated earnings and profits. Report these dividends to shareholders on Form 1099-DIV. Do not report them on Schedule K-1.

Lines 19a and 19b (Schedule K-1 Only)—Recapture of Low-Income Housing Credit

If recapture of part or all of the low-income housing credit is required because: (1) prior year qualified basis of a building decreased, or (2) the corporation disposed of a building or part of its interest in a building, see Form 8611, Recapture of Low-Income Housing Credit. The instructions for Form 8611 indicate when Form 8611 is completed by the corporation and what information is provided to shareholders when recapture is required.

Note: *If a shareholder's ownership interest in a building decreased because of a transaction at the shareholder level, the corporation must provide the necessary information to the shareholder to enable the shareholder to compute the recapture.*

If the corporation posted a bond as provided in section 42(j)(6) to avoid recapture of the low-income housing credit, no entry should be made on line 19 of Schedule K-1.

See Form 8586, Form 8611, and section 42 for more information.

Supplemental Information

Line 20 (Schedule K-1 Only)

Enter in the line 20 Supplemental Information space of Schedule K-1, or on an attached schedule if more space is needed, each shareholder's share of any information asked for on lines 1 through 19 that is required to be reported in detail, and items **1** through **16** below. Please identify the applicable line number next to the information entered in the Supplemental Information space. Show income or gains as a positive number. Show losses in parentheses.

1. Tax-exempt interest income. Include exempt-interest dividends the corporation received as a shareholder in a mutual fund or other regulated investment company.

2. Nondeductible expenses incurred by the corporation.

3. Taxes paid on undistributed capital gains by a regulated investment company. As a shareholder of a regulated investment company, the corporation will receive notice on **Form 2439**, Notice to Shareholder of Undistributed Long-Term Capital Gains, that the company paid tax on undistributed capital gains.

4. Gross income and other information relating to oil and gas well properties that are reported to shareholders to allow them to figure the depletion deduction for oil and gas well properties. See section 613A(c)(11) for details.

The corporation cannot deduct depletion on oil and gas wells. Each shareholder must determine the allowable amount to report on his or her return. See Pub. 535 for more information.

5. Qualified exploratory costs. In order for each shareholder to compute the alternative minimum tax adjustment based on energy preferences, the corporation must identify the portion, if any, of intangible drilling and development costs shown on line 16a that is attributable to qualified exploratory costs. Identify this amount on line 20 as "Qualified exploratory costs included on line 16a." Qualified exploratory costs are intangible drilling and development costs paid or incurred in connection with the drilling of an exploratory well located in the United States. See section 56(h)(6) for more details.

6. Recapture of section 179 expense deduction. For property placed in service after 1986, the section 179 deduction is recaptured at any time the business use of property drops to 50% or less. Enter the amount that was originally passed through and the corporation's tax year in which it was passed through. Inform the shareholder if the recapture amount was caused by the disposition of the section 179 property. See section 179(d)(10) for more information. Do not include this amount on line 4 or 5, page 1, Form 1120S.

Page 19

7. Recapture of certain mining exploration expenditures (section 617).

8. Any information or statements the corporation is required to furnish to shareholders to allow them to comply with requirements under section 6111 (registration of tax shelters) or section 6662(d)(2)(B)(ii) (regarding adequate disclosure of items that may cause an understatement of income tax).

9. If the corporation is involved in farming or fishing activities, report the gross income from these activities to shareholders.

10. Any information needed by a shareholder to compute the interest due under section 453A(c). If an obligation arising from the disposition of property to which section 453A applies is outstanding at the close of the year, each shareholder's tax liability must be increased by the tax due under section 453(c) on the shareholder's pro rata share of the tax deferred under the installment method.

11. Any information needed by a shareholder to compute the interest due under section 453(l)(3). If the corporation elected to report the dispositions of certain timeshares and residential lots on the installment method, each shareholder's tax liability must be increased by the shareholder's pro rata share of the interest on tax attributable to the installment payments received during the tax year.

12. Any information needed by a shareholder to properly capitalize interest as required by section 263A(f). See **Section 263A uniform capitalization rules** on page 9 for additional information. See Notice 88-99 for more information.

13. If the corporation is a closely held S corporation (defined in section 460(b)) and it entered into any long-term contracts after February 28, 1986, that are accounted for under either the percentage of completion-capitalized cost method or the percentage of completion method, it must attach a schedule to Form 1120S showing the information required in items (a) and (b) of the instructions for lines 1 and 3 of Part II for **Form 8697,** Interest Computation Under the Look-Back Method for Completed Long-Term Contracts. It must also report the amounts for Part II, lines 1 and 3, to its shareholders. See the instructions for Form 8697 for more information.

14. Expenditures qualifying for the **(a)** rehabilitation credit not related to rental real estate activities, **(b)** energy credit, or **(c)** reforestation credit. Complete and attach Form 3468 to Form 1120S. See Form 3468 and related instructions for information on eligible property and the lines on Form 3468 to complete. Do not include that part of the cost of the property the corporation has elected to expense under section 179. Attach to each Schedule K-1 a separate schedule in a format similar to that shown on Form 3468 detailing each shareholder's pro rata share of qualified expenditures. Also indicate the lines of Form 3468 on which the shareholders should report these amounts.

15. Recapture of investment credit. Complete and attach **Form 4255,** Recapture of Investment Credit, when investment credit property is disposed of or it no longer qualifies for the credit. State the kind of property at the top of Form 4255, and complete lines 2, 3, 4, and 8, whether or not any shareholder is subject to recapture of the credit. Attach to each Schedule K-1 a separate schedule providing the information the corporation is required to show on Form 4255, but list only the shareholder's pro rata share of the cost of the property subject to recapture. Also indicate the lines of Form 4255 on which the shareholders should report these amounts.

The corporation itself is liable for investment credit recapture in certain cases. See the instructions for line 22c, page 1, Form 1120S, for details.

16. Any other information the shareholders need to prepare their tax returns.

Specific Instructions

Schedule L—Balance Sheets

The balance sheets should agree with the corporation's books and records. Include certificates of deposit as cash on line 1 of Schedule L.

Line 5—Tax-Exempt Securities

Include on this line:

1. State and local government obligations, the interest on which is excludible from gross income under section 103(a), and

2. Stock in a mutual fund or other regulated investment company that distributed exempt-interest dividends during the tax year of the corporation.

Line 24—Retained Earnings

If the corporation maintains separate accounts for appropriated and unappropriated retained earnings, it may want to continue such accounting for purposes of preparing its financial balance sheet. Also, if the corporation converts to C corporation status in a subsequent year, it will be required to report its appropriated and unappropriated retained earnings on separate lines of Schedule L of Form 1120.

Schedule M-1— Reconciliation of Income per Books With Income per Return

Line 3b—Travel and Entertainment

Include on this line: 20% of meals and entertainment not allowed under section 274(n); expenses for the use of an entertainment facility; the part of business gifts in excess of $25; expenses of an individual allocable to conventions on cruise ships in excess of $2,000; employee achievement awards in excess of $400; the cost of entertainment tickets in excess of face value (also subject to 20%

disallowance); the cost of skyboxes in excess of the face value of nonluxury box seat tickets; the part of the cost of luxury water travel not allowed under section 274(m); expenses for travel as a form of education; and other travel and entertainment expenses not allowed as a deduction.

Schedule M-2—Analysis of Accumulated Adjustments Account, Other Adjustments Account, and Shareholders' Undistributed Taxable Income Previously Taxed

Column (a)—Accumulated Adjustments Account

The accumulated adjustments account (AAA) is to be maintained by all S corporations.

At the end of the tax year, if the corporation **does not have accumulated earnings and profits (E&P),** the AAA is determined by taking into account all items of income, loss, and deductions for the tax year (including nontaxable income and nondeductible losses and expenses). See section 1368 for other details. After the year-end income and expense adjustments are made, the account is reduced by distributions made during the tax year. See **Distributions** below for distribution rules.

At the end of the tax year, if the corporation **has accumulated E&P,** the AAA is determined by taking into account the taxable income, deductible losses and expenses, and nondeductible losses and expenses for the tax year. Adjustments for nontaxable income are made to the other adjustments account as explained in the column (b) instruction below. See section 1368. After the year-end income and expense adjustments are made, the AAA is reduced by distributions made during the tax year. See **Distributions** below for distribution rules.

Note: *The AAA may have a negative balance at year end. See section 1368(e).*

Column (b)—Other Adjustments Account

The other adjustments account is maintained only by corporations that **have** accumulated E&P at year end. The account is adjusted for tax-exempt income (and related expenses) of the corporation. See section 1368. After adjusting for tax-exempt income, the account is reduced for any distributions made during the year. See **Distributions** below.

Column (c)—Shareholders' Undistributed Taxable Income Previously Taxed

The shareholders' undistributed taxable income previously taxed account, also called previously taxed income (PTI), is maintained only if the corporation had a balance in this account at the start of its 1991 tax year. If there is a beginning

Page 20

balance for the 1991 tax year, no adjustments are made to the account except to reduce the account for distributions made under section 1375(d) (as in effect before the enactment of the Subchapter S Revision Act of 1982). See **Distributions** below for the order of distributions from the account.

Each shareholder's right to nontaxable distributions from PTI is personal and cannot be transferred to another person. The corporation is required to keep records of each shareholder's net share of PTI.

Distributions

Generally, property distributions (including cash) are applied in the following order to reduce accounts of the S corporation that are used to compute the tax effect of distributions made by the corporation to its shareholders:

1. Reduce AAA (but not below zero). If distributions during the tax year exceed the AAA at the close of the tax year, the AAA is allocated pro rata to each distribution made during the tax year. See section 1368(c).

2. Reduce shareholders' PTI account for any section 1375(d) (as in effect before 1983) distributions. A distribution from the PTI account is tax free to the extent of a shareholder's basis in his or her stock in the corporation.

3. Reduce accumulated E&P. Generally, the S corporation has accumulated E&P only if it has not distributed E&P accumulated in prior years when the S corporation was a C corporation (section 1361(a)(2)) or a small business corporation prior to 1983 (section 1371 of prior law).

See section 312 for information on E&P. The only adjustments that can be made to the accumulated E&P of an S corporation are: **(a)** reductions for dividend distributions; **(b)** adjustments for redemptions, liquidations, reorganizations, etc.; and **(c)** reductions for investment credit recapture tax for which the corporation is liable. See sections 1371(c) and (d)(3).

4. Reduce the other adjustments account.

5. Reduce any remaining shareholders' equity accounts.

If the corporation has accumulated E&P and wants to distribute this E&P before making distributions from the AAA, it may elect to do so with the consent of all its affected shareholders (section 1368(e)(3)). If the corporation has PTI and wants to make distributions from retained earnings before making distributions from PTI, it may elect to do so with the consent of all its shareholders. The statement of election must be attached to a timely filed Form 1120S for the tax year during which the distributions are made. The election must be made separately for each tax year.

In the case of either election, after all accumulated E&P in the retained earnings are distributed, the above general order of distributions applies except that item **3** is eliminated.

Example

The following example for a corporation that has accumulated E&P shows how the Schedule M-2 accounts are adjusted for items of income (loss), deductions, and distributions reported on Form 1120S.

Items per return are:

1. Page 1, line 21 income—$219,000

2. Schedule K, line 2 loss—($3,000)

3. Schedule K, line 4a income—$4,000

4. Schedule K, line 4b income—$16,000

5. Schedule K, line 7 deduction—$24,000

6. Schedule K, line 11a deduction—$3,000

7. Schedule K, line 13 jobs credit—$6,000

8. Schedule K, line 17 distributions—$65,000, and

9. Schedule K, line 18 scheduled items:

a. Tax-exempt income—$5,000, and

b. Nondeductible expense—$6,000 (reduction in salaries and wages for jobs credit).

Based on return items 1 through 9 and starting balances of zero, the columns for the AAA and the other adjustments account are completed as shown in the Schedule M-2 Worksheet below.

Note: *For the AAA account, the worksheet line 3—$20,000 amount is the total of the Schedule K, lines 4a and 4b incomes of $4,000 and $16,000. The worksheet line 5—$36,000 amount is the total of the Schedule K, line 2 loss of ($3,000), line 7 deduction of $24,000, line 11a deduction of $3,000, and the line 18 nondeductible expense item of $6,000. For the other adjustments account, the worksheet line 3 amount is the Schedule K, line 18, tax-exempt income of $5,000. Other worksheet amounts are self-explanatory.*

Schedule M-2   Worksheet

		(a) Accumulated adjustments account	(b) Other adjustments account	(c) Shareholders' undistributed taxable income previously taxed
1	Balance at beginning of tax year . . .	-0-	-0-	
2	Ordinary income from page 1, line 21 .	219,000	/////////	
3	Other additions	20,000	5,000	
4	Loss from page 1, line 21	( )	/////////	
5	Other reductions	(36,000)	( )	
6	Combine lines 1 through 5	203,000	5,000	
7	Distributions other than dividend distributions	65,000	-0-	
8	Balance at end of tax year. Subtract line 7 from line 6	138,000	5,000	

Codes for Principal Business Activity

These codes for the Principal Business Activity are designed to classify enterprises by the type of activity in which they are engaged to facilitate the administration of the Internal Revenue Code. Though similar in format and structure to the Standard Industrial Classification (SIC) codes, they should not be used as SIC codes.

Using the list below, enter on page 1, under B, the code number for the specific industry group from which the largest percentage of

"total receipts" is derived. "Total receipts" means the total of: gross receipts on line 1a, page 1; all other income on lines 4 and 5, page 1; all income on lines 2, 19, and 20a of Form 8825; and income (receipts only) on lines 3a and 4a through 4f of Schedule K.

On page 2, Schedule B, line 2, state the principal business activity and principal product or service that account for the largest percentage of total receipts. For example, if the

principal business activity is "Grain mill products," the principal product or service may be "Cereal preparations."

If, as its principal business activity, the corporation: (1) purchases raw materials, (2) subcontracts out for labor to make a finished product from the raw materials, and (3) retains title to the goods, the corporation is considered to be a manufacturer and must enter one of the codes (2010–3998) under "Manufacturing."

Agriculture, Forestry, and Fishing
Code
0400 Agricultural production.
0600 Agricultural services (except veterinarians), forestry, fishing, hunting, and trapping.

Mining
Metal mining:
1010 Iron ores.
1070 Copper, lead and zinc, gold and silver ores.
1098 Other metal mining.
1150 Coal mining.

Oil and gas extraction:
1330 Crude petroleum, natural gas, and natural gas liquids.
1380 Oil and gas field services.

Nonmetallic minerals, except fuels:
1430 Dimension, crushed and broken stone; sand and gravel.
1498 Other nonmetallic minerals, except fuels.

Construction
General building contractors and operative builders:
1510 General building contractors.
1531 Operative builders.

1600 Heavy construction contractors.

Special trade contractors:
1711 Plumbing, heating, and air conditioning.
1731 Electrical work.
1798 Other special trade contractors.

Manufacturing
Food and kindred products:
2010 Meat products.
2020 Dairy products.
2030 Preserved fruits and vegetables.
2040 Grain mill products.
2050 Bakery products.
2060 Sugar and confectionery products.
2081 Malt liquors and malt.
2088 Alcoholic beverages, except malt liquors and malt.
2089 Bottled soft drinks, and flavorings.
2096 Other food and kindred products.

2100 Tobacco manufacturers.

Textile mill products:
2228 Weaving mills and textile finishing.
2250 Knitting mills.
2298 Other textile mill products.

Apparel and other textile products:
2315 Men's and boys' clothing.
2345 Women's and children's clothing.
2388 Other apparel and accessories.
2390 Miscellaneous fabricated textile products.

Lumber and wood products:
2415 Logging, sawmills, and planing mills.
2430 Millwork, plywood, and related products.
2498 Other wood products, including wood buildings and mobile homes.

2500 Furniture and fixtures.

Paper and allied products:
2625 Pulp, paper, and board mills.
2699 Other paper products.

Printing and publishing:
2710 Newspapers.
2720 Periodicals.
2735 Books, greeting cards, and miscellaneous publishing.
2799 Commercial and other printing, and printing trade services.

Code
Chemicals and allied products:
2815 Industrial chemicals, plastics materials and synthetics.
2830 Drugs.
2840 Soap, cleaners, and toilet goods.
2850 Paints and allied products.
2898 Agricultural and other chemical products.

Petroleum refining and related industries (including those integrated with extraction):
2910 Petroleum refining (including integrated).
2998 Other petroleum and coal products.

Rubber and misc. plastics products:
3050 Rubber products: plastics footwear, hose, and belting.
3070 Misc. plastics products.

Leather and leather products:
3140 Footwear, except rubber.
3198 Other leather and leather products.

Stone, clay, and glass products:
3225 Glass products.
3240 Cement, hydraulic.
3270 Concrete, gypsum, and plaster products.
3298 Other nonmetallic mineral products.

Primary metal industries:
3370 Ferrous metal industries; misc. primary metal products.
3380 Nonferrous metal industries.

Fabricated metal products:
3410 Metal cans and shipping containers.
3428 Cutlery, hand tools, and hardware; screw machine products, bolts, and similar products.
3430 Plumbing and heating, except electric and warm air.
3440 Fabricated structural metal products.
3460 Metal forgings and stampings.
3470 Coating, engraving, and allied services.
3480 Ordnance and accessories, except vehicles and guided missiles.
3490 Misc. fabricated metal products.

Machinery, except electrical:
3520 Farm machinery.
3530 Construction and related machinery.
3540 Metalworking machinery.
3550 Special industry machinery.
3560 General industrial machinery.
3570 Office, computing, and accounting machines.
3598 Other machinery except electrical.

Electrical and electronic equipment:
3630 Household appliances.
3665 Radio, television, and communications equipment.
3670 Electronic components and accessories.
3698 Other electrical equipment.

3710 Motor vehicles and equipment.

Transportation equipment, except motor vehicles:
3725 Aircraft, guided missiles and parts.
3730 Ship and boat building and repairing.
3798 Other transportation equipment, except motor vehicles.

Instruments and related products:
3815 Scientific instruments and measuring devices; watches and clocks.
3845 Optical, medical, and ophthalmic goods.
3860 Photographic equipment and supplies.

3998 Other manufacturing products.

Transportation and Public Utilities
Code
Transportation:
4000 Railroad transportation.
4100 Local and interurban passenger transit.
4200 Trucking and warehousing.
4400 Water transportation.
4500 Transportation by air.
4600 Pipe lines, except natural gas.
4700 Miscellaneous transportation services.

Communication:
4825 Telephone, telegraph, and other communication services.
4830 Radio and television broadcasting.

Electric, gas, and sanitary services:
4910 Electric services.
4920 Gas production and distribution.
4930 Combination utility services.
4990 Water supply and other sanitary services.

Wholesale Trade
Durable:
5008 Machinery, equipment, and supplies.
5010 Motor vehicles and automotive equipment.
5020 Furniture and home furnishings.
5030 Lumber and construction materials.
5040 Sporting, recreational, photographic, and hobby goods, toys and supplies.
5050 Metals and minerals, except petroleum and scrap.
5060 Electrical goods.
5070 Hardware, plumbing and heating equipment and supplies.
5098 Other durable goods.

Nondurable:
5110 Paper and paper products.
5129 Drugs, drug proprietaries, and druggists' sundries.
5130 Apparel, piece goods, and notions.
5140 Groceries and related products.
5150 Farm-product raw materials.
5160 Chemicals and allied products.
5170 Petroleum and petroleum products.
5180 Alcoholic beverages.
5190 Misc. nondurable goods.

Retail Trade
Building materials, garden supplies, and mobile home dealers:
5220 Building materials dealers.
5251 Hardware stores.
5265 Garden supplies and mobile home dealers.

5300 General merchandise stores.

Food stores:
5410 Grocery stores.
5490 Other food stores.

Automotive dealers and service stations:
5515 Motor vehicle dealers.
5541 Gasoline service stations.
5598 Other automotive dealers.

5600 Apparel and accessory stores.

5700 Furniture and home furnishings stores.

5800 Eating and drinking places.

Misc. retail stores:
5912 Drug stores and proprietary stores.
5921 Liquor stores.
5995 Other retail stores.

Finance, Insurance, and Real Estate
Code
Banking:
6030 Mutual savings banks.
6060 Bank holding companies.
6090 Banks, except mutual savings banks and bank holding companies.

Credit agencies other than banks:
6120 Savings and loan associations.
6140 Personal credit institutions.
6150 Business credit institutions.
6199 Other credit agencies.

Security, commodity brokers and services:
6210 Security brokers, dealers, and flotation companies.
6299 Commodity contracts brokers and dealers; security and commodity exchanges; and allied services.

Insurance:
6355 Life insurance.
6356 Mutual insurance, except life or marine and certain fire or flood insurance companies.
6359 Other insurance companies.
6411 Insurance agents, brokers, and service.

Real estate:
6511 Real estate operators and lessors of buildings.
6516 Lessors of mining, oil, and similar property.
6518 Lessors of railroad property and other real property.
6530 Condominium management and cooperative housing associations.
6550 Subdividers and developers.
6599 Other real estate.

Holding and other investment companies, except bank holding companies:
6744 Small business investment companies.
6749 Other holding and investment companies, except bank holding companies.

Services
7000 Hotels and other lodging places.
7200 Personal services.

Business services:
7310 Advertising.
7389 Business services, except advertising.

Auto repair; miscellaneous repair services:
7500 Auto repair and services.
7600 Misc. repair services.

Amusement and recreation services:
7812 Motion picture production, distribution, and services.
7830 Motion picture theaters.
7900 Amusement and recreation services, except motion pictures.

Other services:
8015 Offices of physicians, including osteopathic physicians.
8021 Offices of dentists.
8040 Offices of other health practitioners.
8050 Nursing and personal care facilities.
8060 Hospitals.
8071 Medical laboratories.
8099 Other medical services.
8111 Legal services.
8200 Educational services.
8300 Social services.
8600 Membership organizations.
8911 Architectural and engineering services.
8930 Accounting, auditing, and bookkeeping.
8980 Miscellaneous services (including veterinarians).

☆ U.S. Government Printing Office: 1991-285-274

Form 1120S

Department of the Treasury
Internal Revenue Service

U.S. Income Tax Return for an S Corporation

OMB No. 1545-0130

For calendar year 1991, or tax year beginning ...., 1991, and ending ...., 19 .....
▶ **See separate instructions.**

1991

A Date of election as an S corporation	Use IRS label. Other-wise, please print or type.	Name	**C** Employer identification number
		Number, street, and room or suite no. (If a P.O. box, see page 8 of the instructions.)	**D** Date incorporated
B Business code no. (see Specific Instructions)		City or town, state, and ZIP code	**E** Total assets (see Specific Instructions) $

F Check applicable boxes: (1) ☐ Initial return (2) ☐ Final return (3) ☐ Change in address (4) ☐ Amended return
G Check this box if this S corporation is subject to the consolidated audit procedures of sections 6241 through 6245 (see instructions before checking this box) · · ▶ ☐
H Enter number of shareholders in the corporation at end of the tax year · · · · · · · · · · · · · · · · · · ▶

Caution: *Include **only** trade or business income and expenses on lines 1a through 21. See the instructions for more information.*

Income

1a	Gross receipts or sales |_____| **b** Less returns and allowances |_____| **c** Bal ▶	**1c**	
2	Cost of goods sold (Schedule A, line 8) · · · · · · · · · · ·	**2**	
3	Gross profit. Subtract line 2 from line 1c · · · · · · · · · ·	**3**	
4	Net gain (loss) from Form 4797, Part II, line 18 *(attach Form 4797)* · · ·	**4**	
5	Other income (see instructions) *(attach schedule)* · · · · · · ·	**5**	
6	**Total income (loss).** Combine lines 3 through 5 · · · · · · · · ▶	**6**	

Deductions (See instructions for limitations.)

7	Compensation of officers · · · · · · · · · · · · · · ·	**7**	
8a	Salaries and wages |_____| **b** Less jobs credit |_____| **c** Bal ▶	**8c**	
9	Repairs ·	**9**	
10	Bad debts · · · · · · · · · · · · · · · · · · ·	**10**	
11	Rents ·	**11**	
12	Taxes ·	**12**	
13	Interest ·	**13**	
14a	Depreciation (see instructions) · · · · · · · **14a**		
b	Depreciation claimed on Schedule A and elsewhere on return · **14b**		
c	Subtract line 14b from line 14a · · · · · · · · · · · ·	**14c**	
15	Depletion **(Do not deduct oil and gas depletion.)** · · · · · ·	**15**	
16	Advertising · · · · · · · · · · · · · · · · · ·	**16**	
17	Pension, profit-sharing, etc., plans · · · · · · · · · · ·	**17**	
18	Employee benefit programs · · · · · · · · · · · · ·	**18**	
19	Other deductions *(attach schedule)* · · · · · · · · · ·	**19**	
20	**Total deductions.** Add lines 7 through 19 · · · · · · · · · ▶	**20**	
21	Ordinary income (loss) from trade or business activities. Subtract line 20 from line 6 · · · ·	**21**	

Tax and Payments

22	**Tax:**		
a	Excess net passive income tax *(attach schedule)* · · · · · **22a**		
b	Tax from Schedule D (Form 1120S) · · · · · · · · **22b**		
c	Add lines 22a and 22b (see instructions for additional taxes) · · · · · · · · ·	**22c**	
23	**Payments:**		
a	1991 estimated tax payments · · · · · · · · · **23a**		
b	Tax deposited with Form 7004 · · · · · · · · · · **23b**		
c	Credit for Federal tax on fuels *(attach Form 4136)* · · · · · **23c**		
d	Add lines 23a through 23c · · · · · · · · · · · · · ·	**23d**	
24	Estimated tax penalty (see page 3 of instructions). Check if Form 2220 is attached · · ▶ ☐	**24**	
25	**Tax due.** If the total of lines 22c and 24 is larger than line 23d, enter amount owed. See instructions for depositary method of payment · · · · · · · · · · · · · · · · · ▶	**25**	
26	**Overpayment.** If line 23d is larger than the total of lines 22c and 24, enter amount overpaid ▶	**26**	
27	Enter amount of line 26 you want: **Credited to 1992 estimated tax** ▶	Refunded ▶	**27**	

Please Sign Here

Under penalties of perjury, I declare that I have examined this return, including accompanying schedules and statements, and to the best of my knowledge and belief, it is true, correct, and complete. Declaration of preparer (other than taxpayer) is based on all information of which preparer has any knowledge.

▶ _____   _____   ▶ _____
Signature of officer   Date   Title

Paid Preparer's Use Only	Preparer's signature ▶		Date		Check if self-employed ▶ ☐	Preparer's social security number
	Firm's name (or yours if self-employed) and address ▶				E.I. No. ▶	
					ZIP code ▶	

For Paperwork Reduction Act Notice, see page 1 of separate instructions.   Cat. No. 11510H   Form **1120S** (1991)

| Schedule A | Cost of Goods Sold | (See instructions.) |

1	Inventory at beginning of year	**1**	
2	Purchases.	**2**	
3	Cost of labor	**3**	
4	Additional section 263A costs (see instructions) *(attach schedule)*	**4**	
5	Other costs *(attach schedule)*.	**5**	
6	**Total.** Add lines 1 through 5	**6**	
7	Inventory at end of year	**7**	
8	**Cost of goods sold.** Subtract line 7 from line 6. Enter here and on line 2, page 1	**8**	

9a Check all methods used for valuing closing inventory:

    (i) ☐ Cost

    (ii) ☐ Lower of cost or market as described in Regulations section 1.471-4

    (iii) ☐ Writedown of "subnormal" goods as described in Regulations section 1.471-2(c)

    (iv) ☐ Other (specify method used and attach explanation) ▶ ....

  b Check if the LIFO inventory method was adopted this tax year for any goods *(if checked, attach Form 970).* . . . . . ▶ ☐

  c If the LIFO inventory method was used for this tax year, enter percentage (or amounts) of closing
inventory computed under LIFO . . . . | **9c** | |

  d Do the rules of section 263A (for property produced or acquired for resale) apply to the corporation? . . . . ☐ Yes ☐ No

  e Was there any change in determining quantities, cost, or valuations between opening and closing inventory? . . ☐ Yes ☐ No
If "Yes," attach explanation.

| Schedule B | Other Information |

		Yes	No
1	Check method of accounting: **(a)** ☐ Cash **(b)** ☐ Accrual **(c)** ☐ Other (specify) ▶		
2	Refer to the list in the instructions and state your principal:		
	(a) Business activity ▶ .... **(b)** Product or service ▶		
3	Did you at the end of the tax year own, directly or indirectly, 50% or more of the voting stock of a domestic corporation? (For rules of attribution, see section 267(c).) If "Yes," attach a schedule showing: **(a)** name, address, and employer identification number and **(b)** percentage owned.		
4	Were you a member of a controlled group subject to the provisions of section 1561?		
5	At any time during the tax year, did you have an interest in or a signature or other authority over a financial account in a foreign country (such as a bank account, securities account, or other financial account)? (See instructions for exceptions and filing requirements for form TD F 90-22.1.)		
	If "Yes," enter the name of the foreign country ▶		
6	Were you the grantor of, or transferor to, a foreign trust that existed during the current tax year, whether or not you have any beneficial interest in it? If "Yes," you may have to file Forms 3520, 3520-A, or 926		
7	Check this box if the corporation has filed or is required to file **Form 8264,** Application for Registration of a Tax Shelter . . . . ▶ ☐		
8	Check this box if the corporation issued publicly offered debt instruments with original issue discount . . . ▶ ☐		
	If so, the corporation may have to file **Form 8281,** Information Return for Publicly Offered Original Issue Discount Instruments.		
9	If the corporation: **(a)** filed its election to be an S corporation after 1986, **(b)** was a C corporation before it elected to be an S corporation **or** the corporation acquired an asset with a basis determined by reference to its basis (or the basis of any other property) in the hands of a C corporation, and **(c)** has net unrealized built-in gain (defined in section 1374(d)(1)) in excess of the net recognized built-in gain from prior years, enter the net unrealized built-in gain reduced by net recognized built-in gain from prior years (see instructions) . . . . ▶ $...................		
10	Check this box if the corporation had subchapter C earnings and profits at the close of the tax year (see instructions) . . . . ▶ ☐		

Designation of Tax Matters Person (See instructions.)

Enter below the shareholder designated as the tax matters person (TMP) for the tax year of this return:

Name of
designated TMP ▶ _____   Identifying
number of TMP ▶ _____

Address of
designated TMP ▶ _____

Schedule K   Shareholders' Shares of Income, Credits, Deductions, etc.

	(a) Pro rata share items		(b) Total amount	
Income (Loss)	**1** Ordinary income (loss) from trade or business activities (page 1, line 21)	**1**		
	2 Net income (loss) from rental real estate activities *(attach Form 8825)*	**2**		
	3a Gross income from other rental activities	**3a**		
	b Less expenses *(attach schedule)*.	**3b**		
	c Net income (loss) from other rental activities	**3c**		
	4 Portfolio income (loss):			
	a Interest income	**4a**		
	b Dividend income.	**4b**		
	c Royalty income	**4c**		
	d Net short-term capital gain (loss) *(attach Schedule D (Form 1120S))*	**4d**		
	e Net long-term capital gain (loss) *(attach Schedule D (Form 1120S))*.	**4e**		
	f Other portfolio income (loss) *(attach schedule)*	**4f**		
	5 Net gain (loss) under section 1231 (other than due to casualty or theft) *(attach Form 4797)*	**5**		
	6 Other income (loss) *(attach schedule)*	**6**		
Deductions	**7** Charitable contributions (see instructions) *(attach list)*	**7**		
	8 Section 179 expense deduction *(attach Form 4562)*.	**8**		
	9 Deductions related to portfolio income (loss) (see instructions) (itemize)	**9**		
	10 Other deductions *(attach schedule)*	**10**		
Investment Interest	**11a** Interest expense on investment debts	**11a**		
	b (1) Investment income included on lines 4a through 4f above	**11b(1)**		
	(2) Investment expenses included on line 9 above	**11b(2)**		
Credits	**12a** Credit for alcohol used as a fuel *(attach Form 6478)*	**12a**		
	b Low-income housing credit (see instructions):			
	(1) From partnerships to which section 42(j)(5) applies for property placed in service before 1990	**12b(1)**		
	(2) Other than on line 12b(1) for property placed in service before 1990.	**12b(2)**		
	(3) From partnerships to which section 42(j)(5) applies for property placed in service after 1989	**12b(3)**		
	(4) Other than on line 12b(3) for property placed in service after 1989	**12b(4)**		
	c Qualified rehabilitation expenditures related to rental real estate activities *(attach Form 3468)* .	**12c**		
	d Credits (other than credits shown on lines 12b and 12c) related to rental real estate activities (see instructions).	**12d**		
	e Credits related to other rental activities (see instructions)	**12e**		
	13 Other credits (see instructions)	**13**		
Adjustments and Tax Preference Items	**14a** Accelerated depreciation of real property placed in service before 1987	**14a**		
	b Accelerated depreciation of leased personal property placed in service before 1987 . .	**14b**		
	c Depreciation adjustment on property placed in service after 1986	**14c**		
	d Depletion (other than oil and gas)	**14d**		
	e (1) Gross income from oil, gas, or geothermal properties	**14e(1)**		
	(2) Deductions allocable to oil, gas, or geothermal properties	**14e(2)**		
	f Other adjustments and tax preference items *(attach schedule)*	**14f**		
Foreign Taxes	**15a** Type of income ▶			
	b Name of foreign country or U.S. possession ▶			
	c Total gross income from sources outside the United States *(attach schedule)*	**15c**		
	d Total applicable deductions and losses *(attach schedule)*	**15d**		
	e Total foreign taxes (check one): ▶ ☐ Paid ☐ Accrued	**15e**		
	f Reduction in taxes available for credit *(attach schedule)*	**15f**		
	g Other foreign tax information *(attach schedule)*	**15g**		
Other	**16a** Total expenditures to which a section 59(e) election may apply	**16a**		
	b Type of expenditures ▶			
	17 Total property distributions (including cash) other than dividends reported on line 19 below	**17**		
	18 Other items and amounts required to be reported separately to shareholders (see instructions) *(attach schedule)*			
	19 Total dividend distributions paid from accumulated earnings and profits	**19**		
	20 **Income (loss)** (Required only if Schedule M-1 must be completed.). Combine lines 1 through 6 in column (b). From the result, subtract the sum of lines 7 through 11a, 15e, and 16a	**20**		

Schedule L	Balance Sheets	Beginning of tax year		End of tax year	
	Assets	**(a)**	**(b)**	**(c)**	**(d)**
1	Cash				
2a	Trade notes and accounts receivable . .				
b	Less allowance for bad debts				
3	Inventories				
4	U.S. Government obligations.				
5	Tax-exempt securities				
6	Other current assets *(attach schedule)*. .				
7	Loans to shareholders				
8	Mortgage and real estate loans				
9	Other investments *(attach schedule)* . .				
10a	Buildings and other depreciable assets .				
b	Less accumulated depreciation				
11a	Depletable assets				
b	Less accumulated depletion				
12	Land (net of any amortization)				
13a	Intangible assets (amortizable only). . .				
b	Less accumulated amortization				
14	Other assets *(attach schedule)*				
15	Total assets				
	Liabilities and Shareholders' Equity				
16	Accounts payable				
17	Mortgages, notes, bonds payable in less than 1 year				
18	Other current liabilities *(attach schedule)*				
19	Loans from shareholders				
20	Mortgages, notes, bonds payable in 1 year or more				
21	Other liabilities *(attach schedule)* . . .				
22	Capital stock.				
23	Paid-in or capital surplus				
24	Retained earnings				
25	Less cost of treasury stock		( )		( )
26	Total liabilities and shareholders' equity .				

Schedule M-1	Reconciliation of Income per Books With Income per Return (You are not required to complete this schedule if the total assets on line 15, column (d), of Schedule L are less than $25,000.)

1	Net income per books		5	Income recorded on books this year not included on Schedule K, lines 1 through 6 (itemize):	
2	Income included on Schedule K, lines 1 through 6, not recorded on books this year (itemize):			a Tax-exempt interest $	
	....		6	Deductions included on Schedule K, lines 1 through 11a, 15e, and 16a, not charged against book income this year (itemize):	
3	Expenses recorded on books this year not included on Schedule K, lines 1 through 11a, 15e, and 16a (itemize):			a Depreciation $	
a	Depreciation $			....	
b	Travel and entertainment $				
	....		7	Add lines 5 and 6	
4	Add lines 1 through 3		8	Income (loss) (Schedule K, line 20). Line 4 less line 7	

Schedule M-2	Analysis of Accumulated Adjustments Account, Other Adjustments Account, and Shareholders' Undistributed Taxable Income Previously Taxed (See instructions.)

		(a) Accumulated adjustments account	(b) Other adjustments account	(c) Shareholders' undistributed taxable income previously taxed
1	Balance at beginning of tax year . . .			
2	Ordinary income from page 1, line 21 . .			
3	Other additions			
4	Loss from page 1, line 21.	( )		
5	Other reductions	( )	( )	
6	Combine lines 1 through 5			
7	Distributions other than dividend distributions .			
8	Balance at end of tax year. Subtract line 7 from line 6			

*U.S. GPO:1991-285-273

1991  Department of the Treasury
Internal Revenue Service

Shareholder's Instructions for Schedule K-1 (Form 1120S)
Shareholder's Share of Income, Credits, Deductions, Etc.
(For Shareholder's Use Only)

(Section references are to the Internal Revenue Code unless otherwise noted.)

General Instructions

Purpose of Schedule K-1

The corporation uses Schedule K-1 (Form 1120S) to report your pro rata share of the corporation's income (reduced by any tax the corporation paid on the income), credits, deductions, etc. **Please keep it for your records. Do not file it with your tax return (unless you are required to file it with Form 8271**, Investor Reporting of Tax Shelter Registration Number). A copy has been filed with the IRS.

Although the corporation is subject to a capital gains tax (or built-in gains tax) and an excess net passive income tax, you, the shareholder, are liable for income tax on your share of the corporation's income, whether or not distributed, and you must include your share on your tax return if a return is required. **Your distributive share of S corporation income is not self-employment income and it is not subject to self-employment tax.**

You should use these instructions to help you report the items shown on Schedule K-1 on your tax return.

Where "(attach schedule)" appears next to a line on Schedule K-1, it means the information for these lines (if applicable) will be shown in the "Supplemental Information" space below line 20 of Schedule K-1. If additional space was needed, the corporation will have attached a statement to Schedule K-1 to show the information for the line item.

The notation "(see Instructions for Schedule K-1)" in items A and C at the top of Schedule K-1 is directed to the corporation. You, as a shareholder, should disregard these notations.

Schedule K-1 does not show the amount of actual **dividend** distributions the corporation paid to you. The corporation must report to you such amounts totaling $10 or more during the calendar year on **Form 1099-DIV,** Dividends and Distributions. You report actual dividend distributions on Schedule B (Form 1040).

Basis of Your Stock

You are responsible for maintaining records to show the computation of the basis of your stock in the corporation. Schedule K-1 provides you with information to help you make the computation at the end of each corporate tax year. The basis of your stock is adjusted as follows (this list is not all-inclusive).

Basis is increased by:

1. All income (including tax-exempt income) reported on Schedule K-1. **Note:** *Taxable income must be reported on your tax return (if a return is required) for it to increase your basis.*

2. The excess of the deduction for depletion over the basis of the property subject to depletion.

Basis is decreased by:

1. Property distributions made by the corporation (excluding dividend distributions reported on Form 1099-DIV and distributions in excess of basis) reported on Schedule K-1, line 17.

2. All losses and deductions (including nondeductible expenses) reported on Schedule K-1.

Inconsistent Treatment of Items

Generally, you must treat subchapter S items on your return consistent with the way the corporation treated the items on its filed return. This rule does not apply if your S corporation is within the "small S corporation exception" and does not elect to have the tax treatment of subchapter S items determined at the corporate level.

If the treatment on your original or amended return is inconsistent with the corporation's treatment, or if the corporation has not filed a return, you must file **Form 8082,** Notice of Inconsistent Treatment or Amended Return (Administrative Adjustment Request (AAR)), with your original or amended return to identify and explain the inconsistency (or noting that a corporate return has not been filed).

If you are required to file Form 8082 but fail to do so, you may be subject to the accuracy-related penalty. This penalty is in addition to any tax that results from making your amount or treatment of the item consistent with that shown on the corporation's return. Any deficiency that results from making the amounts consistent may be assessed immediately.

Errors

If you believe the corporation has made an error on your Schedule K-1, notify the corporation and ask for a corrected Schedule K-1. Do not change any items on your copy. Be sure that the corporation sends a copy of the corrected Schedule K-1 to the IRS. If your S corporation does not meet the small S corporation exception, and you are unable to reach agreement with the S corporation regarding the inconsistency, you must file Form 8082.

Tax Shelters

If you receive a copy of **Form 8271,** Investor Reporting of Tax Shelter Registration Number, or if your S corporation is involved in a tax shelter, see the instructions for Form 8271 for the information you are required to furnish the IRS. Attach the completed forms to your income tax return. You can find the tax shelter registration number on line C(1) at the top of your Schedule K-1.

International Boycotts

Every S corporation that had operations in, or related to, a boycotting country, company, or national of a country, must file **Form 5713,** International Boycott Report.

If the corporation cooperated with an international boycott, it must give you a copy of the Form 5713 that it filed. You also must file Form 5713 to report the activities of the corporation and any other boycott operations of your own. You may lose certain tax benefits if the corporation participated in, or cooperated with, an international

Cat. No. 115210

boycott. Please see Form 5713 and the instructions for more information.

Elections

Generally, the corporation decides how to figure taxable income from its operations. For example, it chooses the accounting method and depreciation methods it will use.

However, certain elections are made by you separately on your income tax return and not by the corporation. These elections are made under:

● Section 59(e) (deduction of certain qualified expenditures ratably over the period of time specified in that section—see the instructions for lines 16a and 16b);

● Section 617 (deduction and recapture of certain mining exploration expenditures); and

● Section 901 (foreign tax credit).

Additional Information

For more information on the treatment of S corporation income, credits, deductions, etc., see **Pub. 589,** Tax Information on S Corporations; **Pub. 535,** Business Expenses; **Pub. 550,** Investment Income and Expenses; and **Pub. 925,** Passive Activity and At-Risk Rules.

The above publications and other publications referenced throughout these instructions may be obtained at most IRS offices. To order publications and forms, call our toll-free number, 1-800-TAX-FORM (829-3676).

Limitations on Losses, Deductions, and Credits

Aggregate Losses and Deductions Limited to Basis of Stock and Debt

Generally, the deduction for your share of aggregate losses and deductions reported on Schedule K-1 is limited to the basis of your stock and debt owed to you by the corporation. The basis of your stock is figured at year end. See **Basis of Your Stock** on page1. The basis of your loans made to the corporation is the balance the corporation now owes you, less any reduction for losses in a prior year. See the instructions for line 18. Any loss not allowed for the tax year because of this limitation is available for indefinite carryover, limited to the basis of your stock and debt, in each subsequent tax year. See section 1366(d) for details.

At-Risk Limitations

Generally, if you have:

1. A loss or other deduction from any activity carried on as a trade or business or for the production of income by the corporation, and

2. Amounts in the activity for which you are not at-risk, you will have to complete **Form 6198,** At-Risk Limitations, to figure the allowable loss to report on your return.

The at-risk rules generally limit the amount of loss (including loss on the disposition of assets) and other deductions (such as the section 179 expense deduction) that you can claim to the amount you could actually lose in the activity. However, if you acquired your stock before 1987, the at-risk rules do not apply to losses from an activity of holding real property placed in service before 1987 by the corporation. The activity of holding mineral property does not qualify for this exception.

Generally, you are not at risk for amounts such as the following:

● The basis of your stock in the corporation or basis of your loans made to the corporation if the cash or other property used to purchase the stock or make the loans was from a source covered by nonrecourse indebtedness (except for certain qualified nonrecourse financing, as defined in section 465(b)(6)) or protected against loss by a guarantee, stop-loss agreement, or other similar arrangement, or that is covered by indebtedness from a person who has an interest in the activity or from a related person to a person (except you) having such an interest, other than a creditor.

● Any cash or property contributed to a corporate activity, or your interest in the corporate activity, that is covered by nonrecourse indebtedness (except for certain qualified nonrecourse financing, as defined in section 465(b)(6)) or protected against loss by a guarantee, stop-loss agreement, or other similar arrangement, or that is covered by indebtedness from a person who has an interest in such activity or from a related person to a person (except you) having such an interest, other than a creditor.

Any loss from a section 465 activity not allowed for this tax year will be treated as a deduction allocable to the activity in the next tax year.

To help you complete Form 6198, if required, the corporation should tell you your share of the total pre-1976 losses from a section 465(c)(1) activity (i.e., films or video tapes, leasing section 1245 property, farm, or oil and gas property) for which there existed a corresponding amount of nonrecourse liability at the end of the year in which the losses occurred. Also, you should get a separate statement of income, expenses, etc., for each activity from the corporation.

Passive Activity Limitations

Section 469 provides rules that limit the deduction of certain losses and credits. The rules apply to shareholders who:

● Are individuals, estates, or trusts, and

● Have a passive activity loss or credit for the year.

Passive activities **include:**

1. Trade or business activities in which you do not materially participate, and

2. Activities that meet the definition of rental activities under Temporary Regulations section 1.469-1T(e)(3).

Passive activities **do not include:**

1. Trade or business activities in which you materially participate;

. 2. Qualifying low-income housing activities; and

3. An activity of trading personal property for the account of owners of interests in the activity.

The corporation will identify separately each activity that may be passive to you. If the corporation is conducting more than one activity, it will report information in the line 20 Supplemental Information space, or attach a statement if more space is needed, that: **(a).** identifies each activity (trade or business activity, rental real estate activity, rental activity other than rental real estate, etc.); **(b).** specifies the income (loss), deductions, and credits from each activity; **(c).** provides other details you may need to determine if an activity loss or credit is subject to the passive activity limitations.

If you determine that you have a passive activity loss or credit, get **Form 8582,** Passive Activity Loss Limitations, to figure your allowable passive loss, and **Form 8582-CR,** Passive Activity Credit Limitations, to figure your allowable passive credit. See the instructions for these forms for more information.

Material participation in trade or business activities.—You must determine whether you materially participated in each trade or business activity held through the corporation. All determinations of material participation are made with respect to participation during the corporation's tax year.

Material participation standards for shareholders who are individuals are listed below. Special rules apply to certain retired or disabled farmers and to the surviving spouses of farmers. See the Instructions for Form 8582 for details.

Individuals.—If you are an individual, you are considered to materially participate in a trade or business activity only if:

1. You participated in the activity for more than 500 hours during the tax year; or

2. Your participation in the activity for the tax year constituted substantially all of the participation in the activity of all individuals (including individuals who are not owners of interests in the activity); or

Page 2

3. You participated in the activity for more than 100 hours during the tax year, and your participation in the activity for the tax year was not less than the participation in the activity of any other individual (including individuals who were not owners of interests in the activity) for the tax year; or

4. The activity was a significant participation activity for the tax year, and your aggregate participation in all significant participation activities (including those outside the corporation) during the tax year exceeded 500 hours. A significant participation activity is any trade or business activity in which you participated for more than 100 hours during the year and in which you did not materially participate under any of the material participation tests (other than this test 4); or

5. You materially participated in the activity for any five tax years (whether or not consecutive) during the 10 tax years that immediately precede the tax year; or

6. The activity was a personal service activity and you materially participated in the activity for any three tax years (whether or not consecutive) preceding the tax year. An activity is a personal service activity if it involves the performance of personal services in the fields of health, law, engineering, architecture, accounting, actuarial science, performing arts, consulting, or any other trade or business, in which capital is not a material income-producing factor; or

7. Based on all of the facts and circumstances, you participated in the activity on a regular, continuous, and substantial basis during the tax year.

Work counted toward material participation.—Generally, any work that you or your spouse does in connection with an activity held through an S corporation (in which you own stock at the time the work is done) is counted toward material participation. However, work in connection with an activity is not counted toward material participation if:

1. The work is not the sort of work that owners of the activity would usually do and one of the principal purposes of the work that you or your spouse does is to avoid the passive loss or credit limitations, or

2. You do the work in your capacity as an investor and you are not directly involved in the day-to-day operations of the activity. Examples of work done as an investor which would not count toward material participation include:

a. studying and reviewing financial statements or reports on operations of the activity;

b. preparing or compiling summaries or analyses of the finances or operations of the activity; and

c. monitoring the finances or operations of the activity in a non-managerial capacity.

Effect of determination.—If you determine that you materially participated in a trade or business activity of the corporation, report the income (loss), deductions, and credits from the Schedule K-1 as indicated in either column (c) of Schedule K-1 or the instructions for your tax return.

If you determine that you **did not** materially participate in a trade or business activity, or you have income (loss), deductions, or credits from a rental activity of the corporation, the amounts from that activity are passive. Report passive income (losses), deductions, and credits as follows:

1. If you have an overall gain (the excess of income over deductions and losses, including any prior year unallowed loss) from a passive activity, report the income, deductions, and losses from the activity as indicated on Schedule K-1 or in these instructions.

2. If you have an overall loss (the excess of deductions and losses, including any prior year unallowed loss, over income) or credits from a passive activity, you must report the income, deductions, losses, and credits from **all** passive activities following the Instructions for Form 8582 or Form 8582-CR, to see if your deductions, losses, and credits are limited under the passive activity rules.

Active participation in a rental real estate activity.—If you actively participated in a rental real estate activity, you may be able to deduct up to $25,000 of the loss from the activity from nonpassive income. This "special allowance" is an exception to the general rule disallowing losses in excess of income from passive activities. The special allowance is not available if you were married, file a separate return for the year, and did not live apart from your spouse at all times during the year.

Only individuals and qualifying estates can actively participate in a rental real estate activity. Estates (other than qualifying estates) and trusts cannot actively participate.

You are not considered to actively participate in a rental real estate activity if, at any time during the tax year, your interest (including your spouse's interest) in the activity was less than 10% (by value) of all interests in the activity.

Active participation is a less stringent requirement than material participation. You may be treated as actively participating if you participated, for example, in making management decisions or arranging for others to provide services (such as repairs) in a significant and bona fide sense. Management decisions that can count as active participation include approving

new tenants, deciding on rental terms, approving capital or repair expenditures, and other similar decisions.

An estate is treated as actively participating for tax years ending less than 2 years after the date of the decedent's death if the decedent would have satisfied the active participation requirement for the activity for the tax year the decedent died. Such an estate is a "qualifying estate."

The maximum special allowance that single individuals and married individuals filing a joint return for the tax year can qualify for is $25,000. The maximum is $12,500 in the case of married individuals who file separate returns for the tax year and who lived apart at all times during the year. The maximum special allowance for which an estate can qualify is $25,000 reduced by the special allowance for which the surviving spouse qualifies.

If your modified adjusted gross income (defined below) is $100,000 or less ($50,000 or less in the case of married persons filing separately), your loss is deductible up to the amount of the maximum special allowance referred to in the preceding paragraph. If your modified adjusted gross income is more than $100,000 (more than $50,000 in the case of married persons filing separately), the special allowance is 50% of the difference between $150,000 ($75,000 in the case of married persons filing separately) and your modified adjusted gross income. When modified adjusted gross income is $150,000 or more ($75,000 or more in the case of married persons filing separately), there is no special allowance.

Modified adjusted gross income is your adjusted gross income figured without taking into account any passive activity loss, any taxable social security or equivalent railroad retirement benefits, any deductible contributions to an IRA or certain other qualified retirement plans under section 219, the deduction allowed under section 164(f) for one-half of self-employment taxes, or the exclusion from income of interest from Series EE U.S. Savings Bonds used to pay higher education expenses.

Special rule for low-income housing activities.—Transitional relief from the passive activity limitations is provided in the case of certain losses from qualified low-income housing projects. The corporation will identify losses from qualified low-income housing projects on an attachment to your Schedule K-1. See Pub. 925 for more information.

Specific Instructions

Name, Address, and Identifying Number

Your name, address, and identifying number, the corporation's name, address, and identifying number, and items A and B should have been completed. If the corporation is involved in a tax shelter, items C(1) and C(2) should also be completed.

If applicable, item D should be completed.

Lines 1 Through 20

The amounts on lines 1 through 20 show your pro rata share of ordinary income, loss, deductions, credits, and other information from all corporate activities. These amounts do not take into account limitations on losses, credits, or other items that may have to be adjusted because of:

1. The adjusted basis of your stock and debt in the corporation,

2. The at-risk limitations,

3. The passive activity limitations, or

4. Any other limitations that must be taken into account at the shareholder level in figuring taxable income (e.g., the section 179 expense limitation). The limitations of 1., 2., and 3. are discussed above, and the limitations for 4. are discussed throughout these instructions and in other referenced forms and instructions.

If you are an individual, and your pro rata share items are not affected by any of the limitations, report the amounts shown in column (b) of Schedule K-1 as indicated in column (c). If any of the limitations apply, adjust the column (b) amounts for the limitations before you enter the amounts on your return. When applicable, the passive activity limitations on losses are applied after the limitations on losses for a shareholder's basis in stock and debt and the shareholder's at-risk amount.

Note: *The line number references in column (c) are to forms in use for tax years beginning in 1991. If you are a calendar year shareholder in a fiscal year 1991–92 corporation, enter these amounts on the corresponding lines of the tax form in use for 1992.*

Caution: *If you have losses, deductions, credits, etc., from a prior year that were not deductible or usable because of certain limitations, such as the at-risk rules, they may be taken into account in determining your income, loss, etc., for this year. However, do not combine the prior-year amounts with any amounts shown on this Schedule K-1 to get a net figure to report on your return. Instead, report the amounts on your return on a year-by-year basis.*

Income

Line 1—Ordinary Income (Loss) From Trade or Business Activities

The amount reported on line 1 is your share of the ordinary income (loss) from trade or business activities of the

corporation. Generally, where you report this amount on Form 1040 depends on whether the amount is from an activity that is a passive activity to you. If you are an individual shareholder, find your situation below and report your line 1 income (loss) as instructed after applying the basis and at-risk limitations on losses:

1. Report line 1 income (loss) from trade or business activities in which you materially participated on Schedule E (Form 1040), Part II, column (i) or (k).

2. Report line 1 income (loss) from trade or business activities in which you did not materially participate, as follows:

a. If income is reported on line 1, report the income on Schedule E, Part II, column (h).

b. If a loss is reported on line 1, report the loss following the Instructions for Form 8582 to determine how much of the loss can be reported on Schedule E, Part II, column (g).

Line 2—Net Income (Loss) From Rental Real Estate Activities

Generally, the income (loss) reported on line 2 is a passive activity amount for all shareholders. There is an exception, however, for losses from a qualified low-income housing project. The passive activity loss limitations do not apply to losses incurred by qualified investors in qualified low-income housing projects (see Pub. 925). The corporation will have attached a schedule for line 2 to identify any such amounts.

If you are filing a 1991 Form 1040, use the following instructions to determine where to enter a line 2 amount:

1. If you have a loss (other than from a qualified low-income housing project) on line 2 and you meet **all** of the following conditions, enter the loss on Schedule E (Form 1040), Part II, column (g):

a. You actively participated in the corporate rental real estate activities. (See **Active participation in a rental real estate activity,** on page 3.)

b. Rental real estate activities with active participation were your only passive activities.

c. You have no prior year unallowed losses from these activities.

d. Your total loss from the rental real estate activities was not more than $25,000 (not more than $12,500 if married filing separately and you lived apart from your spouse all year).

e. If you are a married person filing separately, you lived apart from your spouse all year.

f. You have no current or prior year unallowed credits from a passive activity.

g. Your modified adjusted gross income was not more than $100,000 (not more than $50,000 if married filing

separately and you lived apart from your spouse all year).

2. If you have a loss (other than from a qualified low-income housing project) on line 2, and **you do not meet** all of the conditions in **1.** above, report the loss following the Instructions for Form 8582 to determine how much of the loss can be reported on Schedule E (Form 1040), Part II, column (g).

3. If you are a qualified investor reporting a qualified low-income housing project loss, report the loss on Schedule E, Part II, column (i).

4. If you have income on line 2, enter the income on Schedule E, Part II, column (h).

Line 3—Net Income (Loss) From Other Rental Activities

The amount on line 3 is a passive activity amount for all shareholders. Report the income or loss as follows:

1. If line 3 is a loss, report the loss following the Instructions for Form 8582.

2. If income is reported on line 3, report the income on Schedule E (Form 1040), Part II, column (h).

Line 4—Portfolio Income (Loss)

Portfolio income or loss is not subject to the passive activity limitations. Portfolio income includes interest, dividend, annuity and royalty income not derived in the ordinary course of a trade or business, and gain or loss on the sale of property that produces these types of income or is held for investment.

Column (c) of Schedule K-1 tells shareholders where to report this income on Form 1040 and related schedules. Line 4f of Schedule K-1 is used to report income other than that reported on lines 4a through 4e. The type and the amount of income reported on line 4f will be listed in the line 20 Supplemental Information space of Schedule K-1. An example of the type of income that is reported in line 4f is income from a Real Estate Mortgage Investment Company (REMIC) in which the corporation is a residual interest holder. Report your share of any REMIC income on Schedule E (Form 1040), Part IV.

Line 5—Net Gain (Loss) Under Section 1231 (Other Than Due to Casualty or Theft)

Section 1231 gain or loss is reported on line 5. The corporation will identify in the line 20 Supplemental Information space the activity to which the section 1231 gain (loss) relates.

If the amount on line 5 relates to a rental activity, the section 1231 gain (loss) is a passive activity amount. Likewise, if the amount relates to a trade or business activity and you do not materially participate in the activity, the section 1231 gain (loss) is a passive activity amount.

Page 4

- If the amount is **not** a passive activity amount to you, report it on line 2, column (g) or (h), whichever is applicable, of **Form 4797,** Sales of Business Property. You do not have to complete the information called for in columns (b) through (f), Form 4797. Write "From Schedule K-1 (Form 1120S)" across these columns.
- If gain is reported on line 5 and it **is** a passive activity amount to you, report the gain on line 2, column (h) of Form 4797.
- If a loss is reported on line 5 and it **is** a passive activity amount to you, see **Passive Loss Limitations** in the Instructions for Form 4797. You will need to report the loss following the Instructions for Form 8582 to determine how much of the loss is allowed on Form 4797.

Line 6—Other Income (Loss)

Amounts on this line are other items of income, gain, or loss not included on lines 1 through 5. The corporation should give you a description and the amount of your share for each of these items.

Report loss items that are passive activity amounts to you following the Instructions for Form 8582.

Report income or gain items that are passive activity amounts to you as instructed below.

The instructions below tell you where to report line 6 items if such items are **not** passive activity amounts.

Line 6 items include the following:
- Income from recoveries of tax benefit items. A tax benefit item is an amount you deducted in a prior tax year that reduced your income tax. Report this amount on Form 1040, line 22, to the extent it reduced your tax.
- Gambling gains and losses.
  1. If the corporation was not engaged in the trade or business of gambling:
  a. Report gambling winnings on Form 1040, line 22.
  b. Deduct gambling losses to the extent of winnings on Schedule A, line 25.
  2. If the corporation was engaged in the trade or business of gambling:
  a. Report gambling winnings in Part II of Schedule E.
  b. Deduct gambling losses to the extent of winnings in Part II of Schedule E.
- Net gain (loss) from involuntary conversions due to casualty or theft. The corporation will give you a schedule that shows the amounts to be reported in Section B of Form 4684, Casualties and Thefts.
- Net short-term capital gain or loss and net long-term capital gain or loss from Schedule D (Form 1120S) that is **not**

portfolio income (e.g., gain or loss from the disposition of nondepreciable personal property used in a trade or business activity of the corporation). Report a net short-term capital gain or loss on Schedule D (Form 1040), line 4, column (f) or (g), and a net long-term capital gain or loss on Schedule D (Form 1040), line 11, column (f) or (g).
- Any net gain or loss from section 1256 contracts. Report this amount on line 1 of **Form 6781,** Gains and Losses From Section 1256 Contracts and Straddles.

Deductions

Line 7—Charitable Contributions

The corporation will give you a schedule that shows which contributions were subject to the 50%, 30%, and 20% limitations. For further information, see the Form 1040 instructions.

If property other than cash is contributed, and the claimed deduction for one item or group of similar items of property exceeds $5,000, the corporation is required to file **Form 8283,** Noncash Charitable Contributions, and give you a copy to attach to your tax return. Do not deduct the amount shown on Form 8283. It is the corporation's contribution. You should deduct the amount shown on line 7, Schedule K-1.

If the corporation provides you with information that the contribution was property other than cash and does not give you a Form 8283, see the Instructions for Form 8283 for filing requirements. A Form 8283 does not have to be filed unless the total claimed deduction of all contributed items of property exceeds $500.

Charitable contribution deductions are not taken into account in figuring your passive activity loss for the year. Do not enter them on Form 8582.

Line 8—Section 179 Expense Deduction

Use this amount, along with the total cost of section 179 property placed in service during the year from other sources, to complete Part I of **Form 4562,** Depreciation and Amortization. Part I of Form 4562 is used to figure your allowable section 179 expense deduction from all sources. Report the amount on line 12 of Form 4562 allocable to a passive activity from the corporation following the Instructions for Form 8582. If the amount is not a passive activity deduction, report it on Schedule E (Form 1040), Part II, column (j).

Line 9—Deductions Related to Portfolio Income

Amounts on line 9 are deductions that are clearly and directly allocable to portfolio income reported on lines 4a

through 4f (other than investment interest expense and section 212 expenses from a REMIC). Generally, you should enter line 9 amounts on Schedule A (Form 1040), line 20. See the instructions for Schedule A, lines 19 through 25, for more information.

These deductions are not taken into account in figuring your passive activity loss for the year. Do not enter them on Form 8582.

Line 10—Other Deductions

Amounts on this line are other deductions not included on lines 7, 8, 9, and 15e, such as:
- Itemized deductions that Form 1040 filers enter on Schedule A (Form 1040).

Note: If there was a gain (loss) from a casualty or theft to property **not** used in a trade or business or for income-producing purposes, you will be notified by the corporation. You will have to complete your own Form 4684.
- Any penalty on early withdrawal of savings.
- Soil and water conservation expenditures. See section 175 for limitations on the amount you are allowed to deduct.
- Expenditures for the removal of architectural and transportation barriers to the elderly and disabled that the corporation elected to treat as a current expense. The expenses are limited by section 190.
- Interest expense allocated to debt-financed distributions. The manner in which you report such interest expense depends on your use of the distributed debt proceeds. See Notice 89-35, 1989-1 C.B. 675, for details.

If the corporation has more than one corporate activity (line **1, 2, or 3** of Schedule K-1), it will identify the activity to which the expenses relate.

The corporation should also give you a description and your share of each of the expense items. Associate any passive activity deduction included on line 10 with the line **1, 2,** or **3** activity to which it relates and report the deduction following the Instructions for Form 8582 (or only on Schedule E (Form 1040) if applicable).

Investment Interest

If the corporation paid or accrued interest on debts properly allocable to investment property, the amount of interest you are allowed to deduct may be limited.

For more information on the special provisions that apply to investment interest expense, see **Form 4952,** Investment Interest Expense Deduction, and **Pub. 550,** Investment Income and Expenses.

Line 11a—Interest Expense on Investment Debts

Enter this amount on Form 4952 along with investment interest expense from other sources to determine how much of your total investment interest is deductible.

Lines 11b(1) and (2)—Investment Income and Investment Expenses

Use the amounts on these lines to determine the amount to enter on Form 4952.

Caution: *The amounts shown on lines 11b(1) and 11b(2) include only investment income and expenses reported on lines 4 and 9 of Schedule K-1. If applicable, the corporation will have listed in the line 20 Supplemental Information space any other items of investment income and expenses reported elsewhere on Schedule K-1. Combine these items with lines 11b(1) and 11b(2) income and expenses to determine your total investment income and total investment expense from the corporation. Combine these totals with investment income and expenses from other sources to determine the amounts to enter on Form 4952.*

Credits

Caution: *If you have credits that are passive activity credits to you (i.e., the activity that generated the credit was a passive activity), you must complete Form 8582-CR in addition to the credit forms referenced below. See the Instructions for Form 8582-CR for more information.*

Also, if you are entitled to claim more than one general business credit (i.e., investment credit, jobs credit, credit for alcohol used as fuel, research credit, low-income housing credit, enhanced oil recovery credit, and disabled access credit), you must complete Form 3800, General Business Credit, in addition to the credit forms referenced below. If you have more than one credit, see the instructions for Form 3800 for more information.

Line 12a—Credit for Alcohol Used as Fuel

Your share of the corporation's credit for alcohol used as fuel that is related to all trade or business activities is reported on line 12a. Enter this credit on **Form 6478**, Credit for Alcohol Used as Fuel, to determine your allowed credit for the year.

Line 12b—Low-Income Housing Credit

Your share of the corporation's low-income housing credit is shown on lines 12b(1) through (4). Your allowable credit is entered on **Form 8586**, Low-Income Housing Credit, to

determine your allowed credit for the year.

If the corporation invested in a partnership to which the provisions of section 42(j)(5) apply, it will report separately on lines 12b(1) and 12b(3) your share of the credit it received from the partnership.

Your share of all other low-income housing credits of the corporation is reported on lines 12b(2) and 12b(4). You must keep a separate record of the amount of low-income housing credit from these lines so that you will be able to correctly compute any recapture of the credit that may result from the disposition of all or part of your stock in the corporation. For more information, see the instructions for **Form 8611,** Recapture of Low-Income Housing Credit.

Caution: *You cannot claim the low-income housing credit on any qualified low-income housing project if you, or any person, were allowed relief from the passive activity limitations on losses from the project (section 502 of the Tax Reform Act of 1986).*

Line 12c—Qualified Rehabilitation Expenditures Related to Rental Real Estate Activities

The corporation should identify your share of rehabilitation expenditures that are related to each rental real estate activity. The allowable investment credit for qualified rehabilitation expenditures is figured on **Form 3468,** Investment Credit.

Line 12d—Credits (Other Than Credits Shown on Lines 12b and 12c) Related to Rental Real Estate Activities

If applicable, your pro rata share of any other credit (other than on line 12b or 12c) related to rental real estate activities will be shown on line 12d. If more than one credit is involved, the credits will be shown and identified as line 12d credits in the line 20 Supplemental Information space. If the corporation has more than one rental real estate activity, each activity will be separately identified with any credits from the activity, and other information needed to figure the passive activity limitations.

Line 12e—Credits Related to Other Rental Activities

If applicable, your share of any credit related to other rental activities will be reported on line 12e. Income or loss for these activities is reported on line 3 of Schedule K-1. If more than one credit is involved, the credits will be listed separately, each credit identified as a line 12e credit, and the activity to which the credit relates will be identified. This information will be shown in the line 20

Supplemental Information space. The credit may be limited by the passive activity limitations.

Line 13—Other Credits

If applicable, your pro rata share of any other credit (other than on lines 12a through 12e) will be shown on line 13. If more than one credit is reported, the credits will be shown and identified in the line 20 Supplemental Information space. Expenditures qualifying for the **(a)** rehabilitation credit not related to rental real estate activities, **(b)** energy credit, or **(c)** reforestation credit will be reported to you on line 20.

Line 13 credits include the following:

● Nonconventional source fuel credit. Enter this credit on a schedule you prepare yourself to determine the allowed credit to take on your tax return. See section 29 for rules on how to figure the credit.

● Unused investment credit from cooperatives. Enter this credit on Form 3468 to figure your allowable investment credit.

● Credit for backup withholding on dividends, interest income, and other types of income. Include the amount the corporation reports to you in the total that you enter on line 54, page 2, Form 1040. Be sure to check the box on line 54 and write "From Schedule K-1".

● Credit for increasing research activities and orphan drug credit. Enter these credits on **Form 6765,** Credit for Increasing Research Activities.

● Jobs credit. Enter this credit on **Form 5884,** Jobs Credit.

● Disabled access credit. Enter this credit on **Form 8826,** Disabled Access Credit.

● Enhanced oil recovery credit. Enter this credit on **Form 8830,** Enhanced Oil Recovery Credit.

Adjustments and Tax Preference Items

Use the information reported on lines 14a through 14f (as well as adjustments and tax preference items from other sources) to prepare your **Form 6251,** Alternative Minimum Tax—Individuals, or **Form 8656,** Alternative Minimum Tax—Fiduciaries.

Lines 14e(1) and 14e(2)—Gross Income From, and Deductions Allocable to, Oil, Gas, and Geothermal Properties

The amounts reported on these lines include only the gross income from, and deductions allocable to, oil, gas, and geothermal properties that are included on line 1 of Schedule K-1. The corporation should have reported separately any income from or deductions allocable to such properties

Page 6

that are included on lines 2 through 10. This separate information is reported in the line 20 Supplemental Information space. Use the amounts reported on lines 14e(1) and 14e(2) and any amounts reported on a schedule to help you determine the net amount to enter on line 6g of Form 6251.

Line 14f—Other Adjustments and Tax Preference Items

Enter the line 14f adjustments and tax preference items that are shown in the line 20 Supplemental Information space, with other items from other sources, on the applicable lines of Form 6251.

Foreign Taxes

Use the information on lines 15a through 15g, and attached schedules, to figure your foreign tax credit. For more information, see **Form 1116**, Foreign Tax Credit—Individual, Fiduciary, or Nonresident Alien Individual, and the related instructions.

Other

Lines 16a and 16b

The corporation will show on line 16a the total qualified expenditures to which an election under section 59(e) may apply. It will identify the type of expenditures on line 16b. If there is more than one type of expenditure, the amount of each type will be listed on an attachment. Generally, section 59(e) allows each shareholder to elect to deduct certain expenses ratably over the number of years in the applicable period rather than deduct the full amount in the current year. Under the election, you may deduct ratably over a 3-year period circulation expenditures. Research and experimental expenditures and mining exploration and development costs qualify for a writeoff period of 10 years. Intangible drilling and development costs may be deducted over a 60-month period, beginning with the month in which such costs were paid or incurred. If you make this election, these items are not treated as adjustments or tax preference items for purposes of the alternative minimum tax. Make the election on Form 4562.

Because each shareholder decides whether to make the election under section 59(e), the corporation cannot provide you with the amount of the adjustment or tax preference item related to the expenses listed on line 16a. You must decide both how to claim the expenses on your return and how to compute the resulting adjustment or tax preference item.

Line 17

Reduce the basis of your stock in the corporation by the distributions on line 17. If these distributions exceed the basis of your stock, the excess is treated as gain from the sale or exchange of property and is reported on Schedule D (Form 1040).

Line 18

If the line 18 payments are made on indebtedness with a reduced basis, the repayments result in income to you to the extent the repayments are more than the adjusted basis of the loan. See section 1367(b)(2) for information on reduction in basis of a loan and restoration in basis of a loan with a reduced basis. See Revenue Ruling 64-162, 1964-1 (Part 1) C.B. 304 and Revenue Ruling 68-537, 1968-2 C.B. 372, for other information.

Lines 19a and 19b—Recapture of Low-Income Housing Credit

The corporation will report separately on line 19a your share of any recapture of a low-income housing credit attributable to its investment in partnerships to which the provisions of section 42(j)(5) apply. All other recapture of low-income housing credits will be reported on line 19b. You must keep a separate record of recapture attributable to lines 19a and 19b so that you will be able to correctly figure any credit recapture that may result from the disposition of all or part of your corporate stock ownership. Use the lines 19a and 19b amounts to compute the low-income housing credit recapture on Form 8611. See the instructions for Form 8611 and section 42(j) for additional information.

Supplemental Information

Line 20

If applicable, the corporation should have listed in line 20, Supplemental Information, or if additional space was needed, on an attached statement to Schedule K-1, your distributive share of the following:

1. Information for lines 4f, 6, 7, 9, 10, 14f, 15c, 15d, 15f, and 15g of Schedule K-1.

2. Tax-exempt interest income realized by the corporation. Generally, this income increases your basis in stock of the corporation. Tax-exempt interest earned by the corporation is stated separately for the following reasons:

a. If applicable, use this amount to figure the taxable portion of your social security or railroad retirement benefits. See the Instructions for Form 1040 for details.

b. If you are required to file a tax return for 1991, you must report on your return as an item of information the amount of tax-exempt interest income received or accrued during the tax year. Individual shareholders should report this amount on line 8b of Form 1040.

3. Nondeductible expenses paid or incurred by the corporation. These expenses are not deducted on your tax return but decrease the basis of your stock.

4. Taxes paid on undistributed capital gains by a regulated investment company. (Form 1040 filers, enter your share of these taxes on line 59 of Form 1040, check the box for Form 2439, and add the words "Form 1120S". Also reduce the basis of your stock in the S corporation by this tax.)

5. Gross income from the property, share of production for the tax year, etc., needed to figure your depletion deduction for oil and gas wells. The corporation should also allocate to you a proportionate share of the adjusted basis of each corporate oil or gas property. The allocation of the basis of each property is made as specified in section 613A(c)(11). See Pub. 535 for how to figure your depletion deduction. Also reduce your basis in stock by this deduction (section 1367(a)(2)(E)).

6. Your share of the intangible drilling and development costs shown on line 16a that is attributable to qualified exploratory costs. Use this amount to compute the alternative minimum tax adjustment based on energy preferences. See section 56(h) for more details.

7. Recapture of the section 179 expense deduction. The corporation will tell you if the recapture was caused by a disposition of the property.

The recapture amount is limited to the amount you deducted in earlier years. See Form 4797 for additional information.

8. Recapture of certain mining exploration expenditures (section 617).

9. Any information or statements you need to comply with requirements under section 6111 (registration of tax shelters) or 6662(d)(2)(B)(ii) (regarding adequate disclosure of items that may cause an understatement of income tax).

10. Gross farming and fishing income. If you are an individual shareholder, enter this income on Schedule E (Form 1040), Part V, line 41. Do not report this income elsewhere on Form 1040.

For a shareholder that is an estate or trust, report this income to the beneficiaries on Schedule K-1 (Form 1041). Do not report it elsewhere on Form 1041.

11. Any information you need to compute the interest due under section 453A(c) with respect to certain installment sales of property. If you are an individual, report the interest on Form 1040, line 53. Write "453A(c)" and the amount of the interest on the dotted line to the left of line 53. See the instructions for **Form 6252**, Installment Sale Income, for more information. Also see section

Page 7

453A(c) for details on making the computation.

12. Information you need to figure the interest due under section 453(l)(3). If the corporation elected to report the dispositions of certain timeshares and residential lots on the installment method, your tax liability must be increased by the interest on tax attributable to your pro rata share of the installment payments received by the corporation during its tax year. If applicable, use the information provided by the corporation to figure your interest. Include the interest on Form 1040, line 53. Also write "453(l)(3)" and the amount of the interest on the dotted line to the left of line 53.

13. Capitalization of interest under section 263A(f). To the extent that certain production or construction expenditures of the corporation are made from proceeds associated with debt that you incur as an owner-shareholder, you must capitalize the interest on this debt. If applicable, use the information on expenditures the corporation gives to you to determine the amount of interest you must capitalize. See Section XII of Notice 88-99, 1988-2 C.B. 422 for more information.

14. Any information you need to compute the interest due or to be refunded under the look-back method of section 460(b)(2) on certain long-term contracts. Use **Form 8697,** Interest Computation Under the Look-Back Method for Completed Long-Term Contracts, to report any such interest.

15. Your share of expenditures qualifying for the **(a)** rehabilitation credit not related to rental real estate activities, **(b)** energy credit, or **(c)** reforestation credit. Enter the expenditures on the appropriate line of Form 3468 to figure your allowable credit.

16. Investment credit properties subject to recapture. Any information you need to figure your recapture tax on **Form 4255,** Recapture of Investment Credit. See the Form 3468 on which you took the original credit for other information you need to complete Form 4255.

You may also need Form 4255 if you disposed of more than one-third of your stock in the corporation.

17. Preproductive period farm expenses. You may elect to deduct these expenses currently or capitalize them under section 263A. See **Pub. 225,** Farmer's Tax Guide, and Temporary Regulations section 1.263A-1T(c) for more information.

18. Any other information you may need to file with your individual tax return that is not shown elsewhere on Schedule K-1.

SCHEDULE K-1
(Form 1120S)

Department of the Treasury
Internal Revenue Service

Shareholder's Share of Income, Credits, Deductions, etc.

▶ See separate instructions.

For calendar year 1991 or tax year
beginning _____, 1991, and ending _____, 19___

OMB No. 1545-0130

1991

Shareholder's identifying number ▶	Corporation's identifying number ▶
Shareholder's name, address, and ZIP code	Corporation's name, address, and ZIP code

A Shareholder's percentage of stock ownership for tax year (see Instructions for Schedule K-1) . . . . . ▶ _____ %

B Internal Revenue service center where corporation filed its return ▶ ....

C **(1)** Tax shelter registration number (see Instructions for Schedule K-1) . . . . . . ▶ ....

    (2) Type of tax shelter ▶ ....

D Check applicable boxes: **(1)** ☐ Final K-1   **(2)** ☐ Amended K-1

		(a) Pro rata share items		(b) Amount	(c) Form 1040 filers enter the amount in column (b) on:
Income (Loss)	1	Ordinary income (loss) from trade or business activities . .	1		See Shareholder's Instructions for Schedule K-1 (Form 1120S).
	2	Net income (loss) from rental real estate activities	2		
	3	Net income (loss) from other rental activities	3		
	4	Portfolio income (loss):			
	a	Interest	4a		Sch. B, Part I, line 1
	b	Dividends	4b		Sch. B, Part II, line 5
	c	Royalties	4c		Sch. E, Part I, line 4
	d	Net short-term capital gain (loss)	4d		Sch. D, line 4, col. (f) or (g)
	e	Net long-term capital gain (loss)	4e		Sch. D, line 11, col. (f) or (g)
	f	Other portfolio income (loss) (attach schedule)	4f		(Enter on applicable line of your return.)
	5	Net gain (loss) under section 1231 (other than due to casualty or theft)	5		See Shareholder's Instructions for Schedule K-1 (Form 1120S).
	6	Other income (loss) (attach schedule)	6		(Enter on applicable line of your return.)
Deductions	7	Charitable contributions (see instructions) (attach schedule) .	7		Sch. A, line 13 or 14
	8	Section 179 expense deduction	8		See Shareholder's Instructions for Schedule K-1 (Form 1120S).
	9	Deductions related to portfolio income (loss) (attach schedule) .	9		
	10	Other deductions (attach schedule)	10		
Investment Interest	11a	Interest expense on investment debts	11a		Form 4952, line 1
	b	**(1)** Investment income included on lines 4a through 4f above	b(1)		See Shareholder's Instructions for Schedule K-1 (Form 1120S).
		(2) Investment expenses included on line 9 above	b(2)		
Credits	12a	Credit for alcohol used as fuel	12a		Form 6478, line 10
	b	Low-income housing credit:			
		(1) From section 42(j)(5) partnerships for property placed in service before 1990	b(1)		
		(2) Other than on line 12b(1) for property placed in service before 1990 .	b(2)		Form 8586, line 5
		(3) From section 42(j)(5) partnerships for property placed in service after 1989 .	b(3)		
		(4) Other than on line 12b(3) for property placed in service after 1989 . .	b(4)		
	c	Qualified rehabilitation expenditures related to rental real estate activities (see instructions)	12c		
	d	Credits (other than credits shown on lines 12b and 12c) related to rental real estate activities (see instructions) . . .	12d		See Shareholder's Instructions for Schedule K-1 (Form 1120S).
	e	Credits related to other rental activities (see instructions) . .	12e		
	13	Other credits (see instructions)	13		
Adjustments and Tax Preference Items	14a	Accelerated depreciation of real property placed in service before 1987	14a		
	b	Accelerated depreciation of leased personal property placed in service before 1987	14b		See Shareholder's Instructions for Schedule K-1 (Form 1120S) and Instructions for Form 6251
	c	Depreciation adjustment on property placed in service after 1986	14c		
	d	Depletion (other than oil and gas)	14d		
	e	**(1)** Gross income from oil, gas, or geothermal properties . .	e(1)		
		(2) Deductions allocable to oil, gas, or geothermal properties	e(2)		
	f	Other adjustments and tax preference items (attach schedule)	14f		

For Paperwork Reduction Act Notice, see page 1 of Instructions for Form 1120S.   Cat. No. 11520D   **Schedule K-1 (Form 1120S) 1991**

(a) Pro rata share items		(b) Amount	(c) Form 1040 filers enter the amount in column (b) on:
Foreign Taxes	**15a** Type of income ▶		Form 1116, Check boxes
	b Name of foreign country or U.S. possession ▶		
	c Total gross income from sources outside the U.S. (attach schedule) .	15c	} Form 1116, Part I
	d Total applicable deductions and losses (attach schedule) . .	15d	
	e Total foreign taxes (check one): ▶ ☐ Paid ☐ Accrued .	15e	Form 1116, Part II
	f Reduction in taxes available for credit (attach schedule) . .	15f	Form 1116, Part III
	g Other foreign tax information (attach schedule)	15g	See Instructions for Form 1116
Other	**16a** Total expenditures to which a section 59(e) election may apply	16a	} See Shareholder's Instructions for Schedule K-1 (Form 1120S).
	b Type of expenditures ▶		
	17 Property distributions (including cash) other than dividend distributions reported to you on Form 1099-DIV	17	
	18 Amount of loan repayments for "Loans From Shareholders" .	18	
	19 Recapture of low-income housing credit:		
	a From section 42(j)(5) partnerships	19a	} Form 8611, line 8
	b Other than on line 19a	19b	

20 Supplemental information required to be reported separately to each shareholder (attach additional schedules if more space is needed):

Supplemental Information

....

....

....

....

....

....

....

....

....

....

....

....

....

....

....

....

....

....

....

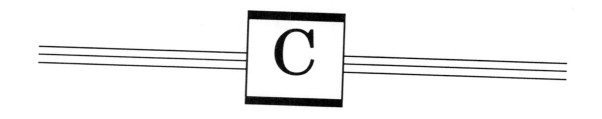

IRS Schedules D and E:
Capital Gains and Losses
and Supplemental Income
and Loss

Instructions for Schedule D, Capital Gains and Losses

A Change You Should Note. *For 1991, the maximum tax rate on net capital gain is 28%. If you have a net capital gain (both lines 16 and 17 of Schedule D are gains), and your taxable income is more than $82,150 ($49,300 if single; $70,450 if head of household; $41,075 if married filing separately), use new Part IV, Tax Computation Using Maximum Capital Gains Rate, to figure your tax.*

Additional Information. Get **Pub. 544,** *Sales and Other Dispositions of Assets,* and **Pub. 550,** *Investment Income and Expenses,* for more details.

General Instructions

Which Form To Use

Use Schedule D to:

• Report the sale or exchange of a capital asset.

• Report gains from involuntary conversions of capital assets not held for business or profit.

• Reconcile Forms 1099-B you got for bartering transactions. (See Part VII.)

• Make a long-term capital gain election for lump-sum pension plan distributions.

Use **Form 4797,** Sales of Business Property, instead of Schedule D, to report the following:

• The sale or exchange of trade or business property, depreciable and amortizable property, oil, gas, geothermal, or other mineral property, and section 126 property.

• The involuntary conversion (other than by casualty or theft) of trade or business property and capital assets held for business or profit.

• The disposition of other noncapital assets not mentioned above.

Use **Form 4684,** Casualties and Thefts, to report involuntary conversions of property due to casualty or theft.

Use **Form 8824,** Like-Kind Exchanges, if you made one or more like-kind exchanges. See **Exchange of Like-Kind Property,** on the next page.

Capital Gain Elections on Lump-Sum Distributions From Qualified Retirement Plans

The amount of a lump-sum distribution that qualifies for capital gain treatment should be shown on Form 1099-R, Box 3. If you qualify to use **Form 4972,** Tax on Lump-Sum Distributions, you can make the 20% capital gain election in Part II of that form. If you do not include the capital gain portion on Form 4972, you can make a long-term capital gain election on Schedule D. To make the election, write "lump-sum distribution" on line 8d, column (a). Enter in column (g) 25% (.25) of the amount from Form 1099-R, Box 3. Enter the remaining amount of the distribution (Form 1099-R, Box 2, minus the amount used on Schedule D) on Form 1040, lines 17a and 17b. However, if you qualify to use Form 4972, you may report the balance on that form instead of Form 1040, lines 17a and 17b.

If you elect to include net unrealized appreciation (NUA) in income, a portion of the amount from Form 1099-R, Box 6, can generally receive capital gain treatment. See Instructions for Form 4972 for details.

Capital Asset

Most property you own and use for personal purposes, pleasure, or investment is a capital asset. For example, your house, furniture, car, stocks, and bonds are capital assets.

A capital asset is any property held by you **except** the following:

a. Stock in trade or other property included in inventory or held for sale to customers.

b. Accounts or notes receivable for services performed in the ordinary course of your trade or business or as an employee, or from the sale of any property described in **a.**

c. Depreciable property used in your trade or business even if it was fully depreciated.

d. Real property (real estate) used in your trade or business.

e. Copyrights, literary, musical, or artistic compositions, letters or memoranda, or similar property: (1) created by your personal efforts; (2) prepared or produced for you (in the case of letters, memoranda, or similar property); or (3) that you received from someone who created them or for whom they were created, as mentioned in (1) or (2), in a way (such as by gift) that entitled you to the basis of the previous owner.

f. U.S. Government publications, including the Congressional Record, that you received from the government, other than by purchase at the normal sales price, or that you got from someone who had received it in a similar way, if your basis is determined by reference to the previous owner's basis.

Short-Term or Long-Term

Separate your capital gains and losses according to how long you held or owned the property. The holding period for long-term capital gains and losses is more than 1 year. The holding period for short-term capital gains and losses is 1 year or less.

To figure the holding period, begin counting on the day after you received the property and include the day you disposed of it. Use the trade dates for date acquired and date sold for stocks and bonds traded on an exchange or over-the-counter market.

Generally, a nonbusiness bad debt must be treated as a short-term capital loss. See Pub. 550 under **Nonbusiness Bad Debts** for what qualifies as a nonbusiness bad debt and how to enter it on Schedule D.

Capital Losses

The amount of capital loss that can be deducted after offsetting capital gains is limited to $3,000 ($1,500 if married filing a separate return).

Losses That Are Not Deductible

Do not deduct a loss from the direct or indirect sale or exchange of property between any of the following:

• Members of a family.

• A corporation and an individual owning more than 50% of the corporation's stock (unless the loss is from a distribution in complete liquidation of a corporation).

• A grantor and a fiduciary of a trust.

• A fiduciary and a beneficiary of the same trust.

• A fiduciary and a beneficiary of another trust created by the same grantor.

• An individual and a tax-exempt organization controlled by the individual or the individual's family.

See Pub. 544 for more details on sales and exchanges between related parties.

If you dispose of (1) an asset used in an activity to which the at-risk rules apply, or (2) any part of your interest in an activity to which the at-risk rules apply, and you have amounts in the activity for which you are not at risk, get the instructions for **Form 6198,** At-Risk Limitations. If the loss is allowable under the at-risk rules, it is then subject to the passive activity rules. Get **Form 8582,** Passive Activity Loss Limitations, and its instructions to see how to report capital gains and losses from a passive activity.

Items for Special Treatment and Special Cases

The following items may require special treatment:

• Transactions by a securities dealer.

• Wash sales of stock or securities (including contracts or options to acquire or sell stock or securities). See Pub. 550 for details.

• Bonds and other debt instruments. See Pub. 550 for details.

• Certain real estate subdivided for sale which may be considered a capital asset.

• Gain on the sale of depreciable property to a more than 50% owned entity, or to a trust of which you are a beneficiary.

• Gain on the disposition of stock in an Interest Charge Domestic International Sales Corporation.

• Gain on the sale or exchange of stock in certain foreign corporations.

Page 53

- Transfer of property to a foreign corporation as paid-in surplus or as a contribution to capital, or to a foreign trust or partnership.
- Transfer of property to a partnership that would be treated as an investment company if it were incorporated.
- Sales of stock received under a qualified public utility dividend reinvestment plan. See Pub. 550 for details.
- Transfer of appreciated property to a political organization.
- Loss on the sale, exchange, or worthlessness of small business (section 1244) stock.
- In general, no gain or loss is recognized on the transfer of property from an individual to a spouse or a former spouse, if the transfer is incident to a divorce. Get **Pub. 504,** Tax Information for Divorced or Separated Individuals.
- Amounts received on the retirement of a debt instrument generally are treated as received in exchange for the debt instrument.
- Any loss on the disposition of converted wetland or highly erodible cropland that is first used for farming after March 1, 1986, is reported as long-term capital loss on Schedule D, but any gain is reported as ordinary income on Form 4797.
- Gifts of property and inherited property. See Pub. 544.
- Amounts received by shareholders in corporate liquidations.
- Cash received in lieu of fractional shares of stock as a result of a stock split or stock dividend. See Pub. 550.
- Mutual fund load charges may not be taken into account in determining gain or loss on certain dispositions of stock in mutual funds if reinvestment rights were exercised. For details, get **Pub. 564,** Mutual Fund Distributions.
- Deferral of gain on conflict-of-interest dispositions under section 1043. See Form 8824.

Inherited Property

If you disposed of property that you acquired by inheritance, report the disposition as a long-term gain or loss, regardless of how long you held the property. Write **"INHERITED"** in column (b), instead of the date you acquired the property.

Gain or Loss From Options

Report on Schedule D gain or loss from the closing or expiration of an option that is not a section 1256 contract, but that is a capital asset in your hands.

If a purchased option expired, enter the expiration date in column (c), and write **"EXPIRED"** in column (d).

If an option that was granted (written) expired, enter the expiration date in column (b), and write **"EXPIRED"** in column (e).

Fill in the other columns as appropriate. See Pub. 550 for more details.

Exchange of Like-Kind Property

A "like-kind exchange" occurs when you exchange business or investment property for property of a like kind. Report on Schedule D (or Form 4797, whichever applies) the exchange of like-kind property, even if no gain

Page 54

or loss is recognized. Also complete and attach Form 8824 to your return for each exchange.

For exchanges reported on Schedule D, write "From Form 8824" in column (a). Skip columns (b) through (e), and enter the gain or loss from Form 8824, if any, in column (f) or (g). If an exchange was made with a related party, write "Related Party Like-Kind Exchange" in the top margin of Schedule D. See Form 8824 and its instructions for details.

Sale or Exchange (Other Than Involuntary Conversion) of Capital Assets Held for Personal Use

Gain from the sale or exchange of this property is a capital gain. Report it on Schedule D, Part I or Part II. Loss from the sale or exchange of this property is not deductible. But if you had a loss from the sale or exchange of real estate held for personal use (other than your main home), you must report the transaction on Schedule D even though the loss is not deductible.

For example, you have a loss on the sale of a vacation home that is not your main home. Report it on line 1a or 8a, depending on how long you owned the home. Complete columns (a) through (e). Since the loss is not deductible, write "Personal Loss" across columns (f) and (g).

Disposition of Partnership Interest

A sale or other disposition of an interest in a partnership may result in ordinary income. Get **Pub. 541,** Tax Information on Partnerships.

Long-Term Capital Gains From Regulated Investment Companies

Include in income as a long-term capital gain the amount on **Form 2439,** Notice to Shareholder of Undistributed Long-Term Capital Gains, that represents your share of the undistributed capital gains of a regulated investment company. Enter on Form 1040, line 59, the tax paid by the company shown on Form 2439. Add to the basis of your stock the excess of the amount included in income over the amount of the credit. See Pub. 550 for more details.

Capital Gain Distributions

Enter on line 12 capital gain distributions paid to you during the year as a long-term capital gain regardless of how long you held your investment. See Pub. 550 for more details.

Sale of Your Home

Use **Form 2119,** Sale of Your Home, to report a gain or loss from the sale of your main home whether or not you bought another one. You must file Form 1040 for the year in which you sell your main home, even if you are not otherwise required to file. For more details, get **Pub. 523,** Tax Information on Selling Your Home.

Installment Sales

If you sold property (other than publicly traded stocks or securities) at a gain, and you will receive a payment in a tax year after the year of sale, you must report the sale on the installment method unless you elect not to do so.

Use **Form 6252,** Installment Sale Income, to report the sale on the installment method. Also use Form 6252 to report any payment received in 1991 from a sale made in an earlier year that you reported on the installment method.

To elect out of the installment method, report the sale as follows on a timely filed return (including extensions):

(1) Report the full amount of the sale on Schedule D.

(2) If you received a note or other obligation and you are reporting it at less than face value (including all contingent payment obligations), complete Part VI. If you received more than one, enter the amounts separately in the spaces in Part VI.

Get **Pub. 537,** Installment Sales, for more details.

Section 1256 Contracts and Straddles

Use **Form 6781,** Gains and Losses From Section 1256 Contracts and Straddles, to report these transactions. See Pub. 550 for more details.

Form 1099-A, Acquisition or Abandonment of Secured Property

If you received a Form 1099-A from your lender, you may have gain or loss to report because of the acquisition or abandonment. See Pub. 544 for details.

Specific Instructions

Column (d)

Sales Price

Enter in this column either the gross sales price or the net sales price from the sale. If you sold stocks or bonds and you received a Form 1099-B or similar statement from your broker that shows gross sales price, enter that amount in column (d). However, if Form 1099-B (or your broker) indicates that gross proceeds minus commissions and option premiums were reported to the IRS, enter that net amount in column (d). If the net amount is entered in column (d), do not include the commissions and option premiums in column (e).

You should not have received a Form 1099-B (or substitute statement) for a transaction merely representing the return of your original investment in a nontransferrable obligation, such as a savings bond or a certificate of deposit. But if you did, report the amount shown on Form 1099-B (or substitute statement) in both columns (d) and (e).

Caution: *Be sure to add all sales price entries on lines 1a and 8a, column (d), to amounts* on lines 1b and 8b, column (d). Enter the totals on lines 1c and 8c.

Column (e)

Cost or Other Basis

In general, the cost or other basis is the cost of the property plus purchase commissions and improvements, minus depreciation, amortization, and depletion. If you inherited the property, got it as a gift, or received it in a tax-free exchange, involuntary conversion, or "wash sale" of stock, you may not be able to use the actual cost as the basis. If you do not use the actual cost, attach an explanation of your basis.

You should not have received a Form 1099-B (or substitute statement) for a transaction merely representing the return of your original investment in a nontransferrable obligation, such as a savings bond or a certificate of deposit. But if you did, report the amount shown on Form 1099-B (or substitute statement) in both columns (d) and (e).

When selling stock, adjust your basis by subtracting all the nontaxable distributions you received before the sale. Also adjust your basis for any stock splits. See Pub. 550 for how to figure your basis in stock that split during the time you owned it.

The basis of property acquired by gift is generally the basis of the property in the hands of the donor. The basis of property acquired from a decedent is generally the fair market value at the date of death.

The cost or other basis of an original issue discount (OID) debt instrument is increased by the amount of OID that has been included in gross income for that instrument.

If a charitable contribution deduction is allowed because of a bargain sale of property to a charitable organization, the adjusted basis for purposes of determining gain from the sale is the amount which has the same ratio to the adjusted basis as the amount realized has to the fair market value.

Increase your cost or other basis by any expense of sale, such as broker's fees, commissions, state and local transfer taxes, and option premiums before making an entry in column (e), unless you reported the net sales price in column (d).

For more details, get **Pub. 551,** Basis of Assets.

Lines 1a and 8a

Enter all sales and exchanges of stocks, bonds, etc., and real estate (if not reported on Form 2119, 4797, or 6252). Include these transactions whether or not you actually received a Form 1099-B or 1099-S (or substitute statement) for the transaction. You can use abbreviations to describe the property as long as the abbreviations are based on the descriptions of the property as shown on Form 1099-B or 1099-S (or substitute statement).

Use **Schedule D-1,** Continuation Sheet for Schedule D (Form 1040), if you need more space to list transactions for lines 1a and 8a. You may use as many Schedules D-1 as you need to list your transactions. Enter on Schedule D, lines 1b and 8b, columns (d), (f), and (g) the combined totals of all your Schedules D-1.

Lines 1d and 8d

Enter sales and exchanges of other capital assets on these lines that are not reported on lines 1a or 8a. Do not include transactions reported on Form 2119, 4797, or 6252.

Part VII

This part enables the IRS to compare amounts of bartering income reported to you on Forms 1099-B with amounts you report on your tax return. For details on bartering income, get **Pub. 525,** Taxable and Nontaxable Income.

Instructions for Schedule E, Supplemental Income and Loss

Use Schedule E to report income or loss from rents, royalties, partnerships, S corporations, estates, trusts, and residual interests in REMICs.

If you attach your own schedule(s) to report income or loss from any of these sources, use the same format as on Schedule E. Enter separately on Schedule E the total income and the total loss for each part. Enclose loss figures in (parentheses).

Parts II and III. Income or Loss From Partnerships, S Corporations, Estates, or Trusts

If you are a member of more than one partnership, a shareholder in more than one S corporation, or a beneficiary of more than one estate or trust, do not report information from more than one entity on the same line.

If you need more space in Parts II and III to list your income or losses, attach a continuation sheet using the same format as shown in Parts II and III. However, be sure to complete the "Totals" columns for lines 28a and 28b, or lines 33a and 33b, as appropriate. If you also completed Part I on more than one Schedule E, use the same Schedule E on which you entered the combined totals in Part I.

Tax Shelter Registration Number. If you are claiming or you are reporting any deduction, loss, credit, or other tax benefit, or reporting income from an interest purchased or otherwise acquired in a tax shelter, you must complete and attach **Form 8271**, Investor Reporting of Tax Shelter Registration Number. This reports the tax shelter registration number as well as other information about the tax shelter. There is a $250 penalty if you fail to report this number on your tax return.

Tax Preference Items. If you are a partner, a shareholder in an S corporation, or a beneficiary of an estate or trust, you must take into account your share of tax preference items and adjustments from these entities on **Form 6251**, Alternative Minimum Tax—Individuals, or **Form 8656**, Alternative Minimum Tax—Fiduciaries.

Partnerships and S Corporations

If you are a member of a partnership or joint venture or a shareholder in an S corporation, use Part II to report your share of the partnership or S corporation income (even if not received) or loss. You should receive a **Schedule K-1** from the partnership or the S corporation. Do not attach Schedules K-1 to your return. Keep them for your records. You should also receive a copy of the Partner's or Shareholder's Instructions for Schedule K-1. If you did not receive these instructions with your Schedule K-1, you can get a copy at most IRS offices. Your copy of Schedule K-1 and its instructions will tell you where on your return to report your share of the items.

Special rules apply that limit losses. Please note the following:

● If you have a current year loss or a prior year unallowed loss from a partnership or an S corporation, see the **At-Risk Rules** explained earlier and the **Passive Activity Loss Rules** on this page.

Partners and S corporation shareholders should get a separate statement of income, expenses, deductions, and credits for each activity engaged in by the partnership and S corporation. If you are subject to the at-risk rules for any activity, use Form 6198 to figure the amount of any deductible loss. If the activity is nonpassive, enter the deductible loss, if any, from Form 6198 in Part II, column (i), of Schedule E.

● If you have a passive activity loss, you generally need to complete Form 8582 to figure the amount of the allowable loss to enter in Part II, column (g), for that activity. But if you are a **general** partner or an S corporation shareholder reporting your share of a partnership or an S corporation loss from a rental real estate activity, **and** you meet **ALL THREE** of the conditions listed in the instructions for line 23, you do not have to complete Form 8582. Instead, enter your allowable loss in Part II, column (g).

● If you have passive activity income, complete Part II, column (h), for that activity.

● If you have nonpassive income or losses, complete Part II, columns (i) through (k), as appropriate.

If you are treating items on your tax return differently from the way the partnership or S corporation treated them on its return, you may have to file **Form 8082**, Notice of Inconsistent Treatment or Amended Return.

Partnerships

If you have other partnership items from a passive activity, or income or loss from any publicly traded partnership, see the Schedule K-1 instructions before entering them on your return.

If you have other partnership items, such as depletion, from a nonpassive activity, show each item on a separate line in Part II. Show unreimbursed partnership expenses from nonpassive activities on a separate line in column (i) of Part II. Unreimbursed expenses that are itemized deductions are entered on Schedule A. Report allowable interest expense paid or incurred from debt-financed acquisitions in Part II, or on Schedule A, depending on the type of expenditure to which the interest is allocated. See Pub. 535 for details.

If you claimed a credit for Federal tax on gasoline or other fuels on your 1990 Form 1040 (based on information received from the partnership), enter as income in column (h) or column (k), whichever applies, the amount of the credit claimed in 1990.

Part or all of your share of partnership income or loss from the operation of the business may be considered net earnings from self-employment that must be reported on **Schedule SE** (Form 1040). Enter the amount from Schedule K-1 (Form 1065), line 15a, on Schedule SE, after you reduce this amount by any allowable expenses attributable to that income.

If you have losses or deductions from a prior year that you could not deduct because of the at-risk or basis rules, and the amounts are now deductible, do not combine the prior year amounts with any current year amounts

to arrive at a net figure to report on Schedule E. Instead, report the prior year amounts and the current year amounts on separate lines of Schedule E.

S Corporations

Your share of the net income is NOT subject to self-employment tax. Distributions of prior year accumulated earnings and profits of S corporations are dividends and are reported on **Schedule B** (Form 1040). For details, get **Pub. 589**, Tax Information on S Corporations.

Interest expense relating to the acquisition of shares in an S corporation may be fully deductible on Schedule E. For details, see Pub. 535.

As a shareholder in an S corporation, your share of the corporation's aggregate losses and deductions (combined income, losses, and deductions) is limited to the adjusted basis of your corporate stock and any debt the corporation owes you. Any loss or deduction not allowed this year because of the basis limitation may be carried forward and deducted in a later year subject to the basis limitation for that year. If you are claiming a deduction for your share of an aggregate loss, attach to your return a computation of the adjusted basis of your corporate stock and of any debt the corporation owes you. See Pub. 589 for more information.

After applying the basis limitation, the deductible amount of your aggregate losses and deductions may be further reduced by the at-risk rules and the passive activity loss rules explained earlier.

If you have losses or deductions from a prior year that you could not deduct because of the basis or at-risk limitations, and the amounts are now deductible, do not combine the prior year amounts with any current year amounts to arrive at a net figure to report on Schedule E. Instead, report the prior year amounts and the current year amounts on separate lines of Schedule E.

Estates and Trusts

If you are a beneficiary of an estate or trust, use Part III to report your part of the income (even if not received) or loss. You should receive a **Schedule K-1** (Form 1041) from the fiduciary. Do not attach that schedule to your return. Keep it for your records. Your copy of Schedule K-1 and its instructions will tell you where on your return to report the items from Schedule K-1.

If you have estimated taxes credited to you from a trust (Schedule K-1, line 13a), write "ES payment claimed" and the amount on the dotted line next to line 36. **Do not** include this amount in the total on line 36. Instead, enter the amount on Form 1040, line 55.

A U.S. person who transferred property to a foreign trust may have to include in income the income received by the trust as a result of the transferred property if, during 1991, the trust had a U.S. beneficiary. For more information, get **Form 3520-A**, Annual Return of Foreign Trust With U.S. Beneficiaries.

SCHEDULE D

(Form 1040)

Department of the Treasury
Internal Revenue Service (o)

Capital Gains and Losses

(And Reconciliation of Forms 1099-B for Bartering Transactions)

▶ Attach to Form 1040. ▶ See Instructions for Schedule D (Form 1040).
▶ For more space to list transactions for lines 1a and 8a, get Schedule D-1 (Form 1040).

OMB No. 1545-0074

1991

Attachment
Sequence No. **12A**

Name(s) shown on Form 1040

Your social security number

Caution: *Add the following amounts reported to you for 1991 on Forms 1099-B and 1099-S (or on substitute statements):* **(a)** *proceeds from transactions involving stocks, bonds, and other securities, and* **(b)** *gross proceeds from real estate transactions not reported on another form or schedule. If this total does not equal the total of lines 1c and 8c, column (d), attach a statement explaining the difference.*

Part I   Short-Term Capital Gains and Losses—Assets Held One Year or Less

(a) Description of property (Example, 100 shares 7% preferred of "Z" Co.)	(b) Date acquired (Mo., day, yr.)	(c) Date sold (Mo., day, yr.)	(d) Sales price (see instructions)	(e) Cost or other basis (see instructions)	(f) LOSS If (e) is more than (d), subtract (d) from (e)	(g) GAIN If (d) is more than (e), subtract (e) from (d)
1a Stocks, Bonds, Other Securities, and Real Estate. Include Form 1099-B and 1099-S Transactions. See instructions.						

1b Amounts from Schedule D-1, line 1b (attach Schedule D-1)			
1c **Total of All Sales Price Amounts.** Add column (d) of lines 1a and 1b ▶	**1c**		

1d Other Transactions (Do NOT include real estate transactions from Forms 1099-S on this line. Report them on line 1a.)

2 Short-term gain from sale or exchange of your home from Form 2119, line 10 or 14c	**2**		
3 Short-term gain from installment sales from Form 6252, line 22 or 30	**3**		
4 Net short-term gain or (loss) from partnerships, S corporations, and fiduciaries .	**4**		
5 Short-term capital loss carryover from 1990 Schedule D, line 29	**5**		
6 Add lines 1a, 1b, 1d, and 2 through 5, in columns (f) and (g).	**6** (	)	
7 **Net short-term capital gain or (loss).** Combine columns (f) and (g) of line 6	**7**		

Part II   Long-Term Capital Gains and Losses—Assets Held More Than One Year

8a Stocks, Bonds, Other Securities, and Real Estate. Include Form 1099-B and 1099-S Transactions. See instructions.

8b Amounts from Schedule D-1, line 8b (attach Schedule D-1)			
8c **Total of All Sales Price Amounts.** Add column (d) of lines 8a and 8b . . ▶	**8c**		

8d Other Transactions (Do NOT include real estate transactions from Forms 1099-S on this line. Report them on line 8a.)

9 Long-term gain from sale or exchange of your home from Form 2119, line 10 or 14c	**9**		
10 Long-term gain from installment sales from Form 6252, line 22 or 30	**10**		
11 Net long-term gain or (loss) from partnerships, S corporations, and fiduciaries .	**11**		
12 Capital gain distributions	**12**		
13 Gain from Form 4797, line 7 or 9	**13**		
14 Long-term capital loss carryover from 1990 Schedule D, line 36.	**14**		
15 Add lines 8a, 8b, 8d, and 9 through 14, in columns (f) and (g)	**15** (	)	
16 **Net long-term capital gain or (loss).** Combine columns (f) and (g) of line 15	**16**		

For Paperwork Reduction Act Notice, see Form 1040 instructions.   Cat. No. 11338H   Schedule D (Form 1040) 1991

Name(s) shown on Form 1040. (Do not enter name and social security number if shown on other side.)   **Your social security number**

Part III   Summary of Parts I and II

17	Combine lines 7 and 16 and enter the net gain or (loss) here. If the result is a gain, also enter the gain on Form 1040, line 13. (**Note:** *If both lines 16 and 17 are gains, see Part IV below.*)	**17**	
18	If line 17 is a (loss), enter here and as a (loss) on Form 1040, line 13, the **smaller** of:		
a	The (loss) on line 17; **or**		
b	($3,000) or, if married filing a separate return, ($1,500)	**18**	( )

     Note: *When figuring whether line 18a or 18b is **smaller**, treat both numbers as positive.*
     Complete Part V if the loss on line 17 is more than the loss on line 18, OR if Form 1040, line 37, is zero.

Part IV   Tax Computation Using Maximum Capital Gains Rate

USE THIS PART TO FIGURE YOUR TAX ONLY IF BOTH LINES 16 AND 17 ARE GAINS, AND:

You checked filing status box:	AND	Form 1040, line 37, is over:	You checked filing status box:	AND	Form 1040, line 37, is over:
1		$49,300	3		$41,075
2 or 5		$82,150	4		$70,450

19	Enter the amount from Form 1040, line 37	**19**	
20	Enter the **smaller** of line 16 or line 17.	**20**	
21	Subtract line 20 from line 19	**21**	
22	Enter: **a** $20,350 if you checked filing status box 1; **b** $34,000 if you checked filing status box 2 or 5; **c** $17,000 if you checked filing status box 3; or **d** $27,300 if you checked filing status box 4 . . .	**22**	
23	Enter the **greater** of line 21 or line 22.	**23**	
24	Subtract line 23 from line 19	**24**	
25	Figure the tax on the amount on line 23. Use the Tax Table or Tax Rate Schedules, whichever applies	**25**	
26	Multiply line 24 by 28% (.28)	**26**	
27	Add lines 25 and 26. Enter here and on Form 1040, line 38, and check the box for Schedule D . .	**27**	

Part V   Capital Loss Carryovers from 1991 to 1992

Section A.—Carryover Limit

28	Enter the amount from Form 1040, line 35. If a loss, enclose the amount in parentheses	**28**	
29	Enter the loss from line 18 as a positive amount	**29**	
30	Combine lines 28 and 29. If zero or less, enter -0-.	**30**	
31	Enter the **smaller** of line 29 or line 30	**31**	

Section B.—Short-Term Capital Loss Carryover to 1992 (Complete this section only if there is a loss on both lines 7 and 18.)

32	Enter the loss from line 7 as a positive amount		**32**	
33	Enter the gain, if any, from line 16.	**33**		
34	Enter the amount from line 31	**34**		
35	Add lines 33 and 34		**35**	
36	**Short-term capital loss carryover to 1992.** Subtract line 35 from line 32. If zero or less, enter -0- .		**36**	

Section C.—Long-Term Capital Loss Carryover to 1992 (Complete this section only if there is a loss on both lines 16 and 18.)

37	Enter the loss from line 16 as a positive amount		**37**	
38	Enter the gain, if any, from line 7	**38**		
39	Enter the amount from line 31	**39**		
40	Enter the amount, if any, from line 32. . .	**40**		
41	Subtract line 40 from line 39. If zero or less, enter -0-	**41**		
42	Add lines 38 and 41		**42**	
43	**Long-term capital loss carryover to 1992.** Subtract line 42 from line 37. If zero or less, enter -0- .		**43**	

Part VI   Election Not To Use the Installment Method (Complete this part only if you elect out of the installment method and report a note or other obligation at less than full face value.)

44	Check here if you elect out of the installment method . . . . ▶	☐
45	Enter the face amount of the note or other obligation . . . . ▶	
46	Enter the percentage of valuation of the note or other obligation . . . . ▶	%

Part VII   Reconciliation of Forms 1099-B for Bartering Transactions
(Complete this part if you received one or more Forms 1099-B or substitute statements reporting bartering income.)

Amount of bartering income from Form 1099-B or substitute statement reported on form or schedule

47	Form 1040, line 22	**47**	
48	Schedule C, D, E, or F (Form 1040) (specify) ▶ _____	**48**	
49	Other form or schedule (identify) (if nontaxable, indicate reason—attach additional sheets if necessary): _____	**49**	
50	**Total.** Add lines 47 through 49. This amount should be the same as the total bartering income on all Forms 1099-B and substitute statements received for bartering transactions	**50**	

*U.S. Government Printing Office: 1991 — 285-176

SCHEDULE E
(Form 1040)

Department of the Treasury
Internal Revenue Service (0)

Name(s) shown on return

Supplemental Income and Loss

(From rents, royalties, partnerships, estates, trusts, REMICs, etc.)
► **Attach to Form 1040 or Form 1041.**
► **See Instructions for Schedule E (Form 1040).**

OMB No. 1545-0074

1991

Attachment
Sequence No. **13**

Your social security number

Part I   Income or Loss From Rentals and Royalties   Note: *Report farm rental income or loss from* **Form 4835** *on page 2, line 39.*

1 Show the kind and location of each **rental property:**

A ....

B ....

C ....

2 For each rental property listed on line 1, did you or your family use it for personal purposes for more than the greater of 14 days or 10% of the total days rented at fair rental value during the tax year? (See instructions.)

	Yes	No
A		
B		
C		

Rental and Royalty Income:

		Properties			Totals
		A	**B**	**C**	(Add columns A, B, and C.)
3 Rents received	3				3
4 Royalties received	4				4

Rental and Royalty Expenses:

5 Advertising	5				
6 Auto and travel	6				
7 Cleaning and maintenance	7				
8 Commissions	8				
9 Insurance	9				
10 Legal and other professional fees	10				
11 Mortgage interest paid to banks, etc. (see instructions)	11				11
12 Other interest	12				
13 Repairs	13				
14 Supplies	14				
15 Taxes	15				
16 Utilities	16				
17 Wages and salaries	17				
18 Other (list) ►	18				
19 Add lines 5 through 18	19				19
20 Depreciation expense or depletion (see instructions)	20				20
21 Total expenses. Add lines 19 and 20	21				
22 Income or (loss) from rental or royalty properties. Subtract line 21 from line 3 (rents) or line 4 (royalties). If the result is a (loss), see instructions to find out if you must file **Form 6198**	22				
23 Deductible rental loss. **Caution:** *Your rental loss on line 22 may be limited. See instructions to find out if you must file* **Form 8582**	23	( )	( )	( )	

24 **Income.** Add rental and royalty income from line 22. Enter the total income here · · · · · | 24 | |

25 **Losses.** Add royalty losses from line 22 and rental losses from line 23. Enter the total losses here | 25 | ( ) |

26 Total rental and royalty income or (loss). Combine lines 24 and 25. Enter the result here. If Parts II, III, IV, and line 39 on page 2 do not apply to you, enter the amount from line 26 on Form 1040, line 18. Otherwise, include the amount from line 26 in the total on line 40 on page 2 · · · · | 26 | |

For Paperwork Reduction Act Notice, see Form 1040 instructions.   Cat. No. 11344L   Schedule E (Form 1040) 1991

Name(s) shown on return. (Do not enter name and social security number if shown on other side.) | Your social security number

Note: *If you report amounts from farming or fishing on Schedule E, you must enter your gross income from those activities on line 41 below.*

Part II　Income or Loss From Partnerships and S Corporations

If you report a loss from an at-risk activity, you MUST check either column **(e)** or **(f)** of line 27 to describe your investment in the activity. See instructions. If you check column **(f)**, you must attach **Form 6198**.

27	(a) Name	(b) Enter P for partnership; S for S corporation	(c) Check if foreign partnership	(d) Employer identification number	Investment At Risk?	
					(e) All is at risk	(f) Some is not at risk
A						
B						
C						
D						
E						

	Passive Income and Loss		Nonpassive Income and Loss		
	(g) Passive loss allowed (attach Form 8582 if required)	(h) Passive income from Schedule K–1	(i) Nonpassive loss from Schedule K–1	(j) Section 179 expense deduction from Form 4562	(k) Nonpassive income from Schedule K–1
A					
B					
C					
D					
E					
28a Totals					
b Totals					

29	Add columns (h) and (k) of line 28a. Enter the total income here	29	
30	Add columns (g), (i), and (j) of line 28b. Enter the total here	30	( )
31	Total partnership and S corporation income or (loss). Combine lines 29 and 30. Enter the result here and include in the total on line 40 below	31	

Part III　Income or Loss From Estates and Trusts

32	(a) Name	(b) Employer identification number
A		
B		
C		

	Passive Income and Loss		Nonpassive Income and Loss	
	(c) Passive deduction or loss allowed (attach Form 8582 if required)	(d) Passive income from Schedule K–1	(e) Deduction or loss from Schedule K–1	(f) Other income from Schedule K–1
A				
B				
C				
33a Totals				
b Totals				

34	Add columns (d) and (f) of line 33a. Enter the total income here	34	
35	Add columns (c) and (e) of line 33b. Enter the total here	35	( )
36	Total estate and trust income or (loss). Combine lines 34 and 35. Enter the result here and include in the total on line 40 below	36	

Part IV　Income or Loss From Real Estate Mortgage Investment Conduits (REMICs)—Residual Holder

37	(a) Name	(b) Employer identification number	(c) Excess inclusion from Schedules Q, line 2c (see instructions)	(d) Taxable income (net loss) from Schedules Q, line 1b	(e) Income from Schedules Q, line 3b

38	Combine columns (d) and (e) only. Enter the result here and include in the total on line 40 below	38	

Part V　Summary

39	Net farm rental income or (loss) from **Form 4835**. (Also complete line 41 below.)	39	
40	**TOTAL** income or (loss). Combine lines 26, 31, 36, 38, and 39. Enter the result here and on Form 1040, line 18　▶	40	
41	**Reconciliation of Farming and Fishing Income:** Enter your **gross** farming and fishing income reported in Parts II and III and on line 39 (see instructions)	41	

★U.S.GPO:1991-0-285-181

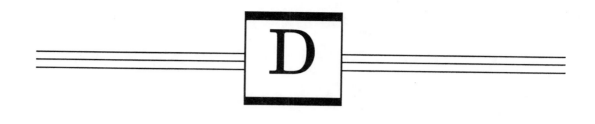

IRS Form 4562:
Depreciation and
Amortization

1991

Department of the Treasury
Internal Revenue Service

Instructions for Form 4562

Depreciation and Amortization

(Section references are to the Internal Revenue Code, unless otherwise noted.)

General Instructions

Paperwork Reduction Act Notice

We ask for the information on this form to carry out the Internal Revenue laws of the United States. You are required to give us the information. We need it to ensure that taxpayers are complying with these laws and to allow us to figure and collect the right amount of tax.

The time needed to complete and file this form will vary depending on individual circumstances. The estimated average time is:

Recordkeeping . . . . 35 hrs., 17 min.

**Learning about the
law or the form** . . . . .3 hrs., 35 min.

**Preparing and sending
the form to the IRS** . . . .4 hrs., 35 min.

If you have comments concerning the accuracy of these time estimates or suggestions for making this form more simple, we would be happy to hear from you. You can write to both the IRS and the Office of Management and Budget at the addresses listed in the instructions for the tax return with which this form is filed.

Purpose of Form

Use Form 4562 to claim your deduction for depreciation and amortization; to make the election to expense certain tangible property (section 179); and to provide information on the business/investment use of automobiles and other listed property.

Who Must File

You must complete and file Form 4562 if you are claiming:

● Depreciation for property placed in service during the 1991 tax year;

● A section 179 expense deduction (which may include a carryover from a previous year);

● Depreciation on any listed property (regardless of when it was placed in service);

● The standard mileage rate (unless **Form 2106**, Employee Business Expenses, is used for this purpose—see the Part V instructions); or

● Amortization of costs that begins during the 1991 tax year.

All corporations (other than S corporations) must also file Form 4562 for any depreciation claimed on assets acquired in previous tax years.

You should prepare and submit a separate Form 4562 for each business or activity on your return. If more space is needed, attach additional sheets. However, complete only one Part I in its entirety when computing your allowable section 179 expense deduction.

Definitions

Depreciation.—Depreciation is the annual deduction allowed to recover the cost or other basis of business or income-producing property with a determinable useful life of more than 1 year. However, land and goodwill are not depreciable.

Depreciation starts when you first use the property in your business or for the production of income. It ends when you take the property out of service, deduct all your depreciable cost or other basis, or no longer use the property in your business or for the production of income. For additional information, see **Pub. 534**, Depreciation, **Pub. 946**, How To Begin Depreciating Your Property, and **Pub. 917**, Business Use of a Car.

Amortization.—Amortization is similar to the straight line method of depreciation in that an annual deduction is allowed to recover certain costs over a fixed period of time. You can amortize such items as the costs of starting a business, reforestation, and pollution control facilities. For additional information, see **Pub. 535**, Business Expenses.

"Listed Property".—For a definition of "listed property" see the Part V instructions.

Recordkeeping

Except for Part V, relating to listed property, the IRS does not require you to submit detailed information with your return regarding the depreciation of assets placed in service in previous tax years. However, the information needed to compute your depreciation deduction (basis, method, etc.) must be part of your permanent records.

Because Form 4562 does not provide for permanent recordkeeping, you may use the depreciation worksheet on page 8 to assist you in maintaining depreciation records. However, the worksheet is designed only for Federal income tax purposes. You may need to keep additional records for accounting and state income tax purposes.

Certification of Business Use Requirement for Aircraft Exempt From Luxury Tax

If you purchased a new aircraft in 1991 with a sales price of more than $250,000, the 10% Federal luxury tax generally imposed on such a sale will not apply if at least 80% of your use of the aircraft (measured in hours of flight time) will be for business purposes. If you purchased an aircraft that was exempt from the luxury tax **solely** for this reason, you must attach a statement to your income tax return for each of the 2 tax years ending after the date the aircraft was placed in service. On this statement, you must certify that at least

Cat. No. 12907Y

80% of your use of the aircraft during the tax year was in a trade or business. If you fail to make this certification, you must pay a tax equal to the luxury tax that would have been imposed on the sale of the aircraft if the business use exemption had not applied. In addition, interest is imposed on the tax from the date of sale of the aircraft.

If you do not pay the tax when due because you failed to meet this requirement, no depreciation may be claimed on the aircraft for any tax year.

See the instructions for **Form 720**, Quarterly Federal Excise Tax Return, for more information on paying the tax and interest due.

Specific Instructions

Part I.—Election To Expense Certain Tangible Property (Section 179)

Note: *An estate or trust cannot make this election. If you are married filing separately, see section 179(b)(4) for special limitations.*

You may make an irrevocable election to expense part of the cost of certain tangible personal property used in your trade or business and certain other property described in Pub. 534. To do so, you must have purchased the property (as defined in section 179(d)(2)) and placed it in service during the 1991 tax year, or have a carryover of disallowed deduction from 1990. If you elect this deduction, the amount on which you figure your depreciation or amortization deduction must be reduced by the amount of the section 179 expense.

Section 179 property does **not** include: **(1)** property used 50% or less in your trade or business; or **(2)** property held for investment (section 212 property). If you are a noncorporate lessor, the property that you lease to others does not qualify as section 179 property unless:
(1) you manufactured or produced the property; or **(2)** the term of the lease is less than 50% of the property's class life, and for the first 12 months after the property is transferred to the lessee, the sum of the deductions related to the property that are allowed to you solely under section 162 (except rents and reimbursed amounts) is more than 15% of the rental income from the property.

The section 179 expense deduction is subject to two separate limitations, both of which are figured in Part I:

1. A dollar limitation; and

2. A taxable income limitation.

In the case of a partnership, these limitations apply to the partnership and each partner. In the case of an

S corporation, these limitations apply to the S corporation and each shareholder. In the case of a controlled group, all component members are treated as one taxpayer.

Line 1.—The maximum amount of section 179 deduction you can claim is $10,000. If you are married filing separately, your maximum deduction is $5,000, unless you and your spouse elect otherwise. However, the total deduction for both of you cannot be more than $10,000. If you are married filing separately, cross out the preprinted "$10,000" on line 1 and enter in the margin "$5,000" (or whatever other amount you elect, not to exceed $10,000 for both spouses).

Line 2.—Enter the cost of all section 179 property placed in service during the tax year. Be sure to include amounts from any listed property from Part V.

Line 5.—If you placed $210,000 or more of section 179 property in service during the 1991 tax year, you cannot elect to expense any property. If line 5 is -0-, skip lines 6 through 11, enter -0- on line 12, and enter the carryover of disallowed deduction from 1990, if any, on line 13.

Line 6.—

Column (a)—Enter a brief description of the property for which you are making the election (e.g., truck, office furniture, etc.).

Column (b)—Enter the cost of the property. If you acquired the property through a trade-in, do not include any undepreciated basis of the assets you traded in. See **Pub. 551**, Basis of Assets, for more information.

Column (c)—Enter the amount that you elect to expense. You do not have to elect to expense the entire cost of the property. Whatever amount is not elected to be expensed can be depreciated. See line 14 and line 15 instructions below.

To report your share of a section 179 expense deduction from a partnership or an S corporation, instead of completing columns (a) and (b), write "from Schedule K-1 (Form 1065)" or "from Schedule K-1 (Form 1120S)" across the columns.

Line 9.—The tentative deduction represents the amount you may expense in 1991 or carry over to 1992. If this amount is less than the taxable income limitation on line 11, you may expense the entire amount. If this amount is more than line 11, you may expense in 1991 only an amount equal to line 11. Any excess may be carried over to 1992.

Line 10.—The carryover of disallowed deduction from 1990 is the amount of section 179 property, if any, elected to be expensed in previous years, but not allowed as a deduction due to the taxable income limitation. If you filed Form 4562 for 1990, enter the amount from line 13 of your 1990 Form 4562. For additional information, see Pub. 534.

Line 11.—The section 179 expense deduction is further limited to the "taxable income" limitation under section 179(b)(3).

For an individual, enter the aggregate taxable income from any active trade or business computed without regard to any section 179 expense deduction or the deduction for one-half of self-employment taxes under section 164(f). Include in aggregate taxable income the wages,

salaries, tips, and other compensation you earned as an employee. If you are married filing a joint return, combine the aggregate taxable incomes for both you and your spouse. For all other entities, enter the taxable income computed without regard to any section 179 expense deduction. In any case, do not enter more than line 5.

Line 12.—The limitations on lines 5 and 11 apply to the taxpayer, and not to each separate business or activity. Therefore, if you have more than one business or activity, you may allocate your allowable section 179 expense deduction among them. To do so, write "Summary" at the top of Part I of the separate Form 4562 you are completing for the aggregate amounts from all businesses or activities. Do not complete the rest of that form. On line 12 of the Form 4562 you prepare for each separate business or activity, enter the amount allocated to the business or activity from the "Summary." No other entry is required in Part I of the separate Form 4562 prepared for each business or activity.

Part II.—MACRS Depreciation For Assets Placed in Service ONLY During Your 1991 Tax Year

Note: *The term "Modified Accelerated Cost Recovery System" (MACRS) includes the General Depreciation System and the Alternative Depreciation System. Generally, MACRS is used to depreciate any tangible property placed in service after 1986. However, MACRS does not apply to films, videotapes, and sound recordings. See section 168(f) for other exceptions.*

Depreciation may be an adjustment for alternative minimum tax (AMT) purposes. See the appropriate AMT form that you are required to file.

Lines 14a through 14h.—General Depreciation System (GDS).—
Note: *Use lines 14a through 14h only for assets placed in service during the tax year beginning in 1991 and depreciated under the General Depreciation System, except for automobiles and other listed property (which are reported in Part V).*

Determine which property you acquired and placed in service during the tax year beginning in 1991. Then, sort that property according to its classification (3-year property, 5-year property, etc.) as shown in column (a) of lines 14a through 14h. The classifications for some property are shown below. For property not shown, see **Determining the Classification** below.

● 3-year property includes: (1) a race horse that is more than 2 years old at the time it is placed in service; and (2) any horse (other than a race horse) that is more than 12 years old at the time it is placed in service.

● 5-year property includes:
(1) automobiles; (2) light general purpose trucks; (3) typewriters, calculators, copiers, and duplicating equipment; (4) any semi-conductor manufacturing equipment; (5) any computer or peripheral equipment; (6) any section 1245 property used in connection with research and experimentation; and (7) certain energy property specified in section 168(e)(3)(B)(vi).

● 7-year property includes: (1) office furniture and equipment; (2) appliances, carpets, furniture, etc. used in residential rental property; (3) railroad track; and (4) any property that does not have a class life and is not otherwise classified.

● 10-year property includes: (1) vessels, barges, tugs, and similar water transportation equipment; (2) any single purpose agricultural or horticultural structure (see section 48(p)); and (3) any tree or vine bearing fruit or nuts.

● 15-year property includes: (1) any municipal wastewater treatment plant; and (2) any telephone distribution plant and comparable equipment used for 2-way exchange of voice and data communications.

● 20-year property includes any municipal sewers.

● Residential rental property is a building in which 80% or more of the total rent is from dwelling units.

● Nonresidential real property is any real property that is neither residential rental property nor property with a class life of less than 27.5 years.

● 50-year property includes any improvements necessary to construct or improve a roadbed or right-of-way for railroad track that qualifies as a railroad grading or tunnel bore under section 168(e)(4). There is no separate line to report 50-year property. Therefore, attach a statement showing the same information as required in columns (a) through (g). Include the deduction in the line 20 "Total" and write "See attachment" in the bottom margin of the form.

Determining the Classification.—If your depreciable property is **not** listed above, determine the classification as follows: First, find the property's class life. The class life of most property can be found in the Table of Class Lives and Recovery Periods in Pub. 534. Next, use the following table to find the classification in column (b) that corresponds to the class life of the property in column (a).

(a) Class life (in years) (See Pub. 534)	(b) Classification
4 or less	3-year property
More than 4 but less than 10 .	5-year property
10 or more but less than 16 .	7-year property
16 or more but less than 20 .	10-year property
20 or more but less than 25 .	15-year property
25 or more	20-year property

Column (b).—For lines 14g and 14h, enter the month and year the property was placed in service. If property held for personal use is converted to use in a trade or business or for the production of income, treat the property as being placed in service on the date of conversion.

Column (c).—To find the basis for depreciation, multiply the cost or other basis of the property by the percentage of business/investment use. From that result, subtract any section 179 expense deduction and the amount of any enhanced oil recovery credit (section 43). See section 50(c) to determine the basis adjustment for investment credit property.

Column (d).—See the "Note" in the line 14, column (f) instructions below, for an election

Page 2

you can make to use the 150% declining balance method of depreciation (for 3-, 5-, 7-, and 10-year property). If you do not elect to use the 150% method, determine the recovery period from the table below:

In the case of:	The applicable recovery period is:
3-year property	3 yrs.
5-year property	5 yrs.
7-year property	7 yrs.
10-year property	10 yrs.
15-year property	15 yrs.
20-year property	20 yrs.
Residential rental property	27.5 yrs.
Nonresidential real property	31.5 yrs.
Railroad gradings and tunnel bores . . .	50 yrs.

If you elect the 150% declining balance method, you must use the recovery period under the Alternative Depreciation System discussed in the line 15 instructions below. You will not have an adjustment for alternative minimum tax purposes on the property for which you make this election.

Column (e).—The applicable convention determines the portion of the tax year for which depreciation is allowable during a year property is either placed in service or disposed of. There are three types of conventions (discussed below). To select the correct convention, you must know:
(a) when you placed the property in service; and (b) the type of property.

Half-year convention (HY).—This convention applies to all property reported on lines 14a through 14f, unless the mid-quarter convention applies. It does not apply to residential rental property, nonresidential real property, and railroad gradings and tunnel bores. It treats all property placed in service (or disposed of) during any tax year as placed in service (or disposed of) on the mid-point of such tax year.

Mid-quarter convention (MQ).—This convention applies instead of the half-year convention if the aggregate bases of property subject to depreciation under section 168 that is placed in service during the last 3 months of your tax year exceeds 40% of the aggregate bases of property subject to depreciation under section 168 that is placed in service during the entire tax year.

The mid-quarter convention treats all property placed in service (or disposed of) during any quarter as placed in service (or disposed of) on the mid-point of such quarter.

In determining whether the mid-quarter convention applies, do not take into account:

● Property that is being depreciated under the pre-1987 rules;

● Any residential rental property, nonresidential real property, or railroad gradings and tunnel bores; and

● Property that is placed in service and disposed of within the same tax year.

Mid-month convention (MM).—This convention applies ONLY to residential rental property, nonresidential real property (lines 14g or 14h), and railroad gradings and tunnel bores. It treats all property placed in service (or disposed of) during any month as placed

in service (or disposed of) on the mid-point of such month.

Enter "HY" for half-year; "MQ" for mid-quarter; or "MM" for mid-month convention.

Column (f).—Applicable depreciation methods are prescribed for each classification of property. For 3-, 5-, 7-, and 10-year property the applicable method is the 200% declining balance method, switching to the straight line method in the first tax year that maximizes the depreciation allowance.

Note: *You may make an irrevocable election to use the 150% declining balance method for one or more classes of property (except for residential rental property, nonresidential real property, any railroad grading or tunnel bore, or any tree or vine bearing fruit or nuts). If you make this election, see "Alternative Depreciation System" below for the recovery period.*

For 15- and 20-year property, and property used in a farming business, the applicable method is the 150% declining balance method, switching to the straight line method in the first tax year that maximizes the depreciation allowance.

For residential rental property, nonresidential real property, any railroad grading or tunnel bore, or any tree or vine bearing fruit or nuts, the only applicable method is the straight line method.

You may also make an irrevocable election to use the straight line method for all property within a classification that is placed in service during the tax year.

Enter "200 DB" for 200% declining balance; "150 DB" for 150% declining balance; or "S/L" for straight line.

Column (g).—To compute the depreciation deduction you may: (a) use the optional Tables A through D on page 7. Multiply the applicable rate from the appropriate table by the property's **unadjusted** basis (column (c)) (see Pub. 534 for complete tables); or (b) compute the deduction yourself. To compute the deduction yourself, complete the following steps:

Step 1.—Determine the depreciation rate as follows:

1. If you are using the 200% or 150% declining balance method in column (f), divide the declining balance rate (use 2.00 for 200 DB or 1.50 for 150 DB) by the number of years in the recovery period in column (d). For example, for property depreciated using the 200 DB method over a recovery period of 5 years, divide 2.00 by 5 for a rate of 40%.

2. If you are using the straight line method, divide 1.00 by the remaining number of years in the recovery period as of the beginning of the tax year (but not less than one). For example, if there are 6½ years remaining in the recovery period as of the beginning of the year, divide 1.00 by 6.5 for a rate of 15.38%.

Note: *If you are using the 200% or 150% DB method, be sure to switch to the straight line rate in the first year that the straight line rate exceeds the declining balance rate.*

Step 2.—Multiply the percentage rate determined in Step 1 by the property's unrecovered basis (cost or other basis reduced by any section 179 expense deduction and all prior years' depreciation).

Step 3.—For property placed in service or disposed of during the current tax year, multiply the result from Step 2 by the applicable decimal amount from the tables below (based on the convention shown in column (e)).

Half-year (HY) convention	0.5

Mid-quarter (MQ) convention

Placed in service (or disposed of) during the:	Placed in service	Disposed of
1st quarter	0.875	0.125
2nd quarter	0.625	0.375
3rd quarter	0.375	0.625
4th quarter	0.125	0.875

Mid-month (MM) convention

Placed in service (or disposed of) during the:	Placed in service	Disposed of
1st month.	0.9583	0.0417
2nd month	0.8750	0.1250
3rd month	0.7917	0.2083
4th month	0.7083	0.2917
5th month	0.6250	0.3750
6th month	0.5417	0.4583
7th month	0.4583	0.5417
8th month	0.3750	0.6250
9th month	0.2917	0.7083
10th month	0.2083	0.7917
11th month	0.1250	0.8750
12th month	0.0417	0.9583

Short Tax Years.—See Pub. 534 for rules on how to compute the depreciation deduction for property placed in service in a short tax year.

Line 15.—Alternative Depreciation System (ADS).—Note: *Lines 15a through 15c should be completed for assets, other than automobiles and other listed property, placed in service ONLY during the tax year beginning in 1991 and depreciated under the Alternative Depreciation System. Depreciation on assets placed in service in prior years is reported on line 16.*

Under ADS, depreciation is computed by using the applicable depreciation method, the applicable recovery period, and the applicable convention. The following types of property **must** be depreciated under ADS:

● Any tangible property used predominantly outside the U.S.;

● Any tax-exempt use property;

● Any tax-exempt bond financed property;

● Any imported property covered by an executive order of the President of the United States; and

● Any property used predominantly in a farming business and placed in service during any tax year in which you made an election under section 263A(d)(3).

Instead of depreciating property under GDS (line 14), you may make an irrevocable election with respect to any classification of property for any tax year to use ADS. For residential rental and nonresidential real property, you may make this election separately for each property.

Note: *See section 168(g)(3)(B) for a special rule for determining the class life for certain property.*

If the property does not have a class life, use line 15b.

Page 3

For residential rental and nonresidential real property, use line 15c.

For railroad gradings and tunnel bores, the recovery period is 50 years.

Column (b).—For 40-year property, enter the month and year it was placed in service, or converted to use in a trade or business, or for the production of income.

Column (c).—See the instructions for line 14, column (c).

Column (d).—Under ADS, the recovery period is generally the class life. However, when looking up the recovery period in Pub. 534, be sure to look under the heading "Alternate MACRS."

Column (e).—Under ADS, the applicable conventions are the same as those used under GDS. See the instructions for line 14, column (e).

Column (f).—Under ADS, the only applicable method is the straight line method.

Column (g).—The depreciation deduction is computed in the same manner as under GDS except you must apply the straight line method over the ADS recovery period and use the applicable convention.

Part III.—Other Depreciation

Note: *Do not use Part III for automobiles and other listed property. Instead, report this property in Part V on page 2 of Form 4562.*

Use Part III for

● ACRS property (pre-'87 rules);

● Property placed in service before 1981;

● Certain public utility property, which does not meet certain normalization requirements;

● Certain property acquired from related persons;

● Property acquired in certain nonrecognition transactions; and

● Certain sound recordings, movies, and videotapes.

Line 16.—GDS and ADS deduction for assets placed in service in tax years beginning before 1991.—For assets placed in service after 1986, and depreciated under post-'86 rules, enter the GDS and ADS deduction for the current year. To compute the deduction, see the instructions for column (g), line 14.

Line 17.—Property subject to section 168(f)(1) election.—Report property that you elect, under section 168(f)(1), to depreciate by the unit-of-production method or any other method not based on a term of years (other than the retirement-replacement-betterment method).

Attach a separate sheet, showing: **(a)** a description of the property and the depreciation method you elect that excludes the property from ACRS or MACRS; and **(b)** the depreciable basis (cost or other basis reduced, if applicable, by salvage value, enhanced oil recovery credit, and the section 179 expense deduction). See section 50(c) to determine the basis adjustment for investment credit property.

Line 18.—ACRS and other depreciation.—Enter the total depreciation attributable to assets, other than automobiles and other listed property, placed in service before 1981 (pre-ACRS), property subject to ACRS, or property that cannot otherwise be

depreciated under ACRS. For ACRS property, unless you use an alternate percentage, multiply the property's unadjusted basis by the applicable percentage as follows:

● *5-year property*—1st year (15%), 2nd year (22%), 3rd through 5th years (21%);

● *10-year property*—1st year (8%), 2nd year (14%), 3rd year (12%), 4th through 6th years (10%), 7th through 10th years (9%);

● *15-year public utility property*—1st year (5%), 2nd year (10%), 3rd year (9%), 4th year (8%), 5th and 6th years (7%), 7th through 15th years (6%);

● *15-year, 18-year, and 19-year real property and low-income housing*—Use the tables in Pub. 534.

If you elected an alternate percentage for any property listed above, use the straight line method over the recovery period you chose in the prior year. See Pub. 534 for more information and tables.

Include any amounts attributable to the Class Life Asset Depreciation Range (CLADR) system. If you previously elected the CLADR system, you must continue to use it to depreciate assets left in your vintage accounts. You must continue to meet recordkeeping requirements.

Prior years' depreciation, plus current year's depreciation, can never exceed the depreciable basis of the property.

The basis and amounts claimed for depreciation should be part of your permanent books and records. **No attachment is necessary.**

Line 20.—A partnership or S corporation does not include any section 179 expense deduction (line 12) on this line. Any section 179 expense deduction is passed through separately to the partners and shareholders on the appropriate line of their Schedules K-1.

Line 21—Section 263A Uniform Capitalization Rules.—If you are subject to the uniform capitalization rules of section 263A, enter the increase in basis from costs that are required to be capitalized. For a detailed discussion of who is subject to these rules, which costs must be capitalized, and allocation of costs among activities, see Temp. Regs. section 1.263A-1T.

Part V.—Automobiles and Other Listed Property

All taxpayers claiming any depreciation for automobiles and other listed property, regardless of the tax year such property was placed in service, must provide the information requested in Part V. However, employees claiming the standard mileage allowance or actual expenses (including depreciation) must use Form 2106 instead of Part V. Listed property includes, but is not limited to:

● Passenger automobiles weighing 6,000 pounds or less.

● Any other property used for transportation if the nature of the property lends itself to personal use, such as motorcycles, pick-up trucks, etc.

● Any property used for entertainment or recreational purposes (such as photographic, phonographic, communication, and video recording equipment).

● Cellular telephones (or other similar telecommunications equipment).

● Computers or peripheral equipment.

Listed property does not include: **(a)** photographic, phonographic, communication, or video equipment used exclusively in a taxpayer's trade or business or regular business establishment; **(b)** any computer or peripheral equipment used exclusively at a regular business establishment and owned or leased by the person operating the establishment; or **(c)** an ambulance, hearse, or vehicle used for transporting persons or property for hire.

Section A.—Depreciation

Lines 23 and 24.—

Qualified business use.—For purposes of determining whether to use line 23 or line 24 to report your listed property, you must first determine the percentage of qualified business use for each property. Generally, a qualified business use is any use in your trade or business. However, it does not include:

● Any investment use;

● Leasing the property to a 5% owner or related person;

● The use of the property as compensation for services performed by a 5% owner or related person; or

● The use of the property as compensation for services performed by any person (who is not a 5% owner or related person), unless an amount is included in that person's income for the use of the property and, if required, income tax was withheld on that amount.

As an exception to the general rule, if at least 25% of the total use of any aircraft during the tax year is for a qualified business use, the leasing or compensatory use of the aircraft by a 5% owner or related person is considered a qualified business use.

Determine your percentage of qualified business use in a manner similar to that used to figure the business/investment use percentage in column (c). Your percentage of qualified business use may be smaller than the business/investment use percentage.

For more information, see Pub. 534.

Column (a).—List on a property-by-property basis all of your listed property in the following order:

1. Automobiles and other vehicles; and

2. Other listed property (computers and peripheral equipment, etc.).

In column (a), list the make and model of automobiles, and give a general description of the listed property.

If you have more than five vehicles used 100% for business/investment purposes, you may group them by tax year. Otherwise, list each vehicle separately.

Column (b).—Enter the date the property was placed in service. If property held for personal use is converted to business/investment use, treat the property as placed in service on the date of conversion.

Column (c).—Enter the percentage of business/investment use. For automobiles and other "vehicles," this is determined by dividing the number of miles the vehicle is driven for trade or business purposes or for the production of income during the year (not to include any commuting mileage) by the total number of miles the vehicle is driven for any purpose. Treat vehicles used by employees as being used 100% for business/investment purposes if the value of personal use is included in the employees' gross income, or the employees reimburse the employer for the personal use.

Employers who report the amount of personal use of the vehicle in the employee's gross income, and withhold the appropriate taxes, should enter "100%" for the percentage of business/investment use. For more information, see Pub. 917. For listed property (such as computers or video equipment), allocate the use based on the most appropriate unit of time the property is actually used. See Temp. Regs. 1.280F-6T.

If you have property that is used solely for personal use that is converted to business/investment use during the tax year, figure the percentage of business/investment use only for the number of months the property is used in your business or for the production of income. Multiply that percentage by the number of months the property is used in your business or for the production of income, and divide the result by 12.

Column (e).—Multiply column (d) by the percentage in column (c). From that result, subtract any section 179 expense deduction and half of any investment credit taken before 1986 (unless you took the reduced credit). For automobiles and other listed property placed in service after 1985 (i.e., "transition property"), reduce the depreciable basis by the entire investment credit.

Column (f).—Enter the recovery period. For property placed in service after 1986 and used more than 50% in a qualified business use, use the table in the line 14, column (d) instructions. For property placed in service after 1986 and used 50% or less in a qualified business use, you must depreciate the property using the straight line method over its ADS recovery period. The ADS recovery period is 5 years for automobiles and computers.

Column (g).—Enter the method and convention used to figure your depreciation deduction. See the instructions for line 14, columns (e) and (f). Write "200 DB," "150 DB," or "S/L," for the depreciation method, and "HY," "MM," or "MQ," for half-year, mid-month, or mid-quarter conventions, respectively. For property placed in service before 1987, write "PRE" if you used the prescribed percentages under ACRS. If you elected an alternate percentage, enter "S/L."

Column (h).—**Caution:** See "Limitations for automobiles" below before entering an amount in column (h).

If the property is used more than 50% in a qualified business use (line 23), and the property was placed in service after 1986, figure column (h) by following the instructions for line 14, column (g). If placed in service before 1987, multiply column (e) by the applicable percentages given in the line 18 instructions for ACRS property. If the recovery period for the property ended before your tax year beginning in 1991, enter your unrecovered basis, if any, in column (h).

If the property is used 50% or less in a qualified business use (line 24), and the

property was placed in service after 1986, figure column (h) by dividing column (e) by column (f) and using the same conventions as discussed in the instructions for line 14, column (e). For automobiles placed in service: (1) during your tax year beginning in 1986, multiply column (e) by 10%; or (2) after June 18, 1984, and before your tax year beginning in 1986, enter your unrecovered basis, if any, in column (h). For computers placed in service after June 18, 1984, and before 1987, multiply column (e) by 8.333%.

For property used 50% or less in a qualified business use, no section 179 expense deduction is allowed.

For property placed in service before 1987 that was disposed of during the year, enter zero.

Limitations for automobiles.—The depreciation deduction plus section 179 expense deduction for automobiles is limited for any tax year. The limitation depends on when you placed the property in service. Use Table E on page 7 to determine the limitation. For any automobile you list on line 23 or 24, the total of columns (h) and (i) for that automobile cannot exceed the limit shown in Table E.

Note: *These limitations are further reduced when the business/investment use percentage (column (c)) is less than 100%. For example, if an automobile placed in service in 1991 is used 60% for business/investment purposes, then the first year depreciation plus section 179 expense deduction is limited to 60% of $2,660, which is $1,596.*

Column (i).—Enter the amount you choose to expense for property used more than 50% in a qualified business use (subject to the limitations for automobiles noted above). Be sure to include the total cost of such property on line 2, page 1.

Recapture of depreciation and section 179 expense deduction.—If any listed property was used more than 50% in a qualified business use in the year it was placed in service, and used 50% or less in a later year, you may have to recapture in the later year part of the depreciation and section 179 expense deduction. Use **Form 4797,** Sales of Business Property, to figure the recapture amount.

Section B.—Information Regarding Use of Vehicles

The information requested in Questions 27 through 33 must be completed for each vehicle identified in Section A.

Employees must provide their employers with the information requested in Questions 27 through 33 for each automobile or vehicle provided for their use.

Employers providing more than five vehicles to their employees, who are not more than 5% owners or related persons, are not required to complete Questions 27 through 33 for such vehicles. Instead, they must obtain this information from their employees, check "Yes" to Question 37, and retain the information received as part of their permanent records.

Section C.—Questions for Employers Who Provide Vehicles for Use by Their Employees

For employers providing vehicles to their employees, a written policy statement regarding the use of such vehicles, if initiated and kept by the employer, will relieve the employee of keeping separate records for substantiation.

Two types of written policy statements will satisfy the employer's substantiation requirements under section 274(d): **(a)** a policy statement that prohibits personal use including commuting; and **(b)** a policy statement that prohibits personal use except for commuting.

Line 34.—Prohibits Personal Use (including commuting):

This policy must meet the following conditions:

● The vehicle is owned or leased by the employer and is provided to one or more employees for use in the employer's trade or business;

● When the vehicle is not used in the employer's trade or business, it is kept on the employer's business premises, unless it is temporarily located elsewhere, for example, for maintenance or because of a mechanical failure;

● No employee using the vehicle lives at the employer's business premises;

● No employee may use the vehicle for personal purposes, other than de *minimis* personal use (such as a stop for lunch between two business deliveries); and

● Except for *de minimis* use, the employer reasonably believes that no employee uses the vehicle for any personal purpose.

Line 35.—Prohibits Personal Use (except for commuting). This policy is NOT available if the commuting employee is an officer, director, or 1% or more owner.

This policy must meet the following conditions:

● The vehicle is owned or leased by the employer and is provided to one or more employees for use in the employer's trade or business and is used in the employer's trade or business;

● For bona fide noncompensatory business reasons, the employer requires the employee to commute to and/or from work in the vehicle;

● The employer establishes a written policy under which the employee may not use the vehicle for personal purposes, other than commuting or *de minimis* personal use (such as a stop for a personal errand between a business delivery and the employee's home);

● Except for *de minimis* use, the employer reasonably believes that the employee does not use the vehicle for any personal purpose other than commuting; and

● The employer accounts for the commuting use by including an appropriate amount in the employee's gross income.

For both written policy statements, there must be evidence that would enable the IRS to determine whether use of the vehicle meets the conditions stated above.

Line 38.—An automobile is considered to have qualified demonstration use if the

Page 5

employer maintains a written policy statement that:

- Prohibits its use by individuals other than full-time automobile salesmen;
- Prohibits its use for personal vacation trips;
- Prohibits storage of personal possessions in the automobile; and
- Limits the total mileage outside the salesmen's normal working hours.

Part VI.—Amortization

Each year you may elect to deduct part of certain capital costs over a fixed period. If you amortize property, the part you amortize does not qualify for the election to expense certain tangible property or depreciation.

For individuals reporting amortization of bond premium for bonds acquired before October 23, 1986, do not report the deduction here. See the instructions for Schedule A (Form 1040).

For taxpayers (other than corporations) claiming a deduction for amortization of bond premium for bonds acquired after October 22, 1986, but before January 1, 1988, the deduction is treated as interest expense and is subject to the investment interest limitations. Use **Form 4952,** Investment Interest Expense Deduction, to compute the allowable deduction.

For taxable bonds acquired after 1987, the amortization offsets the interest income. See **Pub. 550,** Investment Income and Expenses.

Line 39.—Complete line 39 only for those costs for which the amortization period begins during your tax year beginning in 1991.

Column (a).—Describe the costs you are amortizing. You may amortize—

- Pollution control facilities (section 169, limited by section 291 for corporations).
- Certain bond premiums (section 171).
- Research and experimental expenditures (section 174).
- Qualified forestation and reforestation costs (section 194).
- Business start-up expenditures (section 195).

- Organizational expenditures for a corporation (section 248) or partnership (section 709).
- Optional write off of certain tax preferences over the period specified in section 59(e).

Column (b).—Enter the date the amortization period begins under the applicable Code section.

Column (c).—Enter the total amount you are amortizing. See the applicable Code section for limits on the amortizable amount.

Column (d).—Enter the Code section under which you amortize the costs.

Column (f).—Compute the amortization deduction by: (1) dividing column (c) by the number of years over which the costs are to be amortized; or (2) multiplying column (c) by the percentage in column (e).

Attach any other information the Code and regulations may require to make a valid election. See Pub. 535 for more information.

Line 40.—Enter the amount of amortization attributable to those costs for which the amortization period began before 1991.

Table A.—General Depreciation System

Method: 200% declining balance switching to straight line

Convention: half-year

Year	If the recovery period is:			
	3 yrs.	5 yrs.	7 yrs.	10 yrs.
1	33.33%	20.00%	14.29%	10.00%
2	44.45%	32.00%	24.49%	18.00%
3	14.81%	19.20%	17.49%	14.40%
4	7.41%	11.52%	12.49%	11.52%
5		11.52%	8.93%	9.22%

Table B.—General and Alternative Depreciation System

Method: 150% declining balance switching to straight line

Convention: half-year

Year	If the recovery period is:					
	5 yrs.	7 yrs.	10 yrs.	12 yrs.	15 yrs.	20 yrs.
1	15.00%	10.71%	7.50%	6.25%	5.00%	3.750%
2	25.50%	19.13%	13.88%	11.72%	9.50%	7.219%
3	17.85%	15.03%	11.79%	10.25%	8.55%	6.677%
4	16.66%	12.25%	10.02%	8.97%	7.70%	6.177%
5	16.66%	12.25%	8.74%	7.85%	6.93%	5.713%

Table C.—General Depreciation System

Method: Straight line

Convention: Mid-month

Recovery period: 27.5 years

Year	The month in the 1st recovery year the property is placed in service:											
	1	2	3	4	5	6	7	8	9	10	11	12
1	3.485%	3.182%	2.879%	2.576%	2.273%	1.970%	1.667%	1.364%	1.061%	0.758%	0.455%	0.152%
2-8	3.636%	3.636%	3.636%	3.636%	3.636%	3.636%	3.636%	3.636%	3.636%	3.636%	3.636%	3.636%

Table D.—General Depreciation System

Method: Straight line

Convention: Mid-month

Recovery period: 31.5 years

Year	The month in the 1st recovery year the property is placed in service:											
	1	2	3	4	5	6	7	8	9	10	11	12
1	3.042%	2.778%	2.513%	2.249%	1.984%	1.720%	1.455%	1.190%	0.926%	0.661%	0.397%	0.132%
2-7	3.175%	3.175%	3.175%	3.175%	3.175%	3.175%	3.175%	3.175%	3.175%	3.175%	3.175%	3.175%

Table E.—Limitations for automobiles

Year of Deduction	If placed in service—					
after: but before:	6/18/84 1/1/85	12/31/84 4/3/85	4/2/85 1/1/87	12/31/86 1/1/89	12/31/88 1/1/91	12/31/90 1/1/92
1st tax year	4,000	4,100	3,200	2,560	2,660	2,660
2nd tax year	6,000	6,200	4,800	4,100	4,200	4,300
3rd tax year	6,000	6,200	4,800	2,450	2,550	2,550
each succeeding tax year	6,000	6,200	4,800	1,475	1,475	1,575

Depreciation Worksheet

Description of Property	Date Placed in Service	Cost or Other Basis	Business/ Investment Use %	Section 179 Deduction	Depreciation Prior Years	Basis for Depreciation	Method/ Convention	Recovery Period	Rate or Table %	Depreciation Deduction

☆ U.S. GOVERNMENT PRINTING OFFICE: 1992 312-732/54253

Form **4562**

Department of the Treasury
Internal Revenue Service (o)

Depreciation and Amortization
(Including Information on Listed Property)

▶ See separate instructions. ▶ Attach this form to your return.

OMB No. 1545-0172

1991

Attachment
Sequence No. **67**

Name(s) shown on return

Identifying number

Business or activity to which this form relates

Part I **Election To Expense Certain Tangible Property (Section 179)** (Note: *If you have any "Listed Property," complete Part V.*)

1	Maximum dollar limitation (see instructions)	**1**	$10,000
2	Total cost of section 179 property placed in service during the tax year (see instructions) . . .	**2**	
3	Threshold cost of section 179 property before reduction in limitation	**3**	$200,000
4	Reduction in limitation—Subtract line 3 from line 2, but do not enter less than -0-	**4**	
5	Dollar limitation for tax year—Subtract line 4 from line 1, but do not enter less than -0- . . .	**5**	

	(a) Description of property	(b) Cost	(c) Elected cost	
6				

7	Listed property—Enter amount from line 26	**7**	
8	Total elected cost of section 179 property—Add amounts in column (c), lines 6 and 7 . . .	**8**	
9	Tentative deduction—Enter the lesser of line 5 or line 8	**9**	
10	Carryover of disallowed deduction from 1990 (see instructions)	**10**	
11	Taxable income limitation—Enter the lesser of taxable income or line 5 (see instructions) . .	**11**	
12	Section 179 expense deduction—Add lines 9 and 10, but do not enter more than line 11 . .	**12**	
13	Carryover of disallowed deduction to 1992—Add lines 9 and 10, less line 12 ▶	**13**	

Note: *Do not use Part II or Part III below for automobiles, certain other vehicles, cellular telephones, computers, or property used for entertainment, recreation, or amusement (listed property). Instead, use Part V for listed property.*

Part II **MACRS Depreciation For Assets Placed in Service ONLY During Your 1991 Tax Year (Do Not Include Listed Property)**

(a) Classification of property	(b) Mo. and yr. placed in service	(c) Basis for depreciation (Business/investment use only—see instructions)	(d) Recovery period	(e) Convention	(f) Method	(g) Depreciation deduction
14 General Depreciation System (GDS) (see instructions):						
a 3-year property						
b 5-year property						
c 7-year property						
d 10-year property						
e 15-year property						
f 20-year property						
g Residential rental property			27.5 yrs.	MM	S/L	
			27.5 yrs.	MM	S/L	
h Nonresidential real property			31.5 yrs.	MM	S/L	
			31.5 yrs.	MM	S/L	
15 Alternative Depreciation System (ADS) (see instructions):						
a Class life					S/L	
b 12-year			12 yrs.		S/L	
c 40-year			40 yrs.	MM	S/L	

Part III **Other Depreciation (Do Not Include Listed Property)**

16	GDS and ADS deductions for assets placed in service in tax years beginning before 1991 (see instructions)	**16**	
17	Property subject to section 168(f)(1) election (see instructions)	**17**	
18	ACRS and other depreciation (see instructions)	**18**	

Part IV **Summary**

19	Listed property—Enter amount from line 25	**19**	
20	Total—Add deductions on line 12, lines 14 and 15 in column (g), and lines 16 through 19. Enter here and on the appropriate lines of your return. (Partnerships and S corporations—see instructions)	**20**	
21	For assets shown above and placed in service during the current year, enter the portion of the basis attributable to section 263A costs (see instructions)	**21**	

For Paperwork Reduction Act Notice, see page 1 of the separate instructions.   Cat. No. 12906N   Form **4562** (1991)

Part V **Listed Property.—Automobiles, Certain Other Vehicles, Cellular Telephones, Computers, and Property Used for Entertainment, Recreation, or Amusement**

If you are using the standard mileage rate or deducting vehicle lease expense, complete columns (a) through (c) of Section A, all of Section B, and Section C if applicable.

Section A.—Depreciation (Caution: *See instructions for limitations for automobiles.*)

22a Do you have evidence to support the business/investment use claimed? ☐ **Yes** ☐ **No** | 22b If "Yes," is the evidence written? ☐ **Yes** ☐ **No**

(a) Type of property (list vehicles first)	(b) Date placed in service	(c) Business/ investment use percentage	(d) Cost or other basis	(e) Basis for depreciation (business/investment use only)	(f) Recovery period	(g) Method/ Convention	(h) Depreciation deduction	(i) Elected section 179 cost
23 *Property used more than 50% in a qualified business use (see instructions):*								
		%						
		%						
		%						
24 *Property used 50% or less in a qualified business use (see instructions):*								
		%				S/L –		
		%				S/L –		
		%				S/L –		

25 Add amounts in column (h). Enter the total here and on line 19, page 1 . . . . . . | **25** |
26 Add amounts in column (i). Enter the total here and on line 7, page 1 . . . . | **26** |

Section B.—Information Regarding Use of Vehicles—*If you deduct expenses for vehicles:*
- *Always complete this section for vehicles used by a sole proprietor, partner, or other "more than 5% owner," or related person.*
- *If you provided vehicles to your employees, first answer the questions in Section C to see if you meet an exception to completing this section for those vehicles.*

	(a) Vehicle 1		(b) Vehicle 2		(c) Vehicle 3		(d) Vehicle 4		(e) Vehicle 5		(f) Vehicle 6	
27 Total business/investment miles driven during the year (DO NOT include commuting miles).												
28 Total commuting miles driven during the year												
29 Total other personal (noncommuting) miles driven												
30 Total miles driven during the year— Add lines 27 through 29												
	Yes	No	Yes	No	Yes	No	Yes	No	Yes	No	Yes	No
31 Was the vehicle available for personal use during off-duty hours?												
32 Was the vehicle used primarily by a more than 5% owner or related person? . .												
33 Is another vehicle available for personal use?												

Section C.—Questions for Employers Who Provide Vehicles for Use by Their Employees
*(Answer these questions to determine if you meet an exception to completing Section B. **Note:** Section B must always be completed for vehicles used by sole proprietors, partners, or other more than 5% owners or related persons.)*

	Yes	No
34 Do you maintain a written policy statement that prohibits all personal use of vehicles, including commuting, by your employees?		
35 Do you maintain a written policy statement that prohibits personal use of vehicles, except commuting, by your employees? (See instructions for vehicles used by corporate officers, directors, or 1% or more owners.) .		
36 Do you treat all use of vehicles by employees as personal use?.		
37 Do you provide more than five vehicles to your employees and retain the information received from your employees concerning the use of the vehicles?		
38 Do you meet the requirements concerning qualified automobile demonstration use (see instructions)? . .		

Note: *If your answer to 34, 35, 36, 37, or 38 is "Yes," you need not complete Section B for the covered vehicles.*

Part VI **Amortization**

(a) Description of costs	(b) Date amortization begins	(c) Amortizable amount	(d) Code section	(e) Amortization period or percentage	(f) Amortization for this year
39 Amortization of costs that begins during your 1991 tax year:					
40 Amortization of costs that began before 1991			**40**		
41 Total. Enter here and on "Other Deductions" or "Other Expenses" line of your return. . . .			**41**		

*U.S. Government Printing Office: 1991 — 285-329

Index

About the Author

Ted Nicholas is a multifaceted business personality. In addition to being a well-known author and respected speaker, Mr. Nicholas remains an active participant in his own entrepreneurial ventures. Without capital, he started his first business at age 21. Since then, he has started 22 companies of his own.

Mr. Nicholas has written 13 books on business and finance since his writing career began in 1972. The best known is *How To Form Your Own Corporation Without a Lawyer for under $75*. His previous business enterprises include Peterson's House of Fudge, a candy and ice cream manufacturing business conducted through 30 retail stores, as well as other businesses in franchising, real estate, machinery and food.

When the author was only 29, he was selected by a group of business leaders as one of the most outstanding businessmen in the nation and was invited to the White House to meet the President.

Although Mr. Nicholas has founded many successful enterprises, he also has experienced two major setbacks and many minor ones. He considers business setbacks necessary to success and the only true way to learn anything in life, a lesson that goes all the way back to childhood. That's why he teaches other entrepreneurs how to "fail forward."

Mr. Nicholas has appeared on numerous television and radio shows and conducts business seminars in Florida and Switzerland. Presently, he owns and operates four corporations of his own and acts as marketing consultant and copywriter to small as well as large businesses.

If you have any questions, thoughts or comments, Mr. Nicholas loves to hear from his readers! You are welcome to call, write or fax him at the following address:

Nicholas Direct, Inc.
19918 Gulf Boulevard, #7
Indian Shores, FL 34635
Phone: 813-596-4966
Fax: 813-596-6900